D1566754

ECONOMIC JUSTICE AND NATURAL LAW

Gary Chartier elaborates an account of economic justice rooted in the natural law tradition, explaining how it is relevant to economic issues and developing natural law accounts of property, distribution and work. He examines a range of case studies related to ownership, production, distribution, and consumption, using natural law theory as a basis for staking positions on a number of contested issues related to economic life and highlighting the potentially progressive and emancipatory dimension of natural law theory.

GARY CHARTIER is Associate Professor of Law and Business Ethics and Associate Dean of the School of Business at La Sierra University.

ECONOMIC JUSTICE AND NATURAL LAW

GARY CHARTIER

La Sierra University

CAMBRIDGE
UNIVERSITY PRESS

CAMBRIDGE UNIVERSITY PRESS
Cambridge, New York, Melbourne, Madrid, Cape Town, Singapore, São Paulo, Delhi

Cambridge University Press
The Edinburgh Building, Cambridge CB2 8RU, UK

Published in the United States of America by Cambridge University Press, New York

www.cambridge.org
Information on this title: www.cambridge.org/9780521767200

First published 2009

Printed in the United Kingdom at the University Press, Cambridge

A catalogue record for this publication is available from the British Library

Library of Congress Cataloguing in Publication data
Chartier, Gary.
Economic justice and natural law / Gary Chartier.
p.   cm.
Includes index.
ISBN 978-0-521-76720-0 (hardback)   1. Law and economics.
2. Natural law.   I. Title.
K487.E3C474 2009
340'.112–dc22   2009020683

ISBN 978-0-521-76720-0 hardback

For Elenor

CONTENTS

vii

ACKNOWLEDGMENTS

As is surely appropriate for a book about justice, *Economic Justice and Natural Law* reflects the importance in my life of multiple debts of gratitude.

Elenor Webb has offered me many welcome opportunities for dialogue and exchange.

The careful attention four anonymous reviewers gave to my arguments and to the ways in which I express them has substantially improved this book. I have often explicitly noted throughout the text their contributions to the development of my arguments, but they should be confident that I acknowledge, and am grateful for, their assistance even in cases where I have not made direct reference to their suggestions and insights.

Charles Teel, Jr., read an earlier draft of the manuscript and offered many helpful suggestions. I benefited enormously from the editorial assistance of Logan Dirksen, who provided valuable assistance with references.

Fiñola O'Sullivan, Richard Woodham, Dan Dunlavey, Leigh Mueller and Helen Francis of Cambridge University Press all deserve my gratitude as well for their various contributions to the book's development.

Annette Bryson, Jeffrey Cassidy, Aena Prakash, Alexander Lian, Andrew Howe, Anne-Marie Pearson, Bart Willruth, Carole Pateman, Craig R. Kinzer, David B. Hoppe, David R. Larson, Deborah K. Dunn, Donna Carlson, Eva Pascal, Fritz Guy, Jan M. Holden, Jesse Leamon, Joel Sandefur, John Elder, John Thomas, John W. Webster, Julio C. Muñoz, Kenneth A. Dickey, Kimberly Sogioka, Lawrence T. Geraty, Ligia Radoias, Linn Marie Tonstad, Maria Zlateva, Michael Orlando, Miralyn Keske, Nabil Abu-Assal, Patricia Cabrera, Roger E. Rustad, Jr., Ronel Harvey, Ruth E. E. Burke, Sel J. Wahng, W. Kent Rogers, and Wonil Kim have all participated in valued and valuable exchanges for which they deserve continued appreciation.

Other people who participated in discussions with me regarding the material included in this book or who have otherwise contributed to its development or refinement include Carter Wolverton, Cruz Reynoso, DonaJayne King, Elina Camarena, Elsa Sanchez, Imil Coker, Jennifer Oshima, Johanna Schiavoni, Jon Wagner, Karen Perez, Lee H. Reynolds, Melissa Mullen, Michael Henshaw, Moira Rai, Moses Chambi, Pei Pei Tan, Rose Mary Rodrigues, Sarah Fandrich, Sharee Smalling, Shaunette Bigby, Shelly Gilroy, Stephanie Lasker, Stephen Munzer, Stephen R. L. Clark, and Theodore Maya.

I am immensely pleased by the opportunities I have had to learn over the last two decades from the work of contemporary natural law theorists; I thank Germain Grisez, John Finnis, Robert P. George, Joseph M. Boyle, Jr., Chris Tollefsen, Mark C. Murphy, Alfonso Gómez-Lobo, and Timothy Chappell for the insights their work has offered me. My understanding of a range of economic and organizational issues has also been substantially enhanced by Kevin Carson's extremely thoughtful and creative work, even if, like the new classical natural law theorists, he is likely to conclude that I have not yet learned enough.

I hope in this book to honor the memories of Stanley E. Chartier and H. Glenn Chartier, whose arguments decades ago may first have exposed me to some of the issues regarding economic life with which I am still wrestling here, and of Helen Chartier, who regarded my political and economic views with skeptical but genial tolerance even as she gave me more love than I could ever have deserved.

Material from JOHN FINNIS, NATURAL LAW AND NATURAL RIGHTS (1981) appears here by permission of Oxford University Press. I am also thankful to the editors and publishers who authorized my use here of material taken from several of my previously published articles: *Sweatshops, Labor Rights, and Comparative Advantage*, 10 OREGON REV. INT'L L. 149 (2008); *Consumption, Development Aid, and Natural Law*, 13 WASHINGTON & LEE J.C.R. & SOC. JUST. 205 (2007); *Self-Integration as a Basic Good: A Response to Chris Tollefsen*, 52 AM. J. JURIS, 293 (2007); *Toward a Consistent Natural Law Ethics of False Assertion*, 51 AM. J. JURIS. 43 (2006); *Toward a New Employer–Worker Compact*, 9 EMPLOYEE RTS. & EMPL. POL'Y J. 101 (2005); *Urban Redevelopment and Land Reform: Theorizing Eminent Domain after Kelo*, 11 LEG. THEORY 363 (2005); *Consumers, Boycotts, and Non-Human Animals*, 12 BUFF. ENV. L. J. 123 (2005); *Friendship, Identity, and Solidarity: An Approach to Rights in Plant Closing Cases*, 16 RATIO JURIS 324 (2003); *Natural Law, Same-Sex Marriage, and the Politics of Virtue*, Comment, 48 UCLA L. REV. 1593 (2001); *Civil Rights and Economic Democracy*, 40 WASHBURN L. J. 267 (2001). However, readers of articles on which

I draw here will recognize that the articles have undergone significant changes. Many of these changes reflect a shift in my own thinking from a position exhibiting many affinities with a purified corporate liberalism to a more radical opposition to the power of both the large business organization and the state.

~

Introduction

This book develops an account of economic justice rooted in the natural law tradition. In it, I elaborate a particular version of natural law theory, explain how it is relevant to reflection on economic issues, and develop natural law accounts of property, distribution, and work. Then, I go on to examine how, in light of natural law theory, individual and institutional actors might respond to injustice, accident, and economic insecurity. I use natural law theory as a basis for staking positions on a number of contested issues related to economic life while also challenging alternate positions on some of these issues.

Natural law theory offers a provocative alternative to Kantian and consequentialist understandings of morals, politics, and law. It emphasizes substantive rather than formal accounts of human flourishing and a plurality of both (*i*) basic aspects of well being and (*ii*) norms of practical reasonableness. Contemporary natural law theories reflect the influence, of course, of Aristotle and Aquinas. But natural law theorists now employ the techniques and vocabulary of analytic moral and political philosophy. And, despite the theological roots of their position, their characteristic arguments are straightforwardly philosophical.[1]

I draw especially in this book on the so-called "new classical natural law" (NCNL) theory,[2] articulated primarily in the work of Germain Grisez, John Finnis, Joseph M. Boyle, Jr., Robert P. George, and Chris Tollefsen.[3] But I also take seriously the work of other natural law

---

[1] One exception is the discussion of vocation to which I briefly allude below in Chapter 2.

[2] *Cf.* Steven Macedo, *The New Natural Lawyers*, HARV. CRIMSON, Oct. 29, 1993, at 2. The proponents of the position prefer "new classical natural law" to "new natural law" as a label for the focus of their position. I refer to Germain Grisez, John Finnis, Joseph M. Boyle, Jr., Robert P. George, and Chris Tollefsen collectively as the new classical natural law theorists, or, clumsily, NCNLTs.

[3] *See* JOHN FINNIS, NATURAL LAW AND NATURAL RIGHTS (1980); JOHN FINNIS, FUNDAMENTALS OF ETHICS (1983); JOHN FINNIS, AQUINAS: MORAL, POLITICAL, AND LEGAL THEORY (1998); GERMAIN GRISEZ, THE WAY OF THE LORD JESUS: CHRISTIAN MORAL PRINCIPLES (1983); JOHN M. FINNIS, JOSEPH M. BOYLE, JR., & GERMAIN G. GRISEZ, NUCLEAR DETERRENCE, MORALITY, AND REALISM (1987); ROBERT P. GEORGE, IN DEFENSE OF NATURAL LAW (2001); GERMAIN GRISEZ & RUSSELL SHAW, BEYOND THE NEW MORALITY: THE RESPONSIBILITIES OF FREEDOM (3rd ed. 1988); 2 GERMAIN G.

theorists, including Mark Murphy, Alfonso Gómez-Lobo, and Timothy Chappell.[4]

While this book participates, therefore, in a sustained, ongoing scholarly conversation, I believe it is distinctive for at least two reasons. Other treatments of economic justice do not characteristically proceed from natural law premises. And recent discussions of moral, legal, and political issues in the natural law tradition have devoted less attention to economic questions than to topics related to the beginning and the end of life. In addition, of course, my conclusions differ at a variety of points, in what I hope are interesting ways, from those defended by other natural law theorists.

In Part I of the Introduction, I outline the remainder of the book, elaborating its organizational structure and summarizing its individual elements. In Part II, I introduce natural law theory, before going on to explain its conception of well being in Part III and its understanding of practical reasonableness in Part IV.[5] My goal is not to provide a defense of natural law theory, but to explain its central components. In Part V, I contrast the natural law conception of practical reason with the standard social science model of rationality. I focus in Part VI on the maintenance of social order in accordance with natural law theory, emphasizing that communal norms, rules, and institutions are governed by the principles of practical reasonableness; that affirming the importance of social order does not entail regarding the state as essential; and that the principle of subsidiarity is a requirement of justice. I summarize my arguments in Part VII.

I The plan of the book

I begin the book by laying the foundations for a natural law account of economic justice. I develop a natural law account of property, of justice in distribution, and of work. Then, I consider the remedial application

---

GRISEZ, THE WAY OF THE LORD JESUS: LIVING A CHRISTIAN LIFE (1994); John M. Finnis, Germain G. Grisez, & Joseph M. Boyle, ' "Direct' and 'Indirect'": A Reply to Critics of Our Action Theory, 65 THOMIST 1 (2001); Germain Grisez, Joseph M. Boyle, & John Finnis, Practical Principles, Moral Truth, and Ultimate Ends, 32 AM. J. JURIS. 99 (1987).

[4] See MARK C. MURPHY, NATURAL LAW AND PRACTICAL RATIONALITY (2001); MARK C. MURPHY, NATURAL LAW IN JURISPRUDENCE AND POLITICS (2006); ALFONSO GÓMEZ-LOBO, MORALITY AND THE HUMAN GOODS: AN INTRODUCTION TO NATURAL LAW ETHICS (2002); TIMOTHY CHAPPELL, UNDERSTANDING HUMAN GOODS: A THEORY OF ETHICS (1995).

[5] Natural law theorists often speak of the basic aspects of well being as basic *goods*. I use terms like *basic goods, fundamental aspects of well being*, and *authentic dimensions of welfare* interchangeably.

of natural law theory to disputes regarding these same topics, focusing on circumstances which are distorted by injustice or disaster or in which economic conditions undermine freedom and security.

I seek in Chapter 1 to lay the foundation for what follows by outlining a natural law theory of *property*. I emphasize that property systems are contingent societal creations which reflect a diverse array of rationales. I briefly outline seven such rationales, devoting particular attention to the identity-constitutive function of (some instances of) property. I emphasize that property rights are, from a natural law perspective, limited rather than absolute.

In Chapter 2, I suggest that the principles of practical reasonableness generate norms of justice in *distribution*, and elaborate several such norms. I maintain that these norms help to determine what counts as fairness in pricing, and I argue that, in light of these requirements, each of us has some responsibility to use wealth to support valuable projects or to assist other people, though practical reasonableness ordinarily does not dictate which persons or projects we ought to benefit.

I advance an understanding of several normative issues related to *work* in Chapter 3. I maintain that employment at-will violates basic principles of fairness, and that actual or effective termination is just only when due process is available. I argue that employment discrimination is inconsistent with the Golden Rule. And I suggest that natural law theory requires the participatory management of firms and that it provides plausible arguments for the democratic governance of firms by workers. I recognize that natural law theory may unavoidably leave options open; so I do not suppose I have shown that all other possible workplace arrangements are unjust. I do, however, maintain that there is a substantial, if not indefeasible, cumulative natural law argument for real democracy in the workplace. I defend this view against a number of objections.

In Chapter 4, I suggest that the principles of practical reasonableness can at least sometimes justify reassigning property rights to vulnerable and marginal people whose interests may receive limited protection under the current property rights regime. I emphasize that a community's decision to endorse this kind of reassignment need not commit it to permitting abusive expropriation for the benefit of developers.

I turn in Chapter 5 to the implications of the natural law account of justice in *distribution* I offered in Chapter 2 for responses to injustice, disaster, and insecurity. Though natural law theory cannot on its own generate detailed legal rules or communal norms, or determine the exact shape of communal institutions, I defend a basic income scheme and communal support for universal health care as reasonable, if not necessary, developments of natural law theory's norms of justice. I explore a natural law account of a duty of assistance to the global poor. And I spell out a natural law understanding of the circumstances in which justice in distribution does and does not require boycotts as ways of avoiding participation in the harm caused by trading partners.

In Chapter 6, I focus on natural law responses to conditions in which natural law principles regarding *work* are not completely respected or in which background conditions that shape work relationships have been misshaped by choices and structures inconsistent with the requirements of practical reasoning. I stress the value of collective bargaining as a second-best alternative to workplace democracy and as an option to be pursued en route to worker self-government. I suggest that fair collective bargaining can be used to ensure flexible resolution of questions related not only to compensation but also to workplace safety and work hours in investor-governed firms, and outline mechanisms for participation in the governance of such firms, by workers.[6] And I maintain that collective bargaining can help to remedy the abuses associated with sweatshop labor by creating a minimum level of fairness in the determination of working conditions. I argue that a just system of collective bargaining would allow workers in less-developed communities to compete in the global marketplace without being, as they frequently are at present, exploited.

The models of property rights, justice in distribution, and economic democracy that I outline here are accounts of *ideal theory*: my purpose is at least to gesture at the norms, rules, and institutions of a thoroughly just community. By contrast, my discussions of such topics as poverty relief, sweatshops, worker participation in decision-making in investor-governed firms, and the reassignment of property titles are exercises in *non-ideal theory*: they concern "the justice that becomes relevant when there have been breakdowns in" justice or when market processes fail to

---

[6] Obviously, there is good reason to ask how much it is really investors, rather than executive-level managers, who govern many corporations, as I note later when discussing the separation of ownership and control. I refer to "investor-governed" or "investor-dominated" firms throughout the text as a shorthand way of denoting those firms in which executives (who may themselves be investors) are selected by investors or their representatives, whether it is, in any particular case, the executives or the investors who exercise effective control. I tend here to treat sole proprietorships and partnerships in which not all workers are partners as investor-governed firms.

provide a desired level of economic security.[7] I would not want to imply, by engaging in reflection on issues in non-ideal theory, that I necessarily regard features of contemporary economic life which I do not directly critique, to which I do not offer clear alternatives, or which I seem to address in meliorist fashion as all necessarily compatible with justice.

Fighting poverty using direct wealth transfer or challenging workers' disfranchisement by establishing structures affording them limited opportunities to participate in the governance of investor-dominated firms are, in general, second-best options. Poverty and disempowerment are not typically accidental side-effects of otherwise benign economic relationships or inevitable economic processes. They are all too frequently consequences of the abusive employment of force and of legal and political authority to award unfair privileges to some at the expense of others: the dispossession of smallholders; the creation of professional licensing cartels, copyrights, patents, and other monopolies; the erection and maintenance of barriers to market entry that benefit powerful and established interests at the expense of the disfranchised; capitalization requirements that limit the availability of credit and allow wealthy people and institutions to extract substantial profits in return for lending money; tariffs that enhance the wealth of large corporations while harming poor producers and consumers; property rules that leave untouched the results of large-scale past (and present) expropriation by the powerful; subsidies that redirect the money of poor and working-class people toward corporate boondoggles; the essentially automatic availability of the corporate form, offering entity status and limited liability in both tort and contract;[8] laws that impede the activities of unions; and patents that allow pharmaceutical companies to extract monopoly profits

---

[7] The phrases *ideal theory* and *non-ideal theory* are familiar, of course, from the work of John Rawls; *cf.* NICHOLAS WOLTERSTORFF, JUSTICE: RIGHTS AND WRONGS at ix (2008) (spelling out a distinction between *primary* and *rectifying* justice).

[8] Limited liability protections tend to encourage irresponsible behavior by eliminating investors' and executives' individual responsibilities for corporate misdeeds and may make it more likely that genuine victims of such misdeeds remain uncompensated. Of course people could create something amounting to entity status and limited liability for contract damages on a case-by-case contractual basis. But the automatic availability of the option of creating a corporation with predefined characteristics already reduces transaction costs and shifts the burden of opting out of standard patterns of doing business with contract partners who might, for instance, be willing to pay more to avoid dealing with an entity with limited liability. And it is not clear, in any case, how one could create limited liability in tort through private agreement; its availability seems more clearly to be another way in which the state redistributes resources through corporate law. Thanks to Kevin Carson and Stephan Kinsella for observations that have increased my understanding of these matters.

while people go without needed drugs. The fundamental sources of poverty and powerlessness are all too frequently political.[9] When they are intelligently planned, wealth transfers can help to address the problem of poverty at the margins. Participatory management schemes in investor-governed firms can increase the chance that workers' voices will be heard. But a wide range of structural changes is essential if ordinary people are to be economically secure and in charge of their own lives.[10]

Moral theory is insufficient on its own to *generate* communal norms, rules, and institutions. But a natural law account of property, distribution, and work provides a framework within which the relevant aspects of well being can be identified and norms, rules, and institutions evaluated. A thoroughgoing application of natural law analysis in tandem with relevant insights offered by economics and organizational theory would lead, I believe, to a range of structural reforms with the potential to alter the allocation of power in our communities and offer ordinary people long-term economic freedom and well being.

II The core of natural law theory

The basic elements of natural law theory are an account of well being and an account of reasonable action.

[9] While individual aggression and abuse may be inescapable, *systemic* oppression and exclusion are contingent historical phenomena. Kevin Carson makes this point forcefully in *The Subsidy of History*, THE FREEMAN: IDEAS ON LIBERTY, June 2008, at 33; *see generally* PAUL BARAN & PAUL SWEEZY, MONOPOLY CAPITALISM: AN ESSAY IN THE AMERICAN ECONOMIC AND SOCIAL ORDER (1966); GEORGE BECKFORD, PERSISTENT POVERTY: DEVELOPMENT IN PLANTATION ECONOMIES OF THE THIRD WORLD (1972); GABRIEL KOLKO, CONFRONTING THE THIRD WORLD: UNITED STATES FOREIGN POLICY 1945–1980 (1988); FRANZ OPPENHEIMER, THE STATE (1914); CHERYL PAYER, THE DEBT TRAP: THE INTERNATIONAL MONETARY FUND AND THE THIRD WORLD (1974); MICHAEL PERELMAN, CLASSICAL POLITICAL ECONOMY: PRIMITIVE ACCUMULATION AND THE SOCIAL DIVISION OF LABOUR (1984); WILLIAM BLUM, KILLING HOPE: U.S. MILITARY AND CIA INTERVENTIONS SINCE WORLD WAR II (1995); MAURICE DOBB, STUDIES IN THE DEVELOPMENT OF CAPITALISM (1963); ERIC HOBSBAWM & GEORGE RUDÉ, CAPTAIN SWING (1968); MICHAEL PERELMAN, THE INVENTION OF CAPITALISM: CLASSICAL POLITICAL ECONOMY AND THE SECRET HISTORY OF PRIMITIVE ACCUMULATION (2000); CHAKRAVARTHI RAGHAVAN, RECOLONIZATION: GATT, THE URUGUAY ROUND AND THE THIRD WORLD (1990); MARTIN SKLAR, THE CORPORATE RECONSTRUCTION OF AMERICAN CAPITALISM, 1890–1916: THE MARKET, THE LAW, AND POLITICS (1988); E. P. THOMPSON, THE MAKING OF THE ENGLISH WORKING CLASS (1963); 1 IMMANUEL WALLERSTEIN, THE MODERN WORLD SYSTEM (1974); WILLIAM APPLEMAN WILLIAMS, THE TRAGEDY OF AMERICAN DIPLOMACY (1959). Thanks to Kevin Carson for calling my attention to most of these texts.

[10] I am appreciatively indebted here and elsewhere to Kevin Carson's fascinating analyses; *see, e.g.*, KEVIN A. CARSON, STUDIES IN MUTUALIST POLITICAL ECONOMY (2007).

For natural law theorists, a good life is a life lived in accordance with practical reason and marked by openness to an array of basic aspects of well being, welfare, or flourishing (I use these terms interchangeably).[11] Welfare can be specified with reference to a range of aspects or dimensions; responsible moral action is action open to all of these aspects or dimensions.[12]

Human participation in the various aspects of welfare is appropriate to the extent that it is consistent with a set of principles of practical reasonableness. A morally appropriate act is one that is characterized by respect for all real aspects of well being, as realized in our own lives or those of others. Thus, avoiding wrongdoing is not the goal of human life. Neither is trying (impossibly, since there is no such thing) to maximize well-being-in-general. Morality is a second-order affair, governing people's reasonable participation in basic aspects of welfare.

III   Basic aspects of well being

The purpose of a reasonable human action is participation in one or more intelligible, intrinsically valuable aspects of well being. Each of these aspects is equally basic: none can be reduced to any of the others or to something else, like subjective satisfaction. Recognizing that I am bracketing a range of interesting and important questions, I suggest that it might make sense to offer a tentative list of basic aspects of welfare that looked something like this:

1. æsthetic experience
2. creativity
3. friendship and community
4. knowledge
5. life and bodily well being
6. mental health and inner peace
7. play
8. practical reasonableness
9. religion[13]

[11] *Cf.* GRISEZ, PRINCIPLES, *supra* note 3, at 184; John Finnis, *Commensuration and Practical Reason, in* INCOMMENSURABILITY, INCOMPARABILITY, AND PRACTICAL REASON 215, 225–28 (Ruth Chang ed., 1997).
[12] It is important to emphasize that an action can be open to all of the basic aspects of well being even if it does not involve *active participation* in each of these dimensions of welfare. It will be open just so long as the actor does not choose to treat any of the aspects of well being as if it were not fundamentally and inherently valuable.
[13] *See* CHAPPELL, *supra* note 4, at 37–45; MURPHY, RATIONALITY, *supra* note 4, at 96–138; GÓMEZ-LOBO, *supra* note 4, at 6–25; GRISEZ & SHAW, FREEDOM, *supra*

Not everything that is valuable is necessarily a basic good. For something may sometimes be valuable but not *always* or *necessarily* so. A good example is *autonomy*. Autonomy is frequently valuable, and it facilitates participation in many of the aspects of well being. But it is arguably not always fundamentally valuable. Perhaps the same is true of, say, *self-esteem*. Certainly, the Aristotelian point that *happiness* names our satisfaction at participating in intelligible aspects of well being, rather than another good (perhaps the master good), seems entirely on-target.

In Section A, I consider several alternative ways of determining what is to count as a basic aspect of well being. In Section B, I emphasize that the basic aspects of well being, however identified, must be understood as incommensurable, non-fungible, and incapable of being reduced to any underlying substrate.

A   Identifying basic aspects of well being

There are a number of ways in which one might seek to identify basic aspects of well being. These include direct recognition (Subsection 1); critical reflection on actual desires and on the objectives sought by people in different cultures (Subsection 2); analysis of the implications of our experiences of and judgments regarding harm, privation, and loss (Subsection 3); the acknowledgment that recognizing some objectives of action is unavoidable (Subsection 4); and the pursuit of reflective equilibrium among our various practical judgments (Subsection 5).

1   Direct recognition

Natural law theory does not depend on the existence of any peculiar faculty of "intuition"[14] as the means of identifying basic aspects of welfare. But it is certainly imaginable that we might conclude that we simply *recognize* non-inferentially that some things are aspects of well being.[15]

2   Critical reflection on action and inclination

Alternatively, critical reflection on our own inclinations could be seen as offering us insight into the worth of what we desire.[16] We might simply consider how we make decisions, and where our chains of justification seem to stop, maintaining, with Grisez, that "[o]ne can distinguish

---

note 3, at 77–88; Grisez, Principles, *supra* note 3, at 121–25; Finnis, Law, *supra* note 3, at 59–99.

[14] *See* Finnis, Ethics, *supra* note 3, at 51.   [15] *See* Gómez-Lobo, *supra* note 4, at 9–10.

[16] *Cf.* Finnis, Ethics, *supra* note 3, at 51–52; Finnis, Law, *supra* note 3, at 51–99.

human goods by noticing the assumptions implicit in one's practical reasoning," and observing that "deliberation quickly reaches some good which is taken to be not merely a means to an end but an aspect of personal fulfillment."[17] Thus, we might equate a basic aspect of well being with whatever ends a "complete chain of explanation of an action."[18] Certainly, it makes sense to see basic aspects of well being and basic reasons for action as, finally, the same thing (even if something's proving appealing to me doesn't entail that it must be good for me).[19] Similarly, the treatment of various potential aspects of well being *as* final reasons for action in a range of cultures and historical epochs does not prove that they really are aspects of well being, which is, of course, an inescapably normative notion. But for some natural law theorists it may provide further, indirect, evidence of their value.[20]

3   Critical reflection on privation

Consider a related but different approach: we can also ask, when something goes *wrong*, just how it has gone wrong – what it is that has been harmed or frustrated; we can inquire what we judge to be harms and ask what it is that they harm.[21] Put another way, we can "come to understand what aspects of flourishing there are" by seeking "to isolate them by way of imagined malfunctions," an approach which "enables one to render explicit what is known in some implicit way."[22]

4   Undeniability and self-evidence

Alternatively, one might attempt to identify basic aspects of welfare by specifying those reasons for action that "are typically either evident or self-evident goods or both" – that is, "such that no one would normally dream of denying" their status as aspects of welfare *or* "such that it is self-defeating to deny" their value.[23] One could, for instance, grant the plausibility of arguments to the effect that denying the inherent worth of, say, knowledge or practical reasonableness is self-defeating.[24]

---

[17] GRISEZ, PRINCIPLES, *supra* note 3, at 122.   [18] CHAPPELL, *supra* note 4, at 35.
[19] *Cf. id.* at 36.   [20] *Cf.* FINNIS, LAW, *supra* note 3, at 83–85, 97.
[21] GRISEZ, PRINCIPLES, *supra* note 3, at 123: "One can infer the basic human goods from the privations which mutilate them."
[22] MURPHY, RATIONALITY, *supra* note 4, at 40.   [23] CHAPPELL, *supra* note 4, at 36.
[24] *See* FINNIS, LAW, *supra* note 3, at 73–75; FINNIS, AQUINAS, *supra* note 3, at 58–61. Here and subsequently, I treat arguments offered in the latter book regarding matters of substance as Finnis's own unless he notes his disagreement with Aquinas in the text. I do not intend by doing so to imply that Finnis has substituted his own position for that of Aquinas.

5   Reflective equilibrium

One could also simply seek reflective equilibrium among one's – perhaps ungrounded – beliefs about what is or might be worthwhile and one's critical judgments about the character of human welfare. One might begin by accepting, but then subjecting to careful scrutiny, one's beliefs that particular aspects of life are, in fact, dimensions of flourishing and fulfillment, seeking to equilibrate the deliverances of the tradition or traditions responsible for shaping one's judgments and the data of experience (moral and otherwise).[25]

* * *

There will surely be reasonable disagreement about how to identify a basic aspect of well being and about what does and does not count as one.[26] But whatever the approach one employs – and there will likely be merit to more than one – it does not matter precisely for my immediate purposes just which dimensions of welfare are seen as basic. What is most important is the recognition that there are multiple, distinct aspects of flourishing and fulfillment and that they are independently valuable, not that any taxonomy of these dimensions of welfare be exhaustive or final.[27] Just which reasons for action are actually authentic dimensions of well being makes little difference to most of the arguments I want to advance in this book.

B   Basic aspects of well being as irreducible, incommensurable, and non-fungible

The description of these aspects of well being as *basic* means that every one of them is inherently valuable; none is reducible to any other aspect or aspects of well being, or to any imagined substrate – "happiness," say, or "pleasure." I underscore here the irreducible, incommensurable character of basic aspects of welfare (Subsection 1); their non-reducibility to

---

[25] On the notion of reflective equilibrium, *see* JOHN RAWLS, A THEORY OF JUSTICE 18–19, 42–45 (2d ed. 1999). For an analysis and elaboration of an approach to warranting moral judgment by way of the critical appropriation of moral tradition, *see* CHARLES LARMORE, THE MORALS OF MODERNITY 55–64 (1996). DAVID MCNAUGHTON, MORAL VISION: AN INTRODUCTION TO ETHICS 102–3 (1988) offers a provocative account of change in moral judgment in response to the data of moral experience.

[26] For instance, I think there is good reason to argue that *sensory pleasure* and the *imaginative immersion* we experience when caught up in a compelling narrative should be included among the basic aspects of well being. And I am inclined to think that perhaps *self-integration*, regularly included in some form on the NCNLTs' lists, should not be; *see* Gary Chartier, *Self-Integration as a Basic Good: A Response to Chris Tollefsen*, 52 AM. J. JURIS. 293 (2007).

[27] Thus, I agree on this point with Timothy Chappell; see CHAPPELL, *supra* note 4, at 44.

subjective satisfaction and the significance of emotional responses as pointers to well being (Subsection 2); the significance of emphasizing that the various dimensions of welfare are apprehended by means of intelligence (Subsection 3); and the possibility of choice among aspects of well being despite their incommensurability (Subsection 4).

1   Basic aspects of well being as irreducible

Characterizing the aspects of well being as *basic* means that any valuable state of affairs will be seen to embody one or more of them in some appropriate combination. But it also means that none is more fundamental than any of the others. The value of friendship is not explicable in terms of the value of speculative knowledge; the value of practical reasonableness is not explicable in terms of the value of religion. Nor do people seem to seek æsthetic experience or engage in play as a means to some further goal. In particular, they do not seek basic dimensions of welfare as ways of experiencing some independently specifiable kind of *pleasure* or some kind of subjective satisfaction.

Thus, there is no significant, meaningful way of equating the value realized in friendship, the value realized in the contemplation of great art, and the value to be realized in play. The dimensions of well being in which we participate are fundamentally different. They are not rationally substitutable for each other. Even if, *per impossibile*, we could quantify each, it would still be the case that there was no rationally required equivalence between categories of well being. There is no scale we could use to determine how much, objectively speaking, an instance of one good weighs in comparison with an instance of some other good – as if, say, two units of friendship were worth one of practical reasonableness. And the same is true of individual instances of particular kinds of flourishing: there's no rationally required equivalence between one instance of a given aspect of welfare and another instance of the same aspect of welfare. One friendship, for instance, can't meaningfully be exchanged for another. It seems, then, that there is no common substrate to which basic aspects of well being can be reduced, and so no hope of commensurating them and trading them off against each other.

2   The cognitive significance of emotional satisfaction

It would be irrational to understand friendship, say, as a device for producing a discriminable, pleasurable sensation.[28] And we don't pursue

---

[28] *Cf.* ROBERT C. SOLOMON, ABOUT LOVE: REINVENTING ROMANCE FOR OUR TIME 76–82 (1988) (noting that love is not a means of producing such pleasurable sensations as those

speculative knowledge as a means to some independent, enjoyable psychic state. Participating in the basic aspects of well being can and should give rise to positive feelings. But feelings themselves cannot tell us whether our subjective satisfactions evince our participation in real dimensions of well being; good feelings can be unreliable guides to well being. Whether we feel good or not does not affect the status of a basic aspect of well being as inherently valuable.[29] Emotional satisfaction is a conscious or affective register of participation in one or more genuine, intelligible aspects of well being, of apprehended significance or value;[30] it is not an explanation or source of that significance or value. What matters is not whether doing something *feels* good, but whether it *is* good.

3   Basic aspects of well being as objective

Natural law theorists say that we *participate*, rather than that we, say, *experience*, aspects of well being, in order to emphasize that what matters is actually making an aspect of well being a *part of one's life*. Basic aspects of well being, will often be parts of our experience; but there is a meaningful difference between, for instance, participating in the good of friendship and having particular subjective experiences, which might simply be experiences of *imagining* that one was participating in the good of friendship. *Imagining* a relationship of love or friendship is not the same as actually being in such a relationship; neither is undergoing the neurochemical effects of phenylethylamine, which appears to be responsible in our species for some of the experienced physiological changes associated with being in love.[31] Being well is more than our awareness of being well.

4   Choices among basic aspects of welfare

That basic aspects of welfare are incommensurable and non-fungible does not mean, of course, that we do not or cannot make reasonable choices

---

often accompanying it, but that these feelings are, instead, characteristic accompaniments of love).

[29] I bracket here the question whether sensory pleasure is itself inherently worthwhile. I agree with Chappell that it is, but I do not believe any argument in this book turns on whether we are right about this.

[30] Perhaps "apprehended" isn't the best word here. I use it to emphasize that conscious awareness and reflection are not always involved in my response to a basic aspect of well being. *Feelings*, as opposed to emotions, are not necessarily responses to apprehended value or meaning – feelings are bare sensations – but an emotion, by definition, always presents itself as incorporating a cognitive component.

[31] *Cf.* HELEN FISHER, WHY WE LOVE: THE NATURE AND CHEMISTRY OF ROMANTIC LOVE (2004).

among the dimensions of welfare in which we will seek to participate or in which we may help others to participate. We certainly have preferences. But the fact that a person prefers one aspect of the human good to another is a reflection of the contingent features of her own psyche. It provides no support for the view that anyone else would be rationally required to make the same choice. It does not show that a rational commensuration or rank-ordering of basic aspects of well being is possible, because a *preference* does not, as such, purport to be or embody a judgment about what reason requires. (Of course, the various principles of practical reasonableness *do* constrain in various ways the choices one makes about which of one's preferences to satisfy, and in what way. But they do not do so by rendering the aspects of welfare that are the objects of our preferences commensurable or fungible.)

The basic aspects of well being are not instrumental, not ways of reaching some other end; they're ends in themselves. None can be reduced to each other or to any other putative underlying good. And they can neither be measured on a common scale nor substituted for each other in any way that presupposes that they can be rendered rationally equivalent.[32]

IV Requirements of practical reasonableness

Practical reason requires that one act in a way that takes appropriate account of the diverse aspects of well being and the diverse moral subjects who participate in these aspects of well being. Reasonable participation in well being means acting in accordance with several practical

---

[32] Because of the incommensurability of these dimensions of flourishing as categories, and of individual instances of particular aspects of well being, the consequentialist injunction to maximize the good is in principle incoherent. It depends on maximizing the sum of all relevant dimensions of well being, or something similar, and the notion of such a sum makes no sense. Thus, on the natural law view, no variety of consequentialism can be viable. For criticisms of consequentialist approaches, *see, e.g.,* ALAN DONAGAN, THE THEORY OF MORALITY 172–209 (1977); FINNIS, ETHICS, *supra* note 3, at 80–108; FINNIS, LAW, *supra* note 3, at 111–19; FINNIS ET al., DETERRENCE, *supra* note 3, at 177–296; GRISEZ & SHAW, FREEDOM, *supra* note 3, at 111–14, 131–33; ALASDAIR C. MACINTYRE, AFTER VIRTUE: A STUDY IN MORAL THEORY 61–63, 67–68, 185 (2d ed. 1984); DAVID S. ODERBERG, MORAL THEORY: A NON-CONSEQUENTIALIST APPROACH 65–76, 97–101, 132–33 (2000); NEL NODDINGS, CARING: A FEMININE APPROACH TO ETHICS AND MORAL EDUCATION 86–87, 151–54 (1984); BERNARD WILLIAMS, MORALITY: AN INTRODUCTION TO ETHICS (2d ed. 1993); Bernard Williams, *A Critique of Utilitarianism, in* UTILITARIANISM: FOR AND AGAINST 77–150 (J. J. C. Smart & Bernard Williams, 1973); Stephen R. L. CLARK, *Natural Integrity and Biotechnology, in* HUMAN LIVES 58–76 (Jacqueline A. Laing & David S. Oderberg eds., 1997); Germain Grisez, *Against Consequentialism*, 23 AM. J. JURIS. 21 (1978).

principles.[33] These requirements may be summarized in something like the following way:[34]

1. avoid arbitrary partiality among moral subjects[35]
2. do not make *harm* a part of the proposal one adopts when one acts,[36] and do not act out of hostility[37]
3. given reasonable objectives, pursue these objectives efficiently[38]
4. do not lightly abandon reasonable commitments (to oneself and to others) and attachments.[39]

In general, these principles exclude what is putatively inappropriate without determining that any of a number of possible good choices

---

[33] For different lists of these "modes of responsibility," see GRISEZ & SHAW, FREEDOM, *supra* note 3, at 117–53; GRISEZ, PRINCIPLES, *supra* note 3, at 205–28; FINNIS, LAW, *supra* note 3, at 100–33; FINNIS, ETHICS, *supra* note 3, at 75–76; MURPHY, RATIONALITY, *supra* note 4, at 198–208. I omit consideration of several further potential principles: avoid incoherent life-plans; recognize each instance of each basic dimension of welfare or well being, and each requirement of practical reasonableness, as reason-giving, and do *not* treat illusory or imaginary goods as reason-giving; cooperate appropriately with others and facilitate the common good; do not treat any particular project one pursues as absolute in value; and avoid being swayed by feelings, and avoid acting on feelings for their own sake. *See* MURPHY, RATIONALITY, *supra* note 4, at 198–201, 212; FINNIS, LAW, *supra* note 3, at 103–6, 125–26, 134–60; FINNIS, ETHICS, *supra* note 3, at 75–6; GÓMEZ-LOBO, *supra* note 4, at 42–44; GRISEZ & SHAW, FREEDOM, *supra* note 3, at 121–26; GRISEZ, PRINCIPLES, *supra* note 3, at 206–11. In some cases, I regard these further principles as superfluous, in others as questionable. But I do not believe that anything of great substance in what follows turns on my judgments regarding their appropriateness.

[34] I state principles of practical reasonableness in summary form here. Except as I note explicitly, I do not intend to challenge the formulations offered by other authors in the natural law tradition.

[35] *See* GRISEZ & SHAW, FREEDOM, *supra* note 3, at 119–20; GRISEZ, PRINCIPLES, *supra* note 3, at 211–14; FINNIS, LAW, *supra* note 3, at 106–9; FINNIS, ETHICS, *supra* note 3, at 75; GÓMEZ-LOBO, *supra* note 4, at 44. *Cf.* MURPHY, RATIONALITY, *supra* note 4, at 201–4; THOMAS NAGEL, THE POSSIBILITY OF ALTRUISM (1980).

[36] As, for instance, by purposefully or instrumentally killing. MURPHY, RATIONALITY, *supra* note 4, at 204–7; GRISEZ & SHAW, FREEDOM, 129–39; GRISEZ, PRINCIPLES, at 216–21; FINNIS, LAW, *supra* note 3, at 118–25; FINNIS, ETHICS, *supra* note 3, at 75; GÓMEZ-LOBO, *supra* note 4, at 46. Any act of purposeful or instrumental harm is precluded absolutely; one may sometimes, however, reasonably accept a harmful outcome as a foreseen but unintended side-effect or by-product of a good act. Grisez develops and defends a version of this principle with specific reference to the good of life in *Toward a Consistent Natural-Law Ethics of Killing*, 15 AM. J. JURIS. 64 (1970).

[37] GRISEZ & SHAW, FREEDOM, *supra* note 3, at 121; GRISEZ, PRINCIPLES, *supra* note 3, at 215–16.

[38] *See* MURPHY, RATIONALITY, *supra* note 4, at 207–8; FINNIS, LAW, *supra* note 3, at 111–18; FINNIS, ETHICS, *supra* note 3, at 75.

[39] *See* MURPHY, RATIONALITY, *supra* note 4, at 210–12; GÓMEZ-LOBO, *supra* note 4, at 42; FINNIS, LAW, *supra* note 3, at 109–10; FINNIS, ETHICS, *supra* note 3, at 75.

is to be preferred to any other. Their function is not to provide a strait-jacket that determines precisely what people ought to do. They leave open a diverse array of options while ruling out those putatively inconsistent with reason. The sensible notion that self-regarding and other-regarding considerations cannot always readily be distinguished is clearly among their implications.

In Section A, I spell out the nature of the first principle of practical reasonableness, the Golden Rule. In Section B, I discuss the second, the Pauline Principle.[40] In Section C, I examine the other two principles, which I label the Efficiency Principle and the Integrity Principle. In Section D, I explain how the principles of practical reasonableness generate rights.

A   The Golden Rule

The first practical principle mandates fairness; it precludes "arbitrary preferences"[41] among moral subjects because "intelligence and reasonableness can find no basis in the mere fact that A is A and is not B (that I am I and am not you) for evaluating his (our) well being differentially."[42] In Grisez's most developed formulation: "One should not, in response to different feelings toward different persons, willingly proceed with a preference for anyone *unless the preference is required by intelligible goods themselves.*"[43] Or, in Finnis's: "do not leave out of account, or arbitrarily discount or exaggerate, the goodness of other people's participation in human good."[44]

The Golden Rule excludes as unreasonable two distinguishable kinds of arbitrariness. Preferences among persons as objects of harm or benefit that are not themselves reasonably ways of participating in authentic aspects of well being are unreasonable (Subsection 1). So are acts or omissions in relation to similarly situated others that one would not regard as acceptable in relation to oneself (Subsection 2).

---

[40] For the phrase, "the Pauline Principle," *see* FINNIS, ETHICS, *supra* note 3, at 109; DONAGAN, Theory, *supra* note 31, at 149. The use of "Pauline" reflects St. Paul's passionate rejection, in *Romans* 3:8, of the injunction, "Let us do evil, that good may come."

[41] FINNIS, LAW, *supra* note 3, at 106.

[42] *Id.* at 107; *cf.* FINNIS, AQUINAS, *supra* note 3, at 140: "the basic goods are good for *any* human being, ... [so] I must have a reason for preferring their instantiation in *my own* or *my friends'* existence" (my italics).

[43] GRISEZ, PRINCIPLES, *supra* note 3, at 220 (my italics).

[44] FINNIS, ETHICS, *supra* note 3, at 75.

1   No discrimination except in pursuit of basic aspects of well being

The Golden Rule does not preclude "reasonable self-preference." For "it is through *my* self-determination and self-realizing participation in the basic goods that I can do what reasonableness suggests and requires, *viz.* favour and realize" the basic aspects of well being in accordance with the principles of practical reasonableness.[45] So one "has no general responsibility to give the well being of other people as much care and concern as one gives one's own; the good of others is as really good as one's own good, but is not one's primary responsibility, and to give one's own good priority is not, as such, to violate the requirement of impartiality."[46]

Nor does the Golden Rule preclude preference for persons other than oneself – preference for friends, family members, or particular communities.[47] Respect for the basic dimensions of well being themselves may require discrimination between persons – in the interest of friendship, say, or play. The Golden Rule

> by no means excludes all forms and corresponding feelings of preference for oneself and those who are near and dear (for example, parental responsibility for, and consequent prioritizing of, their own children). It excludes, rather, all those forms of preference which are motivated only by desires, aversions, or hostilities that do not correspond to intelligible aspects of the real reasons for action, the basic human goods instantiated in the lives of other human beings as in the lives of oneself or those close to one's heart.[48]

Acting on the basis of particular preferences and special relationships is partly a matter of regard for oneself (because friendship and community are shared goods, and because honoring one's commitments and attachments is an appropriate expression of care for oneself as well as for persons to whom one is attached), partly a matter of regard for particular others, and partly a matter of regard for one's community. Ultimately, the shared well being of one's community just "*is* the good of individuals, living together and depending upon one another in ways that favour the well being of each."[49]

The Golden Rule does not, then, require an alienating impartiality. Nonetheless, it offers "a pungent critique of selfishness, special pleading, double standards, hypocrisy, indifference to the good of others whom

---

[45] FINNIS, LAW, *supra* note 3, at 107.   [46] *Id.* at 304.   [47] *Id.* at 108.

[48] Finnis, *Commensuration, supra* note 10, at 227.

[49] FINNIS, LAW, *supra* note 3, at 305.

one could easily help . . ., and all the other manifold forms of egoistic and group bias."[50]

2   No treating others as one would not want to be treated

The application of the Golden Rule requires the agent to ask what *she*, personally, would and would not find acceptable: "to apply the Golden Rule, one must know what burdens one considers *too great* to accept. And this knowledge, constituting a premoral commensuration, cannot be a commensurating by reason."[51] There is in this sense an unavoidably subjective aspect to the application of the Golden Rule.

This understanding of the Golden Rule seems unavoidable, given the incommensurability of the basic aspects of well being and the diverse priorities of particular people. While it will be perfectly possible to ask what will be good for a particular person, it will usually be mistaken to suppose that there is some one option or a narrow range of options or preferences capable of being described as *best* or better than all others.[52] Thus, in applying the Golden Rule one cannot but rely on one's preferences. When one does, one will not be engaged in "a rational and objective commensuration of goods and bads." However, "once established," a subjective commensuration based on one's preferences "enables one to measure one's options by a rational and objective standard of interpersonal impartiality."[53] Not everyone might regard a certain cost as too great to bear in particular circumstances. But if *I* thus regard it, I cannot rationally impose it on others in those circumstances.

> Is it fair to impose on others the risks inherent in driving at more than 10 mph . . . ? Yes, in our community, since our community has . . . *decided* to treat those risks and harms as *not too great*. Have we a rational critique of a community which decided to limit road traffic to 10 mph and to accept all the economic and other costs of that decision? . . . No, we have no rational critique of such a community. . . . [T]he decision to permit road traffic to proceed faster than 10 mph . . . was rationally underdetermined.
>
> But we do have a rational critique of someone who drives at 60 mph but who, when struck by someone driving 45 mph complains that the speed is per se negligent. . . . And, in general, we have a rational critique of those who accept the benefits of this and other communal decisions but reject the correlative burdens as they bear on them and those in whom they feel interested.[54]

[50] *Id.* at 107.   [51] Finnis, *Commensuration, supra* note 10, at 227.
[52] It is important to emphasize that this subjective test takes its place along with a variety of other norms of practical reasonableness that undermine the position of the fanatic or the Nazi.
[53] *Id.* at 227.   [54] *Id.* at 228.

And the same point obviously applies at the interpersonal level: "Jane who wants her husband Jack to be faithful plainly violates ... [the Golden Rule] by sleeping with Sam":[55] she wants different standards to apply to herself and to Jack.[56]

The Golden Rule does not seem to mandate a mechanical egalitarianism, since it leaves room for distinctions among persons reflective of concern for basic aspects of well being. However, it enjoins respectful consideration of others' interests (and so, for instance, promise-keeping).[57] It requires that we treat others as fundamentally equal in moral worth. And it demands that we not impose on others burdens we would not be willing that they impose on us or our loved ones. It clearly prescribes active concern for others and it provides a credible basis for resisting oppression and subordination.

B   *The Pauline Principle*

The second norm of practical reasonableness, the Pauline Principle, is the ground of the absolute prohibitions that form the hard core of any reasonable human rights regime – prohibitions of purposeful killing

---

[55] FINNIS ET AL., DETERRENCE, *supra* note 3, at 284.

[56] *Cf.* FINNIS, ETHICS, *supra* note 3, at 91–92: "If we have decided to build a highway through the desert, ... we can use cost-benefit computations to select among materials and methods of leveling and road-building. But it was not, and could not rationally have been, cost-benefit computations which guided our prior commitment to the level of economic activity (trade) and personal mobility which calls for highways of this sort. We know that the building and use of highways of this sort involves the death of tens of thousands of persons, and the horrible injury of hundreds of thousands more, each year. But we have not made any computation which shows that the goods participated in and attained by that level of trade and mobility exceed, outweigh, are proportionately greater, than the goods destroyed and damaged by that level, or any level, of deaths and injuries. Nor, on the other hand, could any computation yield the conclusion that the deaths and injuries are an evil which objectively outweighs, exceeds, etc., the good of mobility, etc. ... The justification, and equally the critique, of any basic commitment [in light of which a choice like this might be assessed] must be in terms of the requirements of practical reasonableness, which give positive direction even though they do not include any principle of optimizing ... , and even though they permit indefinitely many different commitments (as well as, also, excluding indefinitely many other possible commitments!)." According to data from the United States Department of Transportation, "[a] total of 42,643 people died [on United States highways], and 2.89 million were injured in 2003. The fatality rate per 100 million vehicle miles traveled ... was 1.48 in 2003. ..." *Historical Lows for Highway Fatality Rates*, http://www.roadandtravel.com/safetyandsecurity/highwayfatalityrates.htm (last visited Mar. 4, 2005).

[57] *See* FINNIS, LAW, *supra* note 3, at 298–308; FINNIS, AQUINAS, *supra* note 3, at 196–99. *Cf.* THOMAS M. SCANLON, WHAT WE OWE TO EACH OTHER 295–317 (1998).

and torture, for instance. One way to understand it is as an inescapable entailment of the intrinsic value and incommensurability of the various dimensions of well being.

Suppose I adopt an attack on a basic aspect of well being as the purpose of my action. *Ex hypothesi*, this cannot be, because the aspect of well being in question isn't *really* an aspect of well being. So the only other obvious alternative may seem to be that some *other* good is more important, and that concern for this good justifies disregard for the good I propose to attack. But if basic aspects of well being are incommensurable and non-fungible, and if they are not lexically ordered (with the result that goods of one sort always trump goods of another sort), as there is no reason to think they are, then no other dimension of welfare – and, indeed, no alternative *instance* of the same aspect of well being – could play the required role. So the choice to subordinate one basic aspect of welfare to another will always be irrational.[58]

So, too, will be any choice to act out of hostility, or, indeed, to nourish feelings of hostility. For to act out of hostility will be to make harm to some basic good an element of the proposal one adopts when one acts. Since this kind of purpose cannot be rational, for the reasons I have just indicated, this element of the Pauline Principle is clearly defensible as well.

Practical reasonableness does not mean that one must seek to participate in all aspects of well being in the same way and to the same degree.[59] Opting for one good in preference to another is no sign of unreasonableness; indeed, given the range of possible human goods, attempting to embrace all aspects of well being would be a recipe for insanity. But one should act in such a way that one acknowledges the value of each dimension of well being – even if one opts not to participate in it – and of each person's participation in it: thus, one should not will, and so identify oneself with, harm to any basic aspect of well being. It is one thing, for instance, to opt for scholarly monasticism out of a love of learning; it is another to do so out of hostility toward others and a rejection of the value of friendship. In both cases one may have few friends; but one will be a quite different sort of person depending on one's motive – a person open or closed to the value of friendship.

The Pauline Principle is in many ways similar to what is sometimes called the "non-aggression principle," precluding the initiation of force

---

[58] See MURPHY, RATIONALITY, *supra* note 4, at 204–7 for a more detailed defense of this principle in light of the incommensurability thesis.

[59] I owe this example to FINNIS, LAW, *supra* note 3, at 105.

against another. But the Pauline Principle is both more restrictive and more permissive. It is more restrictive because it precludes choosing to *cause harm* purposefully or instrumentally, not just choosing to *initiate* a harm-producing action. It does clearly permit a reasonable actor to cause harm as a side-effect or by-product of otherwise reasonable action, and so to use force to defend herself or others, if necessary. But adhering to the Pauline Principle would not be consistent with the use of *retaliatory* force intended not, per se, to defend but rather to punish or to "teach a lesson," since to use force in this way would be to cause harm instrumentally.[60]

The Pauline Principle is also more permissive than typical versions of the non-aggression principle. The non-aggression principle is characteristically understood to preclude the initiation of force against property. By contrast, the Pauline Principle precludes purposeful or instrumental attacks only on basic aspects of well being. An attack on a basic aspect of well being may sometimes take the form of an attack on property – an attack on a painting might be an attack on someone's æsthetic experience, for instance. But the fact that a person owns something isn't enough to make it an aspect of well being. An incursion on property rights might potentially be inconsistent with the Golden Rule or another principle of practical reasonableness. However, because an item of property isn't, just as such, an instance of a basic aspect of well being, the Pauline Principle *itself* won't uniformly rule out interference with people's property as the non-aggression principle would do. And while the Pauline Principle can be derived from the premise that basic aspects of well being are incommensurable and non-fungible, this sort of derivation is not available for the non-aggression principle (when it is understood as precluding all purposeful or instrumental harm to people's property as well as to basic aspects of their well being), unless it is argued that property is a basic aspect of well being in the same way that friendship, knowledge, or practical reasonableness is. It is obvious why property is instrumentally valuable, but to argue that all property interests are fundamental in the same way as these basic aspects of well being is likely to be, at minimum, quite difficult.

C   *The Efficiency and Integrity Principles*

The third requirement of practical reasonableness, the Efficiency Principle, is a minimum requirement of prudence. Though it has

---

[60] The NCNLTs *would* read the Pauline Principle as permitting retributive punishment; I would not.

implausibly been elevated by neoclassical economists into the sole norm of rational action, *abusus non tollit usum*: it remains a crucial element in our care for others and for ourselves. (Of course, if one seeks to realize multiple aspects of well being, this principle does not require – or permit – one to pursue any of them in ways that involve purposeful or instrumental attacks on others.)

The fourth requirement, the Integrity Principle, states a basic condition for the possession of a stable identity over time. Sitting light to one's serious commitments tends to undermine one's selfhood. To treat one's commitments lightly "would mean, in the extreme case, that one would fail ever to really participate in any of the basic values."[61]

The NCNLTs would frame this principle as an injunction simply to take one's commitments seriously; I prefer to refer to "attachments" as well as "commitments." Focusing solely on "commitments," I think, tends to place too much weight on volitional affiliation with a person or community or volitional identification with a project. Talk of "attachment" certainly overlaps with talk about commitment, but it is broader, rightly (as it seems to me) underscoring the fact that some aspects of our identities, some of the things that are important to us, simply *happen* to us, and that it is reasonable to accept the fact that they do.[62] Our "identity-forming attachments are the organising principles of our ... [lives]." They confer "shape as well as meaning" on our lives, and so "are among the determinants of our individuality." And these attachments "are normative because they engage our integrity."[63]

Honoring commitments and attachments facilitates effective agency. Effective agency requires an awareness of continuous identity over time, and so a measure of predictability and stability. "Some things must remain stationary if anything is to move; some points of reference must be constant, or thought and action are not possible." Meaningful action presupposes the existence of long-term projects within which particular choices can make sense. Thus, attachments and commitments help to make meaningful agency and meaningful life possible.[64]

---

[61] *Id.* at 110.

[62] Joseph Raz reflects insightfully on the moral significance of attachment in VALUE, RESPECT, AND ATTACHMENT 12–40 (2001).

[63] *Id.* at 34. Raz suggests that perhaps "only the more abstract of one's attachments are identity-forming," but notes that "this is only a matter of degree." *Id.* I'm not sure I'm convinced: I think quite particular attachments can, to varying degrees, be genuinely identity-constitutive.

[64] MARGARET RADIN, REINTERPRETING PROPERTY 64 (1993).

D   The status of rights

I have a right against someone not to be treated in a certain way if it would be wrong for her to treat me in that way; I have a right against her to receive some benefit if it would be wrong for her not to confer the benefit on me. Talk about rights doesn't itself *justify* particular moral claims; rather, it is a way of signaling that these claims are justified.

Natural law theory justifies talk about both *absolute* and *relative* rights. It is always, *absolutely*, wrong for someone to harm another – to injure a basic aspect of the other's well being – purposefully or instrumentally. In virtue of the Pauline Principle, purposeful or instrumental harm is always unreasonable. So everyone has an absolute right not to be purposefully or instrumentally harmed. Most obviously, this rules out any purposeful or instrumental attack on someone's life or bodily well being (though not the use of proportionate defensive force).[65]

Moral subjects have rights in virtue of the other principles of practical reasonableness, too. Each has an absolute right to be treated as each principle prescribes. But because the other principles themselves do not (at least typically) generate exceptionless prohibitions of specific kinds of actions, they do not ground absolute rights in the same way that the Pauline Principle does. Instead, they ground a range of *relative* rights, rights that vary, often quite substantially, with circumstances.

Thus, for instance, in accordance with the Golden Rule, everyone has an absolute right to be treated with respectful consideration: no moral subject's well being may be arbitrarily excluded from the scope of an actor's concern. But how this well being is taken into account is unavoidably a function of the circumstances of everyone involved, including the preferences of the actor and the various aspects of well being at stake. It may be, therefore, that you have an unequivocal right that *I* keep *this promise* to *you*, but the Golden Rule does not show that everyone has a right that every promise made to her or him should be kept.

At the same time, however, while absolute moral rights do not typically flow from – for instance – the Golden Rule, legal systems might still *treat* as exceptionless rights that flow from the Golden Rule. A community might decide, and might have good reason to decide, that, say, written, spoken, and symbolic expression should never be subject to prior restraint. The reasons for this decision would presumably be reasons cognizable in accordance with the Golden Rule – a principle that on its own does not ground absolute prohibitions. But the community might still

[65]   *Cf.* FINNIS ET al., DETERRENCE, *supra* note 3.

reasonably decide that *its* courts will enforce an exceptionless right on the part of each of *its* members to express herself freely, and might do so in virtue of the Golden Rule (and perhaps the Efficiency Principle and the Integrity Principle as well).

Practical reason grounds both absolute and relative rights. In general, absolute rights flow from the Pauline Principle, relative rights from the others. Within and in response to the constraints of all the principles of practical reasonableness, an individual legal system can treat what would otherwise – just in virtue of the principles of practical reasonableness – be a relative right as exceptionless, and so, de facto, as absolute.

V   The shape of practical reason in the natural law view

Natural law theory takes a robust view of practical reason that contrasts sharply with models dominant in much of contemporary social science. The natural law view emphasizes the diversity and objectivity of the dimensions of well being, the freedom of human action, and the capacity of the rational actor to take others' welfare into account.

What I will label, I hope not too tendentiously, the *standard social science model* of rational decision-making has consisted of several key elements. Obviously, not all proponents of this model would endorse all of these claims, but I offer them here to delineate an ideal type that serves as a clear foil for the natural law view.

1. *The homogeneity of goals.* Our goals are unified: they can be represented as functions of some quantity that can at least be reasoned about as if it were scalar.[66]
2. *The subjectivity of goals.* This quantity is purely subjective: what we seek when we act is psychic satisfaction of one sort or another, and under that description (at least if we stop to reflect).
3. *Rational action as maximization.* Rational decision-making means maximizing this quantity.
4. *Rational action as deterministic.* Rational decision-making is deterministic. We *necessarily* choose the option that maximizes this scalar quantity.
5. *Goals as immune to reflective criticism.* What we finally prefer is simply a contingent matter of fact, a consequence of our physical and psychic constitutions. Thus, reason must treat our preferences as givens.

---

[66] This might be some discriminable psychological state, but it is more likely to be a formal category (preference-satisfaction, say).

We can ask rationally about alternate means of achieving our ends, and we can ask whether pursuing one end will help or hinder our pursuit of another. But reason can provide us with no guidance regarding the question whether one end is preferable to another.

6. *The necessity of self-interest.* The object of our preferences is our *own* well being. We seek our own psychic satisfaction; therefore, even when we seem to seek the welfare of others, our ultimate motive for doing so is that furthering their well being will improve *our* satisfaction. Rational action is necessarily selfish action.

Social scientists themselves are increasingly suspicious of this sort of view at the margins. The notion that people are best understood as rational utility maximizers seems not to be borne out by the facts. Behavioral economics, like its cousins in such cognate areas as law and finance, has emphasized the extent to which inefficient, and so economically irrational, behavior is common.[67] And the notion that agents are necessarily self-interested has been challenged by behavioral research.[68] But more central features of the standard social science account of things, like the equation of rationality with efficiency, seem to persist. Natural law theory embodies a very different conception of human action; it offers alternatives to each of the key elements of the standard social science model.[69]

1. *The heterogeneity of goals.* Natural law theory emphasizes the irreducible diversity of the aspects of welfare. There is no one thing we seek when we act.

2. *The objectivity of goals.* Natural law theory acknowledges that we may sometimes reasonably choose among options that embody different aspects of welfare in light of our subjective responses to those options. But when one chooses among authentic aspects of human flourishing, what one chooses is *inherently* worthwhile. Its value is not

---

[67] *Cf.* DAN ARIELY, PREDICTABLY IRRATIONAL: THE HIDDEN FORCES THAT SHAPE OUR DECISIONS (2008).

[68] *See, e.g.,* FRANS B. M. DE WAAL, GOOD NATURED: THE ORIGINS OF RIGHT AND WRONG IN HUMANS AND OTHER ANIMALS (1997); ROBERT H. FRANK, WHAT PRICE THE MORAL HIGH GROUND? ETHICAL DILEMMAS IN COMPETITIVE ENVIRONMENTS (2004); ALFIE KOHN, THE BRIGHTER SIDE OF HUMAN NATURE: ALTRUISM AND EMPATHY IN EVERYDAY LIFE (1992); KRISTEN RENWICK MONROE, THE HEART OF ALTRUISM: PERCEPTIONS OF A COMMON HUMANITY (1996); ELLIOTT SOBER & DAVID SLOAN WILSON, UNTO OTHERS: THE EVOLUTION AND PSYCHOLOGY OF UNSELFISH BEHAVIOR (1997).

[69] Obviously, the natural law theorists are not alone in criticizing the rational-choice model of human action. *See, e.g.,* JOHN DUPRÉ, HUMAN NATURE AND THE LIMITS OF SCIENCE 117–53 (2001); MICHAEL TAYLOR, RATIONALITY AND THE IDEOLOGY OF DISCONNECTION (2006).

reducible to one's appreciation for it or one's satisfaction in obtaining or experiencing it. And satisfaction is not as such the *goal* of one's action but a by-product of success in achieving one's goal.[70]

3. *Rational action as constrained choice among incommensurables.* One can and does order one's preferences on the basis of one's contingent desires. But this kind of ordering does not amount to any *rationally necessary* ranking. When we pursue narrowly defined goals, we can pursue those goals more or less efficiently. However, if there *is* no single goal we seek, if our actions cannot helpfully be represented simply as ways of achieving subjective satisfaction, if our goals are diverse and incommensurable, then it will not make sense to understand our actions as concerned with the rational maximization of any particular quantity. We do not, in any case, need to be able to see our actual goals as aspects of some particular, unified subjective state, and so as capable of being rank-ordered, in order to choose among them. Rather, we simply select which ones we will pursue. At the same time, of course, not just any choice will be consistent with the demands of reason: genuinely rational decisions are those consistent with the principles of practical reasonableness.

4. *Rational action as free.* The incommensurability of basic aspects of well being – as they are, and as we apprehend them – rules out the possibility that (except in a very narrow range of contexts[71]) one option could be, or could be seen as, rationally superior to another insofar as choosing that option maximized some scalar quantity. Thus, it cannot be the case that I necessarily select "the best option" when confronted with a range of options which I understand satisfactorily – for, again, there is in most cases no single best option. Because it cannot be explained as a matter of putatively rational utility maximization, my selection of one option or another can only be intelligible if it is free in a fairly strong sense. It is not surprising, then, that the natural law theory's account of rational action is an account of such action as free – constrained but not determined by reason.[72]

---

[70] Thus here, as in its specification of principles of practical reasonableness, natural law theory is a variant of moral realism. For a defense of realism from within the natural law tradition, *see* FINNIS, ETHICS, *supra* note 3, at 56–66. Among the most impressive recent statements of the case for moral realism are TERENCE CUNEO, THE NORMATIVE WEB: AN ARGUMENT FOR MORAL REALISM (2007) and RUSS SHAFER-LANDAU, MORAL REALISM: A DEFENCE (2004).

[71] *See* FINNIS, LAW, *supra* note 3, at 111–12.

[72] *See* JOSEPH M. BOYLE, JR., GERMAIN GRISEZ & OLAF TOLLEFSEN, FREE CHOICE: A SELF-REFERENTIAL ARGUMENT 76–77 (1976).

5. *Goals as subject to reflective criticism.* Our preferences can be defective. We can perfectly well subject them to critical scrutiny. We can ask whether we seek, in fact, to pursue authentic aspects of welfare or whether we are treating merely instrumental goods – say, wealth and power – as if they were fundamental dimensions of well being. And we can ask, if we *are* pursuing intelligible aspects of our own welfare or others', whether we are doing so in a reasonable manner – by giving due regard to the welfare of others, avoiding hostility, not purposefully or instrumentally harming any basic aspect of well being, proceeding efficiently, and so forth.

6. *The possibility of genuine concern for others.* If we can recognize real aspects of well being, we can recognize them as aspects of others' well being as well as of our own; recognizing them as valuable, we can act to help realize them in others' lives.[73] Our reasons and desires are our own, but that doesn't show that acting in accordance with these reasons and desires is acting only or always *for the purpose of* benefiting ourselves.

Natural law theory builds on a distinctive conception of practical reason. Its disagreements with common social scientific conceptions of rationality are reflected in its responses to economic issues.

VI   Natural law and social order

Well being requires social order. Communal norms, rules, and institutions facilitate the coordination of agents' activities, protect people against aggression, and help them to fulfill their obligations to each other. In Section A, I stress the importance of seeing norms, rules, and institutions as reasonable just to the extent that they flow from the principles of practical reasonableness. In Section B, I argue that the state need not be among the institutions required to maintain social order and justice. In Section C, I argue that the principle of subsidiarity points to an important feature of just social organization, suggesting that, for multiple reasons, individuals and small groups should have as much opportunity as possible for self-direction.

A   *Practical reasonableness and communal and societal norms, rules, and institutions*

Throughout this book, I make three kinds of related claims: claims about how it is reasonable for particular persons to behave, claims about how

[73] *See* GRISEZ & SHAW, FREEDOM, *supra* note 3, at 63.

it is reasonable for organizations to behave, and claims about the norms, rules, and institutions it is reasonable for people to support and help to implement as members of their communities. The standards at all three levels are the principles of practical reasonableness because, at each level, every choice – reasonable or unreasonable – is finally the choice of a particular person. The difference, of course, is that at the organizational and communal levels, people are cooperating with others, at least sometimes coordinating their actions in ways that reflect (*i*) *their* awareness of what *others* are doing or will likely do; (*ii*) *others'* awareness of what *they*, in turn, are doing; and (*iii*) the awareness on the part of *each* of the other's *awareness* and *responsive behavior.*

This awareness affects the *context* of reasonable action. How one applies the principles of practical reasonableness will depend on what others are doing and are likely to do. Thus, for instance, what kind of behavior is consistent with the Golden Rule or the Efficiency Principle can be determined only in light of others' choices. But it is *not* the case that *new* principles of practical reason come into play. Actors in groups have new facts to consider about the contexts and consequences of their actions. Clearly, the same physical performance may have a quite different meaning when undertaken as part of a cooperative activity than when engaged in by an individual acting alone. Still the rational requirements for purposive action are the same at every level of social organization. So, for example, the adoption of purposes in coordination with others will be reasonable to the extent that it conforms to the Pauline Principle, just like the adoption of purposes on one's own. The coordinative context of organizational or communal life may reduce or enlarge someone's capacities for action, but it cannot introduce new principles of practical reasonableness.

B   Mechanisms for maintaining social order

Practical reason requires that people support and, if necessary, establish or reform just institutions for the purpose of maintaining social order. Natural law theory has often provided qualified support for the authority of the state as a mechanism for performing this task. But there is nothing about natural law theory itself that requires the belief that the state is preferable to other forms of social organization. If it is, this will be a function of facts about the fairness and effectiveness of state and non-state institutions as sources of just social order. And it is not obvious that either history or experience supports the judgment that the state *is* more effective as source of just social order than the non-state alternatives, or that it can be expected to behave fairly.

A state is an entity that claims, at least, a legitimate monopoly over the use – or the adjudication of questions regarding people's actual and potential use – of force within a given territory, and that enforces its claim with relative success. If there is a reasonable argument for the legitimacy of this claim that derives from the state's capacity to serve as a source of social order, this will have to be because the nature of the order effected by the state's use of its monopoly of force will – probably or necessarily – be superior to the order that might be expected to be maintained by non-state institutions.

The incommensurability of the basic aspects of well being means that decisions – for organizations and communal institutions as well as for individuals – cannot be purely technical or instrumental in nature. Reason leaves open an enormous variety of social forms as well as individual life-plans. So coordination is particularly crucial. Finnis maintains that political authority is (at least in part) rooted in the solution authority can provide for societal coordination problems.[74] The fact that a given person's or entity's judgments regarding these coordination problems will likely be respected gives people a reason to acknowledge the authority of those judgments, since the relevant coordination problems will not otherwise be resolved satisfactorily.

It is not clear, however, that the need to coordinate the realization of incommensurable aspects of well being requires the existence of an entity with an effective monopoly over the use of force.[75] Custom and convention may be capable of resolving many such problems.[76] Consciously

---

[74] See FINNIS, LAW, supra note 3, at 245–52. Murphy hints at this approach in MURPHY, RATIONALITY, supra note 4, at 252–54, and discusses it extensively in MURPHY, JURISPRUDENCE, supra note 4, at 105–11.

[75] See (on the left) MICHAEL TAYLOR, COMMUNITY, ANARCHY, AND LIBERTY (1982); TAYLOR, RATIONALITY, supra note 68; LAW AND ANARCHISM (Thom Holterman & Henc van Maarseveen eds., 1984). See (on the right) ANARCHY AND THE LAW: THE POLITICAL ECONOMY OF CHOICE (Edward P. Stringham ed., 2007); ANARCHY, STATE AND PUBLIC CHOICE (Edward P. Stringham ed., 2009); DAVID D. FRIEDMAN, THE MACHINERY OF FREEDOM: GUIDE TO A RADICAL CAPITALISM (2d ed. 1989). See generally ANARCHY/ MINARCHISM: IS GOVERNMENT PART OF A FREE COUNTRY? 87–188 (Roderick T. Long & Tibor R. Machan eds., 2008); SAMUEL CLARK, LIVING WITHOUT DOMINATION: THE POSSIBILITY OF AN ANARCHIST UTOPIA (2007); STEPHEN R. L. CLARK, THE POLITICAL ANIMAL: BIOLOGY, ETHICS AND POLITICS 23–39, 75–91 (1999); CRISPIN SARTWELL, AGAINST THE STATE AN INTRODUCTION TO ANARCHIST POLITICAL THEORY (2008).

[76] But cf. FINNIS, LAW, supra note 3, at 245–46.

planned non-state communal institutions (including courts) may respond successfully to many others.[77]

If this is so, then concern for the value of community need not count in favor of the state, since states can tend to undermine communal life and personal well being. The putative advantages of the state's activities do not render unimportant the propensity of states to foster organized violence in the form of war, to engage in rapacious plunder and pork-barrel spending, or to undermine non-state institutions; nor do they alter the objectionable nature of authority exercised (as state authority almost always is) without the consent of the governed.[78] Communal norms, rules, and institutions are essential to the achievement of economic justice; but it is not so obvious that the *particular set* of institutions making up the state is as well. If a stateless society could preserve justice and maintain order – perhaps by way of a polycentric legal system[79] – such a society would seem to meet natural law theory's requirements for a political (in the broad sense) order worth supporting.[80]

C   Subsidiarity and social order

Whatever the precise nature of the institutions which help to order a community, practical reason requires respect for the integrity of the various groups of which people are members and calls for providing people with the opportunity to pursue their well being within these groups. The refusal to allow the functions of smaller groups to be unnecessarily usurped by more comprehensive institutions is encapsulated in the principle of *subsidiarity*. This principle holds "that it is unjust for more extensive associations to assume functions which can be performed efficiently by individuals or by less extensive associations . . . ."[81]

This principle has multiple moral foundations.[82] Absent legal distortions and subsidies, smaller organizations tend to be more efficient than

---

[77] *Cf.* 1 Friedrich A. Hayek, Law, Legislation and Liberty: Rules and Order (1978).

[78] Finnis dismisses the notion that any sort of original contract or similar deliberate act of consent lies at the foundation of legal or political authority; *see* Finnis, Law, *supra* note 3, at 248.

[79] *See, e.g.*, Tom W. Bell, *Polycentric Law in a New Century*, Policy, Autumn 1999, at 34.

[80] Mark Murphy has argued that standard moral and epistemological arguments for anarchism could not be successful; *see* Mark C. Murphy *Philosophical Anarchisms, Moral and Epistemological*, Can J. L. & Juris. 95 (2007); I have attempted to respond to Murphy in *In Defence of the Anarchist*, 29 Ox. J. Legal Stud. 115 (2009).

[81] Finnis, Aquinas, *supra* note 3, at 237 n.82.

[82] *Cf.* Chapter 3, Part IV, *infra*.

larger ones, and concern for efficiency is, of course, a requirement of practical reason. Information costs are lower, and decisions can be made without the involvement of organizational hierarchies that may lack information about relevant processes and challenges.

Subsidiarity is also important because, in a small organization, there is a greater chance that each member will be heard and will be able to help in shaping organizational decisions. People who are able more directly to contribute to shaping organizational decisions that affect their lives are more likely to find that their own needs are actually met.[83] This includes, of course, the need simply to be treated not only as worth of respect as a person but also as someone with something of value to *contribute*. And it includes, in addition, any specific needs that fall within the purview of the group: they know what will make for their own welfare better than others are likely to do, and in a small group each member can make it more likely that her well being in particular is addressed – even as, at the same time, engagement within a small group can help a member to see when, given what will contribute to the welfare of other members, her own objectives cannot be met immediately or in the manner she might prefer. Subsidiarity thus fosters both attention to individual needs and respect among those who disagree.

The good of an organization is finally the good of its members. A participant in a smaller organization will often be better able to realize her good in the organization than she will as a participant in a larger group. Someone "who is never more than a cog in big wheels turned by others is denied participation in one of the important aspects of well being."[84] She is not treated with the respect she deserves as a person. Thus, smaller organizations are preferable to larger ones, and there is good reason for organizational hierarchies to cede authority to people who might otherwise be treated as subordinates.

Respecting subsidiarity also fosters the well being of communities by increasing the diversity of approaches to addressing social problems. A diverse array of smaller organizations can often explore a wider range of problem-solving strategies than a smaller group of large institutions, and it can give people more options than they would otherwise have.[85]

The principle of subsidiarity does not in any way preclude the development of norms, rules, and institutions at multiple levels. It simply calls for providing people with as much opportunity as possible to participate in

---

[83] *See* FINNIS, LAW, *supra* note 3, at 358.
[84] *Id.* at 147; *cf. id.* at 159 and GRISEZ, LIVING, *supra* note 3, at 357.
[85] *See* GRISEZ, LIVING, *supra* note 3, at 357.

making decisions regarding the standards, practices, and structures that affect their lives.

VII   Natural law and economic life

Rational reflection – whether on human inclinations, our sense of what harms human beings, diverse cultural practices, our own moral tradition, or the self-defeating character of denying the value of, say, knowledge or practical rationality – can give us some reason to identify various aspects of well being as basic, incommensurable, irreducible, and non-fungible. It also points us toward the recognition that we reasonably participate in these dimensions of welfare to the extent that we do so in accordance with a range of practical principles, which include fairness, respect, efficiency, and integrity, and which lie at the foundation of human rights.

Acknowledging the force of these practical principles puts the natural law tradition at odds with the model of human action often affirmed by contemporary social scientists. Natural law theorists maintain that a richer account of deliberation, motivation, and decision can help us to understand human behavior more adequately and to link moral reflection with behavioral analysis more effectively.

The principles of practical reason apply to behavior in social institutions as much as to choices made by individuals on their own. They constrain communal norms, rules, and institutions, while leaving communities free to craft a variety of reasonable strategies for resolving the challenges they face. These principles do not require that communities create or maintain states, but they do require that communities respect the principle of subsidiarity, which calls for significant autonomy for persons and small groups.

Whatever the shape of the relevant norms, rules, and institutions, they should be shaped in accordance with a satisfactory account of basic aspects of well being and fundamental requirements of practical reasonableness, which should also guide individual actors as they structure and participate in economic life. An understanding of the dimensions of well being and the principles of practical reasonableness lays a helpful groundwork for a natural law account of property, to which I turn in Chapter 1.

1

Foundations: property

Property systems are constrained but contingent products of communal norms, rules, and institutions. Law, convention, and custom determine what does and does not count as property and shape the transactions in which people acquire and dispose of property. While practical reason can and should constrain property-related rules, there is still substantial latitude for different communities to craft morally appropriate structures and practices.

In Part I, I elaborate on the idea that a community's property system is contingent, rooted in communal norms, rules, and institutions, and that it is designed to benefit the community and reasonable to the extent that it does so. In Part II, I suggest that a range of underlying rationales serve as touchstones for a just property system: autonomy, compensation, generosity, productivity, reliability, stewardship, and identity. In Part III, I emphasize that, while a property system is contingent, the requirements of practical reason and the underlying rationales for property rights constrain the property rules a community can reasonably adopt, while leaving communities free to adopt a variety of arrangements in light of their circumstances and priorities. I offer an overview of my arguments in Part IV.

I Property regimes as contingent but constrained social strategies

While some system of property rights will be necessary in most circumstances, this is not because any single system is an inescapable requirement of justice. Rather, a community's system of property rights is justified to the extent that it serves the well being of the community's members and acknowledges the importance of several overlapping rationales for such rights. "Property should be in a certain sense common, but, as a general rule, private," Aristotle wrote, suggesting that separate property rights could and should serve the benefit of the community: "for, when everyone has a distinct interest, men will not complain of one another, and they will make more progress, because every one will be attending

32

to his own business. And yet by reason of goodness, and in respect of use, 'Friends,' as the proverb says, 'will have all things common.'"[1] It will not do simply to inquire about the fairness of particular features of particular transactions, considered in the abstract. Rather, property norms and rules must be crafted with the good of interdependent persons-in-community in mind.[2]

The fact that explicit rules and implicit conventions shape property rights in each community and that these rights are warranted to the extent that they benefit the community's members – as particular persons and in the course of their relationships and shared projects – is a function of the *roots* of property.[3] The land and tangible objects that are our focal instances of property did not arrive in the world with title deeds attached.[4] In significant part, constrained but contingent rules and conventions were (and still are) *necessary* to govern their acquisition and distribution. The operation of these rules and conventions does not amount, then, to a disruption of a purportedly natural property system; rather, it provides a valuable foundation for a complete, well-functioning scheme of property rights.

II Rationales for property rights

The structure of a just property system reflects sensitivity to a variety of distinct but mutually reinforcing and overlapping values. These values can be understood as *rationales* for the system.[5] From another perspective, they can be seen as pointing to different sorts of *interests* someone might be thought to have in a piece of property. From yet another, because a system that ignored one or more of these values would be incomplete, they can be seen as *constraints* on any just property regime. Thus, they may also be seen as *factors (i)* which members of a community might

[1] ARISTOTLE, POLITICS II.5 (Benjamin Jowett trans., 1905). The Aristotelian tradition seems to me to be right that there is good reason to treat much property as ultimately everyone's but in need of allocation. But a property rights regime will satisfactorily reflect the significance of a number of the underlying rationales that rightly shape such regimes only if it treats many property interests as sufficiently sticky that the conception of property as, at root, common will rarely figure reasonably in case-by-case deliberation.
[2] *See* JOHN FINNIS, NATURAL LAW AND NATURAL RIGHTS 169–71 (1980).
[3] Which means *neither* that they serve some imagined collective rather than particular persons, *nor* that, given the aptness of a set of property rules, it is consistently appropriate to reevaluate *particular* transactions in light of their consequences.
[4] *Cf.* FINNIS, LAW, *supra* note 2, at 187 n.30.
[5] *Cf. id.* at 170 ("the explanation of social institutions, and of the terms appropriate for talking about them, is primarily a matter of grasping their rationale").

consider when assessing the justice of their property regime, *or (ii)* which they might weigh or prioritize when refining their property rules and conventions, *or (iii)* which a court might take into account (in light of the relevant community's weights and priorities) when deciding a particular property-related dispute.

I focus here on seven such values: autonomy, compensation, generosity, productivity, reliability, stewardship, and identity. A community's property rules and the resolutions of individual property disputes within a community will be reasonable to the extent that they take account of the various values in light of the principles of practical reasonableness. These values are obviously relevant to individual property claims. However, acknowledging the force of the reliability rationale, in particular (along, probably, with the autonomy and stewardship rationales), will generally mean taking the various rationales directly into account in shaping a community's *system* of property rules, rather than in adjudicating individual cases. None of the rationales warrants belief in absolute property rights, though several can ground quite strong protections for people's property interests.

In Sections A through G, I seek briefly to show how these rationales flow from the basic aspects of well being and the basic principles of practical reasonableness, and to outline some of the general constraints imposed on a property system by the various rationales. In Section H, I briefly note the impact of the principles of practical reasonableness on decisions regarding the contours of property rights.

A   Autonomy

In general, a just property system will be one that facilitates people's autonomy – their freedom to determine the contours of their own lives and make major life choices without coercive intrusion. Someone can sometimes reasonably offer the fact that a piece of property does or could help her to maintain her autonomy in support of her claim to the property.[6]

Autonomy is not itself among the fundamental aspects of human well being, but it is nonetheless important because persons are equal and inherently valuable, and because none, therefore, can rightly be expected to live solely "for the benefit and convenience of others."[7] It is an essential

---

[6] *Cf.* 2 GERMAIN G. GRISEZ, THE WAY OF the LORD JESUS: LIVING A CHRISTIAN LIFE 794–95 (1994).

[7] FINNIS, LAW, *supra* note 2, at 261.

prerequisite to the exercise of practical reasonableness and the free development of the self, and it increases the likelihood that each person's flourishing and fulfillment will be enhanced – since people are often, even if not always, especially well situated to gauge what will contribute to their own well being, and since personally chosen commitments and personally owned attachments to particular goods (attachments and commitments they likely understand better than others, and which they will thus likely be best equipped to nourish) help to *determine* the content of their well being.[8]

Primary control over some real and personal property furthers autonomy because it gives one the ability to act with relative independence from others' influence and control, and the capacity to conduct a significant portion of one's life in private, away from their potentially judgmental scrutiny.[9] The rights created by a fair property system serve the appropriate purpose of giving each "owner freedom to expend his own creativity, inventiveness, and undeflected care and attention upon the goods in question, to give him security in enjoying them or investing or developing them, and to afford him the opportunity of exchanging them for some alternative item(s) of property seeming to him more suitable to his life-plan."[10] Property rights matter because they equip people to control their own lives.

The autonomy rationale will establish a presumption against interfering with people's property to the extent that doing so would significantly reduce autonomy. But it does not warrant the use of property rights to interfere with the autonomy of others. Indeed, the value of autonomy might sometimes be served precisely when one person's use of her property is constrained in the interests of someone else's autonomy, or when property is awarded to someone who previously lacked it in a way that enhances her autonomy. (To be sure, adjustments of particular people's property rights, even in the interest of autonomy, may tend to undermine the capacity of autonomous action generally unless they adhere to reasonable, general, public norms and rules.)

B   Compensation

In general, a just property system will be one that makes it possible for people to receive, and likely that they will receive, compensation for the

---

[8] Finnis indicates that "individual autonomy" is "an aspect of human flourishing," FINNIS, LAW, *supra* note 2, at 192; *cf. id.* at 168–69.
[9] *Cf. id.* at 169.   [10] *Id* at 172.

goods and services they provide to others. Someone can sometimes reasonably offer the fact she is entitled to compensation in support of her claim to a piece of property.

Compensation is arguably a requirement of justice *not only* because it gives people incentives to benefit others, and thus fosters productivity (see Section D, *infra*), *but also* because it would be unfair not to reward them for their efforts and contributions. At minimum, if one would expect compensation for one's own efforts in a given situation, one owes it to others in a comparable situation. Compensation may be given in the form of real or personal property or of money. But money must be exchangeable for property or services if it is to be useful.[11] So the practical requirements of fairness and efficiency, and the derivative value of productivity, all make it reasonable for a community's legal system to recognize the importance of compensation and to allow for and, when necessary, require transfers of property in compensation for goods and services or in exchange for money paid, in turn, in compensation for goods and services.

The compensation rationale could warrant a broad range of property rights. On the one hand, it would certainly encourage recognition of people's rights to money or property received in fair compensation for their contribution to some shared activity. On the other hand, it would also provide some support for conferring on squatters and homesteaders rights to property they have improved, developed, maintained, or cultivated.

C   *Generosity*

In general, a just property system will be one that makes it possible for people to be generous. Someone can sometimes reasonably offer the fact that a piece of property does or could help her to be generous in support of her claim to the property.

Generosity is an important aspect of the basic value of friendship and community, and perhaps also the value of religion. To be generous, a person must have some property rights and must be able to transfer these rights.[12] So the need to make room for generosity also helps to shape the contours of a property system. The generosity rationale grounds a

---

[11] *Cf.* STEPHEN R. MUNZER, A THEORY OF PROPERTY 254–91 (1991).

[12] *See* ARISTOTLE, *supra* note 1, at II.5 ("there is the greatest pleasure in doing a kindness or service to friends or guests or companions, which can only be rendered when a man has private property"; "No one, when men have all things in common, will any longer set an example of liberality or do any liberal action; for liberality consists in the use which is made of property").

presumption of legitimacy for uncompensated transfers by gift. It warrants the existence of stable property rights, but it doesn't justify anyone's claim to anything in particular – except, of course, what is given to her, since there would be no point in giving gifts if they couldn't ordinarily be retained and used by the recipients.

D   Productivity

In general, a just property system will be one that facilitates people's contributions to the productivity of a community's economy. Someone can sometimes reasonably offer the fact that her ownership and use of a piece of property does or could contribute to the productivity of a community's economy in support of her claim to the property.

It is clear, often enough, that "the prospect of having something of their own motivates people to work, to invent, and thus to create wealth,"[13] encouraging the efficient and creative use of "natural resources, and the capital resources and consumer durables derivable therefrom."[14] Thus, there is good reason for a community to structure a system that will "give the owner [of a piece of property] first use and enjoyment of it and its fruits."[15] While economic growth can obviously involve destructive and inefficient use of resources, it can clearly enhance opportunities for people to participate in all of the basic aspects of well being. In addition to this general supportive, instrumental relationship between productivity and participation in the dimensions of welfare, fairness will often require wider sharing of resources, and the burdens associated with such sharing can be reduced if communal resources are increased. Further, making more effective use of resources, in a way that enhances productivity, is a prima facie implication of the Efficiency Principle.

Relatively free transferability is probably an implication of the productivity rationale. This is so both because transferability will help each piece of property to find its most efficient use and because the freedom to transfer will tend to increase the value to the owner of a given item of property and therefore her investment in its maintenance.

The productivity rationale warrants property rights to the extent that they foster the creation of wealth in a community. Given the negative impact on productivity associated with greater uncertainty on the part of property-owners regarding their holdings, the productivity rationale may

---

[13] Grisez, Living, *supra* note 6, at 794.
[14] Finnis, Law, *supra* note 2, at 170.   [15] *Id.* at 173.

lend support to a presumption in favor of respecting existing holdings. But it might also help, for instance, to justify the reassignment of fallow land from owners of large agricultural estates to peasants to the extent that the peasants were likely to be more productive than absentee landlords.

E Reliability

In general, a just property system will enable people to rely on their reasonable expectation that just property rules will continue in force, that decisions made about individual claims in light of such rules will be respected, and that otherwise just property titles will be respected. Someone can sometimes reasonably offer the fact that she has relied on continued entitlement to a piece of property in support of her claim to the property.

The Golden Rule, the Efficiency Principle and the autonomy, stewardship, and productivity rationales for property all provide good reason for a significant measure of reliability in a property system. Property rights can sometimes be extinguished or reassigned in the interests of justice, but it is important – to ensure fairness, to allow people to plan, and to honor people's attachments and expectations – that this ordinarily happen, if at all, for very good reasons, expressed in comprehensible, accessible, predictable rules.[16] Most people don't like it when their own reasonable expectations are disappointed, and the Golden Rule thus dictates that they show due regard for the expectations of others. Further, if frequent reassignment or extinction were a live possibility, people would be less likely to invest in the enhancement and efficient use of their property. And constant reassignment or extinction of property rights is likely to reduce people's autonomy and their ability to plan and complete personal projects. Thus, the reliability rationale justifies protecting present possessory interests, all other things being equal.

F Stewardship

In general, a just property system will facilitate stewardship – taking good care of property, cultivating and developing it responsibly, and preventing it from falling into disrepair. Someone can sometimes reasonably

---

[16] Charles Fried, who rightly emphasizes the contingent character of specific property rights, nonetheless stresses the importance of maintaining existing rights regimes and not upsetting settled expectations unnecessarily. *See* CHARLES FRIED, MODERN LIBERTY AND the LIMITS OF GOVERNMENT 156–60 (2007); *cf.* MUNZER, *supra* note 11, at 191–226. Concern with *reliability* is related to, though distinguishable from, *reliance*; *cf.* Joseph William Singer, *The Reliance Interest in Property*, 40 STAN. L. REV. 611 (1988).

offer the fact that she is likely to be an effective steward of a piece of property in support of her claim to the property.[17]

If no one in particular is responsible for something, experience suggests that it will likely not be taken care of well. But if someone in particular is responsible for something, especially if she is able to realize – whether in the interest of her own welfare or in that of others – some specific benefits associated with ownership, it is likely to be cared for more effectively than it would be if everyone were responsible for it. The value of stewardship is an implication of both the Golden Rule – since particular things typically benefit people other than their owners, and may in any case do so subsequently – and the Efficiency Principle – since if things are well cared for they will not need to be replaced, and since assigning responsibility for particular things to particular people allows individuals to allocate their time and energy less wastefully.

The stewardship rationale warrants property rights to the extent that they ensure that things are cared for at a satisfactory level. Thus, it will sometimes provide support for the reassignment of title to someone likely to care more effectively for a particular piece of property than the putative owner. But it will also support a stable system of property rights, and therefore count against some reassignments, because people are most likely to care for property when they are able to retain it or to dispose of it at their discretion.

G   Identity

In general, a just property system will take reasonable account of people's identity-constitutive attachments to pieces of property. Someone can sometimes reasonably offer the fact that she has an identity-constitutive attachment to a piece of property in support of her claim to the property.

Some relationships with potential elements of real and personal property deserve protection because they help to constitute people's identities.[18] Margaret Radin's characterization of the link between property and personhood helps us to understand the real, if limited, significance

---

[17] *Cf.* FINNIS, LAW, *supra* note 2, at 170.
[18] *Cf.* MARGARET RADIN, REINTERPRETING PROPERTY 35-71 (1993). In general, property rights are instrumental. But I am inclined to think that there is something to be said for a relatively porous view of selfhood that allows the self to incorporate realities outside the bounds of one's skin. Relationships with persons and institutions can help to constitute the self; so, too, I suggest, can ties with at least some instances of real and personal property.

of such attachments.[19] In Subsection 1, I outline the distinction between personal and fungible property. In Subsection 2, I suggest that someone's interest in a given piece of property will be non-fungible, roughly, to the degree that her relationship with the property is a significant, one might say *identity-constitutive*, attachment. In Subsection 3, I suggest that it is worth taking attachments seriously in virtue of the Integrity Principle and the Golden Rule. In Subsection 4, I note some of the potential implications of regarding identity-constitution as a factor to be considered when determining the disposition of property.

1   Property as fungible and personal

Radin's account builds on the awareness that some kinds of property are fungible while some are not. Money in a bank account is a paradigmatic case of fungible property. Cash moves constantly in and out of banks. No one characteristically notices or cares what particular bills or coins might be involved in particular transactions – if, indeed, bills or coins are involved at all. My bank guarantees that I will have access not to any particular physical objects, but to a certain amount of money. One unit of currency is ordinarily regarded as being no more or less valuable than any other. One can usually replace another without loss. If I surreptitiously remove one unit of currency from your bank account and immediately substitute another, then (ignoring exceptional cases) I have not stolen a thing from you.

Sometimes something is non-fungible, however. It cannot be replaced. The relevant description of such an item, the description under which it is valued and desired and appreciated, will typically incorporate *historical* information. The item has a particular history which is significant in determining its meaning. The lover's claim to *this* wedding ring, the heir's claim to *that* farm, differs from the claim of the jeweler or the real estate speculator. It is possible to be mistaken about such claims: the discovery that I have misidentified a ring, or misremembered the location of a family farm on which I grew up but from which I have long been absent, changes the meaning of the ring or the farm in question: it may cause my interest to dissipate in a flash.[20]

---

[19] *See id.* at 35–71.

[20] My interest, that is, in the misidentified object, though not in the ring or farm with which I *intend* to be concerned. Thanks to Margaret Radin for the examples: *see* RADIN, *supra* note 18.

2   Non-fungible property as identity-constitutive

In the cases I have imagined, the property is non-fungible. Part of what matters to the owner is that it be the thing it is, with the particular history it has, and not something else. And in each case, we can say that the owner is attached to the property, that it is attached to her, that it is *part* of her. Non-fungible, identity-constitutive property is strictly irreplaceable, and, if it is alienated, the owner suffers a significant loss that is not monetarily compensable.

What makes a piece of property identity-constitutive is not that one *feels* a certain way about it but that it plays a significant role in shaping who one actually *is*, just as a relationship with another person, with an activity, or with a region or community can do. The identity-constitutive role that a non-fungible piece of property plays in a person's life is grounded in her history in particular ways. I might, to continue with the earlier example, be given another ring – indeed, many other rings – but none of them will be *that* ring, with the particular history it has and the particular links it has to my history. But the loss will also be significant, varying with the degree to which the property in question is identity-constitutive.

3   Grounds for the identity rationale

The notion that some property can be identity-constitutive reflects the attractiveness of an account of the self like that of Raziel Abelson: "one's self," he suggests, "is what one identifies oneself with, what a person cares most about, the loss of which amounts, for him, to self-destruction, either partial or total."[21] The self need not be *bounded* by the body. Certainly other things could play important roles in constituting our identities.

Identity-constitutive attachments may, of course, be unreasonable; and they must be assessed in light of the principles of practical reasonableness. But the Integrity Principle encourages us to give reasonable weight to identity-constitutive attachments. Such attachments matter because they help to make us who we are, and because they help to shape rational planning that gives our lives coherence and intelligibility. And if practical reason means honoring one's own commitments and attachments, the Golden Rule requires that we show reasonable respect to those of others, including their commitments and attachments to their property.

[21] RAZIEL ABELSON, PERSONS: A STUDY IN PHILOSOPHICAL PSYCHOLOGY 91 (1977).

4   The implications of recognizing the significance of identity-constitution.

Acknowledging the significance of identity-constitutive relationships with property[22] can serve to strengthen some property claims and weaken others. When, for instance, two claimants both seek title to the same piece of property, it seems reasonable to suppose that a claimant for whom the property is fungibly valuable should often be less entitled to the property, all other things being equal, than one for whom it is identity-constitutive. By contrast, acknowledging the significance of identity-constitution may sometimes provide particular reason for protecting the privacy of the home to the extent that a person's home *is* integrated tightly with her personhood.

The absence of an identity-constitutive relationship between a person and a piece of property means that the property is, for her, fungible. Thus, for instance, she has less reason than she would if it were non-fungible to object to its court-ordered sale at market rates. And recognizing the special significance of identity-constitutive relationships with property might undermine limitations on commercial owners' rights to exclude others who wish to use their property to engage in public expressive activity: most commercial property is *not* identity-constitutive, and to the extent that it is not, there is perhaps some reason to think that rights in such property ought to be protected less rigorously than ones in personal residential property.[23]

The identity rationale for property can serve to strengthen people's claims to property they hold on other grounds. But it can also provide some independent justification for recognizing people's rights to property they do not already hold. It might thus, for instance, provide some support for squatters' and homesteaders' rights, and some basis for giving at least limited weight to the interests of residential tenants in their homes.[24]

Practical reason offers some justification for treating identity-constitution as a distinct rationale for property rights. People have identity-constitutive attachments to pieces of property, and protecting those attachments is a matter of showing regard for their identities and for their capacities for agency. That a piece of property is identity-constitutive does not automatically trump appeals framed with reference to the other rationales for property rights, which may tug in other directions. However, the special importance of people's non-fungible, identity-constitutive interests suggests that these interests should receive

[22] *See* RADIN, *supra* note 18, at 57.
[23] *See id.* at 68–69.   [24] *See id.* at 59–63.

meaningful weight when they come into conflict with fungible property rights.[25] At the same time, to the extent that a given piece of property does not play an identity-constitutive role in the life of the current owner, her claim to the property itself (as opposed to its monetary value) will be proportionately weaker.

H The impact of the practical principles

These diverse, overlapping factors do not yield a calculus that can determine just what property rights there should be, how strong they should be, which others they should trump, and by which others they are likely to be overridden.[26] There is no rational way of commensurating the goods realized by different schemes of property rights. Communities can reasonably make decisions about property norms, rules, and institutions in light of their own judgments and priorities.[27] A relatively broad range of standards regarding the acquisition, retention, abandonment, forfeiture, deprivation, and voluntary transfer of property may be consistent with the principles of practical reasonableness and respectful of the multiple rationales for property rights. Thus, there is no one right set of property rules.

At the same time, not only the rationales but also the principles of practical reasonableness will constrain the number of possible systems. In accordance with the Pauline Principle, systemic features cannot reasonably be endorsed or sustained out of hostility, for instance. Those defining and applying legal norms will need to take proper account of the Efficiency Principle as well as particular communal commitments that might implicate the Integrity Principle. And, of course, in accordance with the Golden Rule, it will be vital for people to ask, when endorsing general norms or resolving particular disputes, whether they themselves could live with the costs and risks their decisions impose on others.

III The limits of property

Taken together, the various rationales for property rights justify the existence of a property system and constrain the contours of such a system. The characteristics of the property system in a given community will be

---

[25] See id. at 71.   [26] Cf. MUNZER, supra note 11, at 292–314.

[27] See John Finnis, Commensuration and Practical Reason, in INCOMMENSURABILITY, INCOMPARABILITY, AND PRACTICAL REASON 215, 225–28 (Ruth Chang ed., 1997). This will essentially take the form of a Golden Rule test.

shaped by that community's norms, rules, and institutions, which must, in turn, respect the principles of practical reasonableness and acknowledge the force of the various rationales for property rights.

While property regimes are to some extent contingent and conventional, a just property system will almost certainly feature certain elements. The rationales provide very strong reason for the existence of stable property rights (Section A). Communal legal systems consistent with the principles of practical reasonableness will not confer monopoly privileges or sanction workplace subordination (Section B). They will acknowledge rights of immediate emergency use or consumption of others' property (Section C). And they will provide for transfer of title when property is underutilized or actually abandoned (Section D).

A   The requirement that there be dependable property rights

All of the various rationales make the maintenance of some kind of property rights regime eminently reasonable. And concerns related to autonomy, compensation, generosity, reliability, and identity – as well, perhaps, as generosity – will all give a community good reason to create a network of property rights that functions in part as a *given* from the perspective of the legal system. Respect for these basic values will impose limits on the extent to which it is just or reasonable for morally responsible persons, communities, or institutions to interfere with these rights. Whether particular rights are vested in persons, families, or other groups will be a function of each community's legal system, though there is clearly good reason for a legal system to limit authority over and responsibility for particular pieces of property.

B   The preclusion of monopolies and workplace abuses

A reasonable set of property rules will preclude the abuse of property rights. Thus, it will rule out the use of legal authority to create monopolies, which simultaneously increase costs to members of the public to the benefit of the monopolists – thus violating both the Golden Rule and the Efficiency Principle – and interfere substantially with potential competitors' autonomous and creative use of their property. And it will not sanction people's employment of property rights to dominate workers or to treat them unfairly.[28]

---

[28]   *Cf.* Chapter 3, *infra*.

C   Need-based claims to others' property

In virtue of the Golden Rule, property systems will recognize that what might otherwise qualify as theft might be permissible under emergency circumstances – a point made with great bluntness by St. Thomas Aquinas. St. Thomas emphasizes that a property system is designed to meet human needs, and therefore does not serve its own purpose if it keeps people's needs from being met. Thus, when a need is

> so manifest and urgent, that it is evident that the present need must be remedied by whatever means be at hand (for instance when a person is in some imminent danger, and there is no other possible remedy), then it is lawful for a man to succor his own need by means of another's property, by taking it either openly or secretly: nor is this properly speaking theft or robbery.[29]

Similarly, John Locke is clear that "charity gives every man a title to so much out of another's plenty, as will keep him from extreme want, where he has no means to subsist otherwise."[30] Obviously, unpredictable claims on others' property can be disruptive not only to individual lives but to a community's system of property rights. But a property system can preclude such claims in cases of great need only if it ignores the Golden Rule and the underlying point of property rights.

D   Claims based on abandonment and underutilization

Just property rules will also likely acknowledge the legitimacy of some claims by homesteaders and squatters to abandoned or unowned property. This will reflect the importance of the Golden Rule and of the compensation, productivity, stewardship, and identity rationales for property, in light of all of which it seems reasonable to acknowledge the efforts of those who homestead and the value of encouraging their contribution to the creation of communal wealth.

Given the importance of reliability, there will obviously be reason not to acknowledge every claim based on homesteading and squatting. But a system which tended on the whole to, for instance, confer on large

---

[29] THOMAS AQUINAS, SUMMA THEOLOGIÆ II-II q. 94 a. 7c (Fathers of the English Dominican Province trans., 2d ed., 1920).

[30] JOHN LOCKE, FIRST TREATISE OF GOVERNMENT ch. IV, §42 (1689). To be clear, Locke's concern here is to show that no one "could ever have a just power over the life of another by right of property in land or possessions"; and there is nothing here to show that he necessarily believed that a poor person could enforce the right in question as a matter of self-help.

landowners the right to withhold uncultivated property from the market and to deny homesteaders access to such land would be at odds with the well being of the community, and the maintenance of such a system would likely prove inconsistent with the Golden Rule. (There is no reason for a community's legal system to regard deliberate conservation and consequent non-development of land as underutilization in this sense.) Such a system would tend to undermine productivity and it would also seem to condone disregard for the importance of stewardship. Thus, squatters' and homesteaders' interests clearly do deserve some recognition in communities' property rights regimes.

IV   Property and justice

Systems of property rights are constrained by the principles of practical reasonableness and the basic aspects of welfare. But they can still take many forms. Just what their characteristics might be in a given community will be a function of that community's norms, rules, and institutions.

Property regimes are contingent but constrained social strategies designed to yield a variety of communal benefits. A range of factors – autonomy, compensation, generosity, productivity, reliability, stewardship, and identity – help to provide rationales for a just system of property rights, as well as for individual property claims within such a system, and to limit the system's possible contours. The identity rationale provides some reason to recognize a special class of identity-constitutive property that cannot, at least not as easily, be treated, like other property, as fungible.

Provided they conform to the requirements of practical reasonableness and acknowledge the force of these rationales, different property systems can qualify as alternative, but reasonable, responses to the demands of justice. What matters is not that all communities' property systems take the same form but that – however personal, group, or community property is defined – property systems reasonably serve people's well being, take reasonable account of all the relevant overlapping rationales that underlie property rights, and provide the regularity and predictability economic actors need in order to plan. Communities can certainly affirm legal norms that do not afford their members with undisturbable rights. But rights should be constrained in a manner consistent with general rules rather than with arbitrary or ad hoc individual decisions.

A property system is necessarily dynamic. Property is constantly distributed and redistributed through innumerable personal and institutional transactions. In Chapter 2, I seek to clarify the demands of justice with regard to these transactions.

2

Foundations: distribution

Justice in distribution is fundamentally a responsibility of particular persons. Each time we buy, sell, give, retain, or receive goods or services, we either respect the requirements of justice or we do not. Criteria of justice in distribution reflect the implications of the basic principles of practical reasonableness and the character of property rights as justified by their contributions to well being.

Practical reasonableness does not require any overall pattern of wealth distribution. Neither particular persons nor organizations nor communal institutions have any duty to envision and implement an overall distributional pattern, and the responsibility to promote economic security and address the problem of poverty does not flow from any such imagined duty. Rather, each person has a general distributive duty which communal norms, rules, and institutions may help her to perform. This obligation is to *treat as a public trust* resources one does not need in order to fulfill specific duties and which one cannot reasonably use to participate in authentic aspects of well being through personal consumption.

In Part I, I seek to show how the criteria of justice in distribution flow from the principles of practical reasonableness. In Part II, I highlight the implications of these criteria for our responsibilities to contribute to communal projects and assist other people. I recap my arguments in Part III.

I Distribution and practical reasonableness

People have responsibilities to themselves, to other individuals in interpersonal relationships, and as participants in cooperative ventures with others. But the economy of a community as a whole is not, and could not be, a single cooperative venture managed by a realistically conceivable finite intelligence. Thus, it is a mistake to think of justice in distribution as a matter of determining the overall shape or magnitude of the economy. No individual person or organized cooperative group is morally responsible for the overall shape of wealth distribution in the economy of a community, nor is anyone responsible for shaping her own personal choices *for the purpose* of creating a particular overall wealth distribution. But that does not mean that economic actors are simply responsible for their own well being. Justice (or injustice) can't be predicated of the distribution of wealth as a whole, of the actions of some imagined single actor parceling out the contents of the economy. It is, however, a property of the actions of particular persons. Each person has responsibilities to distribute her wealth justly.

In Section A, I explicate the notion that justice is something with which each person has reason to be concerned. In Section B, I attempt to show how multiple criteria of justice in distribution flow from the requirements of practical reasonableness.

A   Justice as a personal responsibility

Justice in distribution is the responsibility of particular persons.[1] This does not mean that individuals should be expected unilaterally to bring about just end-states or to take personal responsibility for the overall level or distribution of wealth in their community. However, they ought to acknowledge the just claims of others and just limits on their own choices. Thus, they will have good reason to support just systems of separate property rights. At the same time, they will recognize that they cannot conform their conduct to the norms of justice in distribution simply by upholding the putative rights acknowledged by the legal system of their community, even if the acknowlegments of these rights is itself consistent with the demands of justice.

Property is not, per se, a basic aspect of well being; it is instrumentally valuable. In general, it serves to *further* people's participation in the various dimensions of well being. So both the underlying rationale for a just property system and specific requirements of practical reasonableness, including the Golden Rule and the Efficiency Principle, render it unreasonable for someone to claim that her property rights entitle her to do whatever she pleases with her property and excuse her from concern for other people or shared communal projects.[2] Someone who holds a valuable asset acts unreasonably if she simultaneously keeps it from playing a role in the market and does not use it herself.[3] Similarly, justice precludes unproductive speculation, the failure to maintain valuable assets,

[1] *See* John Finnis, Natural Law and Natural Rights 185–88 (1980).
[2] *See* 3 Germain G. Grisez, The Way of the Lord Jesus: Difficult Moral Questions 504 (1997).
[3] *See* Finnis, Law, *supra* note 1, at 172.

and the forcible exclusion of others from the market (as by tariffs and the creation of professional licensing cartels and others sorts of monopolies or oligopolies), among other practices that preclude the fulfillment of the legitimate purposes of the property system.[4]

More broadly, practical reasonableness places a fluid and imprecise limit on the property and wealth one can rightly use just for one's own benefit and that of one's dependents or business partners. One has a responsibility to use resources in excess of this limit – I'll call it the *public trust threshold* – to benefit other people or to support valuable communal projects.[5] One may fulfill one's responsibility to use wealth in excess of the threshold appropriately "by investing … in [the] production of more goods for later distribution and consumption; by providing gainful employment to people looking for work; by grants or loans for hospitals, schools, cultural centres, orphanages, etc., or directly for the relief of the poor." And communal norms and rules may reasonably facilitate owners' performance of these duties.[6] The location of the threshold is particular to each person, and requires a good-faith judgment about the requirements of practical reasonableness, though communities may make reasonable assumptions about people's responsibilities and articulate expectations regarding their support of other people and shared projects accordingly.

Communities can reasonably expect that their members will participate – in accordance with the principles of practical reasonableness and the standards of justice in distribution they imply – in the process of helping others and supporting shared goods. But while communal norms may reasonably call for shared support of common projects, people's duties in justice in distribution are logically prior to any enunciation of a community's distributive expectations. Thus, the failure of the members of a community in general to support norms of justice in distribution does not absolve particular persons of responsibility for acting in distributively just ways. Of course, because of the incommensurability of the basic aspects of well being and the incoherence of the notion of a "greatest overall good," the partial subjectivity of the Golden Rule test, the context-specificity and goal-dependence of the Efficiency Principle's implications in particular situations, and so forth, there will typically be numerous ways in which any person can meet the demands of justice in distribution.

---

[4] *See id.* at 172–73.   [5] *See id.* at 173.

[6] *Cf. id.* The relevant norms and rules might be enforced using multiple mechanisms, including, but not limited to, public shaming, the use of certification systems, coordinated boycotts, and a variety of informal but real and effective norm maintenance stratgies.

If persons are individually responsible for meeting the demands of justice in distribution by sharing or investing resources beyond the public trust threshold, then this means that each individual has a derivative responsibility as well – to avoid shirking in ways that increase the burdens of those who are attempting to comply with these demands. The Golden Rule surely requires that one avoid contributing at such a level that others who are attempting to be responsible will be expected to give excessively. Communal norms, and other persons, may thus rightly call for people to donate or invest resources at a reasonable level in support of individuals and groups in need of help, and of various valuable projects.[7]

B   Criteria of justice in distribution

There is no algorithm that will determine definitively whether an action of a given type will count as an instance of justice in distribution in a given situation.[8] But several factors are relevant, including need, function, commitments and attachments, efficiency, capacity, reward, productivity, and the creation or anticipation and acceptance of avoidable risks, and the avoidance of unreasonable harm.

The criteria of justice in distribution point first toward distributional responsibilities that will be fulfilled using resources that fall below the public trust threshold. Indeed, one's public trust threshold is defined with reference to the resources one cannot reasonably use to further one's own participation in the basic aspects of well being. Unavoidably, these criteria overlap with the underlying rationales that constrain a just property system and the corresponding interests particular persons, organizations, and communities might have in individual items of property. But the requirements of justice in distribution are not alternatives or supplements to the rationales for property or the requirements of

---

[7] Thanks to an anonymous reviewer for helping me to see this point.

[8] By speaking about "justice in distribution," I am deliberately avoiding taking a position regarding the analytical distinction between "distributive" and "commutative" justice; see FINNIS, LAW, *supra* note 1, at 165–84. "Justice in distribution" as I conceive of it here includes those elements of distributive and commutative justice that are directly related to the transfer of property and money. It also includes both what Nicholas Wolterstorff terms "primary justice" and what he labels "rectifying justice"; see NICHOLAS WOLTERSTORFF, JUSTICE: RIGHTS AND WRONGS at ix (2008). I am inclined to share Finnis's judgment that "[t]he effort to understand and work with the distinctions – say, between 'distributive' and 'commutative' – sheds little light on the substantive issues of justice." JOHN FINNIS, AQUINAS: MORAL, POLITICAL, and LEGAL THEORY 188 (1998).

practical reasonableness. Rather, they serve as pointers to what practical reason requires given the nature of well being and the deliverances of experience.

Several of the criteria of distributive justice flow from the Golden Rule: need; function; commitments like those to family members, friends, and those to whom one has made promises; efficiency; capacity; reward; the encouragement of productivity; risk acceptance; and the avoidance of harm.[9] Declining to cause harm purposefully or instrumentally is, of course, mandated by the Pauline Principle. Treating function, capacity, reward, the encouragement of productivity, risk acceptance, and, perhaps, need as criteria of justice in distribution also receives support from the Efficiency Principle, as, of course, does the distributional criterion of efficiency itself. Giving distributional weight to function and to our commitments and attachments is part of what it means to respect the Integrity Principle. Individual aspects of well being also help to generate distributional responsibilities: the fact that friendship is a basic dimension of welfare, for instance, is among the factors that render consistent with the Golden Rule the acceptance of special distributive obligations that not only permit but even, sometimes, require partiality.

1   Need

The Golden Rule requires us to assist others just because of their vulnerability to our actions, when we can readily do so; it is unreasonable to show "indifference to the good of others whom one could easily help."[10] For instance: a golfer confronted with a drowning child "has a moral obligation to interrupt his game to save the child."[11] Of course none of us wishes to be simply a component of the universal satisfaction system, or to be devoured by the needs of others, so none of us would expect it, in fairness, of anyone else. Thus, the Golden Rule, which builds on our expectations of each other, is best understood as requiring moderate, rather than overwhelming, beneficence.[12] At the same time, the failure

---

[9] *Cf.* 2 Germain G. Grisez, The Way of the Lord Jesus: Living a Christian Life 328 (1994).

[10] Finnis, Law, *supra* note 1, at 107.

[11] Robert P. George, In Defense of Natural Law 95 (2001).

[12] This is a point recognized by other moral theories that employ versions of the Golden Rule, or one of its cousins. They characteristically spell out the responsibility to offer aid in a way that tends to agree, at least in this way, with a plausible natural law understanding of this implication of the Golden Rule's non-arbitrariness requirement. *Cf.* Onora

to respond to the needs of those one *can* easily help is clearly inconsistent with the demands of practical reasonableness.

2   Function

It is reasonable to allocate resources to people in light of their *functions* within associations and institutions.[13] This is a reflection of the importance of, at least, the Golden Rule – both in ensuring that, for the benefit of everyone in a community or an association, communal roles are performed and in recompensing those who perform these roles; the Efficiency Principle – to the extent that it is served by specialization (which of course it sometimes is not); and regard for the basic aspect of well being that is *community* – to the extent that a community depends upon people's assumption of specific operational roles. This may be a matter of transferring to them ownership – especially if the point is to compensate them – or control – if they can act effectively on behalf of the association or institution.

3   Commitments and attachments

Commitments and attachments – our own and, in virtue of the Golden Rule, other people's – shape distributional choices because of the respect for both reflected in the Integrity Principle. They are also relevant because of the Golden Rule's requirement that we honor promises and relationships of dependence and vulnerability.

All sorts of commitments matter for justice in distribution – from ordinary commercial contracts, both implicit and explicit, to commitments made to ourselves to pursue particular life-plans, to the open-ended promises of faithfulness exchanged by life-partners. Once made, a reasonable commitment affects one's distributional responsibilities.

> In light of a reasonable personal ... commitment I have made, it may be perfectly reasonable for me to treat, and, indeed, it may be patently unreasonable for me to fail to treat, certain basic values or certain possible instantiations of a single basic value as superior to others in their directive force (for me). Choosing in harmony with one's past reasonable commitments, and, thus, establishing or maintaining one's personal integrity ... constitutes an important moral reason which often guides our choices between rationally grounded options.[14]

O'NEILL, TOWARDS JUSTICE AND VIRTUE: A CONSTRUCTIVE ACCOUNT OF PRACTICAL REASON 196–200 (1996); T. M. SCANLON, WHAT WE OWE TO EACH OTHER 224 (1998).
[13] *See* FINNIS, LAW, *supra* note 1, at 175.   [14] GEORGE, DEFENSE, *supra* note 11, at 94.

Thus, actions fulfilling reasonable commitments or honoring reasonable attachments can be distributively just even though they do not treat all possible beneficiaries of one's actions equally.

4   Efficiency

The Efficiency Principle obligates each actor to choose efficient means for the achievement of her goals, and requires that those engaged in a cooperative venture do the same. And adhering to the Golden Rule means making efficient use of goods and services that are or could be shared. Thus, taken in tandem, these principles entail the requirement that we contribute to the shaping of communal norms, rules, and institutions in ways that render them as efficient as possible (given, obviously, their multiple purposes and the multiple constraints on the achievement of these purposes).

They also require that we *consume* efficiently. When aspects of welfare are pursued inefficiently, resources and time that could be used for their benefit are wasted; others may reasonably object that they could have benefited had one acted with greater efficiency. Suppose I can meet the same objective more or less efficiently, with no meaningful loss with respect to other aspects of well being, and that meeting it more efficiently lowers my public trust threshold. In this case, if I give appropriate consideration to the benefits others will reap if I am more efficient, I have good reason to chose the more efficient over the less efficient option.[15]

Thus, for instance, someone who is not committed to being a collector[16] might reasonably buy a *print* of a painting rather than an original – thus furthering her own and others' æsthetic experience efficiently. Someone might reasonably frequent a café as a comfortable place in which to write and think, or to socialize; but she would likely be consuming inefficiently if she purchased a drink there out of force of habit, seeking neither to write and think nor to engage with friends.

5   Capacity

Efficiency, fairness, and regard for the particular aspects of well being that can be realized through specialized activity all make it reasonable to base some distributional decisions on people's *capacities*.[17] For instance: those who make decisions about how the resources of an institution that educates health care providers are spent will ordinarily be *fairest* to those

---

[15] *See* GRISEZ, QUESTIONS, *supra* note 2, at 808.
[16] *Cf. id.* at 840–44.   [17] *See* FINNIS, LAW, *supra* note 1, at 175.

served by the institution if they devote those resources to preparing health care providers selected in light of their ability to deliver these services, rather than on nepotistic grounds.[18] And limited resources will be spent more *efficiently* to the extent that the institution uses capacity as a guide to admission (though it is, of course, no more a trump than any of the other criteria),[19] since fewer resources will often be required to educate a more capable student to a given level of competence.

6   Reward

Taking desert or merit seriously as a feature of justice in distribution is a function of, at least, the practical requirement of fairness and the value of friendship.[20] At minimum, the basic equality of persons and the prevalent psychological preference for reciprocity in social relations – which one must apply to others as well as to oneself – suggest that "the meaning and effect of the Golden Rule includes the thought[] that one good turn deserves another . . . ."[21] And "the friendliness that is expressed by manifested gratitude is a great human good, for both giver and receiver."[22] Acknowledging others' desert and the value of compensating them for their work is thus a reasonable basis for distributional decisions.

7   Productivity

We have good reason to distribute resources in ways that will encourage *productivity* (given, of course, that what is being produced is valuable and that a higher production level would be more valuable). The increased availability of goods and services is widely beneficial: if there are more of them, they will often be easier to obtain and less costly. Seeking this kind of benefit seems to be a matter of adherence to the Golden Rule: one would doubtless want similar benefits from others. And encouraging

---

[18] *See id.*

[19] It does not seem to me that the Golden Rule would necessarily prevent an educational institution from (*i*) admitting less qualified children of former students (*a*) in order to secure donations that will enhance its programs or (*b*) as an expression of loyalty to and solidarity with alums, or from (*ii*) taking membership in disfranchised groups into account in admission decisions (*a*) to respond to applicants' needs, (*b*) to contribute to its community's well being, or (*c*) to compensate for past discrimination on its part. Doing either of these things would make sense only, of course, within the limits imposed by the institution's indirect responsibility to those whom its graduates will serve.

[20] *See id.*; FINNIS, AQUINAS, *supra* note 8, at 196.

[21] FINNIS, AQUINAS, *supra* note 8, at 197. This kind of Golden Rule analysis provides no license for revenge, since the Pauline Principle precludes acting out of hostility.

[22] FINNIS, LAW, *supra* note 1, at 175.

productivity may also, though not necessarily, be a way of encouraging efficiency.

We often benefit our communities when we incentivize others to be productive.[23] But perhaps someone might argue that we ought to incentivize ourselves to be productive as well. To be sure, the fact that I am able to consume may sometimes be a useful spur to my productivity, which in turn benefits other persons and shared projects. Nonetheless, it seems obvious that thinking in this way will often serve, if unchecked by other principles, as a license for unreasonable behavior. So this kind of reasoning must play, at best, a limited role in one's determination of one's own responsibilities in justice.

8   Risk

Expecting those who create or deliberately accept *risks* to bear the costs associated with those risks is a matter of following both the Golden Rule and the Efficiency Principle.[24] It is a matter of following the Golden Rule because most people would resent being held responsible for harms they did not cause and over which they had little or no control. It is a matter of following the Efficiency Principle because arranging a common task or enterprise so that loss is distributed this way will increase incentives to avoid it (up to whatever level is reasonable) and assign the risk to a party effectively situated to prevent the loss.

9   Avoidance of harm

It would be a violation of the Pauline Principle to distribute goods or services for the purpose of causing harm to a basic aspect of well being. And it would be a violation of the Golden Rule to do so in a manner that caused harm unfairly to others or that imposed an unfair risk of harm on others. To the extent that causing harm is a result or a cause of inefficiency, distributing goods or services in a way that results in harm may also violate the Efficiency Principle.

II   Commercial exchange and justice in distribution

A principal means by which goods and services are distributed when people have separate property rights is commercial exchange. The decision to offer or accept contract terms must comport with the principles

---

[23] *Id.* at 170, 173; *cf.* FINNIS, AQUINAS, *supra* note 8, at 190 (noting "the incentive-based advantages which make ownership useful and necessary").

[24] See FINNIS, LAW, *supra* note 1, at 174–75.

of practical reasonableness. In particular, it must be consistent with the Golden Rule (though not, of course, only with the Golden Rule). Thus, for example, a commercial agreement may be unjust if the process leading to the conclusion of the agreement involves decisions inconsistent with the Golden Rule, or if acceptance of the agreement's outcome would contravene the Golden Rule (Section A). Alternatively, the agreement's terms may strongly suggest that it is, in another sense, unjust – because the background conditions of the exchange embody or result from injustice – even though the actual traders may do nothing unjust, and may be entitled to behave as they have (Section B). Justice in pricing is a function of both individual choices and background social conditions (Section C).

A   Process, outcome and market price

The *process* by which a commercial agreement is reached must be consistent with the requirements of practical reasonableness and so with the various criteria of justice in distribution (Subsection 1). And the distinguishable choice to *accept the agreement's terms* must itself be reasonable (Subsection 2). Whether a trader is offering or accepting terms similar to those which others in her market-space are offering or accepting is not necessarily relevant to the fairness of her offer (Subsection 3).

1   Process

Whether a commercial transaction is conducted reasonably is a separate question from whether accepting the outcome of the transaction is reasonable. Thus, for instance, a seller might lie about a product's merits before selling it at an objectively fair price – say, barely above cost. Had the buyer been fully aware of the product's qualities, she might have had no reason to object to the price. But she could still reasonably object to the seller's deception.

Fairness requires that one trader not take advantage of a significant difference in bargaining power between herself and another trader – whether acquired through deception or economic advantage – to press terms on the other. Whether the terms are themselves reasonable matters, but so does the simple fact of having been forced or manipulated. For, at minimum, the offeror would not likely wish to be compelled or coerced into accepting an agreement, and so should not compel the offeree to do so.

Perhaps what the seller has to offer is needed immediately to ensure the buyer's economic survival or physical safety, or perhaps it is a non-fungible item of great importance to the buyer but not to the seller. Perhaps, alternatively, the seller is a participant in a monopoly. In any case, if the seller is aware of a relevant and significant inequality in bargaining power, she acts inconsistently with the Golden Rule if she uses this inequality to *force* an outcome. What will count as forcing, of course, will be the use of tactics and bargaining advantages she would – on honest, self-critical reflection – regard as unreasonable were she their target.

2   Outcome

Even if traders bargain without compulsion, accepting some trading *outcomes* may be unreasonable. For instance, sometimes when a trader is aware of pressing need for something essential she has to sell, fairness might require that she sell at, or perhaps even below, cost. For she herself would want her special need to be considered when she confronted desperate circumstances. In any event, the trader will need to ask whether she would regard the terms as objectionable if roles were reversed (and also, of course, whether accepting them meets the other requirements of practical reasonableness).

3   The relevance of market price

The issue of whether an individual trader's acceptance of a commercial agreement's terms is reasonable typically arises only when she is aware that the *process* leading to the agreement has been unfair *or* that her trading partner's special circumstances would make accepting certain terms unfair. Absent such awareness, traders are entitled to assume that their trading partners have reasonable market power and do not desperately need the products or services being sold or the profits from the transactions. Given this assumption, traders do not act unfairly by seeking to sell for as much as possible and buy for as little as possible. Presuming that a good or service is an instance of, or conduces to participation in, a basic aspect of well being, and presuming it is the sort of thing it is appropriate to buy or sell at all (as art is and friendship is not), then it is worth buying.[25] But how much it is worth to the buyer and the seller will vary with their circumstances, commitments, and preferences.

Thus, there is no reason for the individual buyer or seller in an otherwise presumptively just transaction to ask or offer for a good or service just what it "would currently fetch ... in deals between any willing sellers

---

[25] Obviously, other principles of practical reason may rule out the purchase of an item that is, in the abstract, priced reasonably. And the fact that it is reasonable to ask a certain price of a given buyer does not mean that the buyer will be able to afford it.

and buyers in the same locality and time-frame, each party being aware of the thing's merits and defects."[26] Trying to determine what price to charge in light of other prices charged in the market in which one is operating seems to lead to a recursion problem. A single seller or buyer can certainly opt to determine what she will ask or offer with reference to the market, and avoid charging more or offering less than others. But the market cannot function effectively if all sellers behave this way. In general, sellers will need to set sale prices in light of their own costs and desires and buyers' willingness to pay, and buyers will need to determine what they will offer in light of their own costs and desires and what sellers will accept.

B   Contract terms as pointers to unjust background conditions

What counts as a just commercial agreement will in one sense be transaction-specific. But there is another sense in which it is possible to say rather more about justice in setting contract terms. That a price diverges significantly from a seller's cost (allowing for the impact of non-coercive scarcity rents) suggests strongly that the background conditions of the relevant transaction are marred by injustice.

Pricing in any given case occurs against a background of property rules, of power relations, of economic conditions, all of which may themselves be more or less just. To the extent that they *are* just, barriers to market entry are minimal, rentiers are not able to extract monopoly profits, capital for entrepreneurial ventures is readily available at low rates, and the kind of manipulative distraction involved in much brand competition is absent. In this case, competition will unavoidably be focused on price and, under focused competitive pressure, *price* will tend toward *cost*. And, if workers have not been victimized by unjust dispossession (suffered by themselves or by their ancestors) and are currently able to negotiate freely then – apart from cases in which highly specialized, non-fungible items are involved – it seems apparent that *cost* will tend toward *labor cost*.

In a real-world market, of course, a range of factors will complicate any transaction, so that price will diverge from cost, and cost from labor cost, in a variety of ways. And prices set in light of these divergences need not be set unfairly. But this theoretical model, by highlighting the trajectory of price toward labor cost in a market free from monopolistic domination, provides a further way of giving content to the notion of the just price.

---

[26] FINNIS, AQUINAS, *supra* note 8, at 202 (footnote omitted).

This analytical model does not show that any particular price is significantly affected by background injustice; whether it is or not is, of course, a factual inquiry. The Golden Rule will often demand that people contribute their fare shares of effort or resources or both to remedying background injustices in which they participate. But individually adjusting prices is neither necessary nor often even feasible as a way of remedying these injustices, and it is not reasonable to expect individual traders to charge the prices they would charge had no background injustices occurred (even presuming they could know what prices would be in this case).

Nonetheless, when market prices tend to diverge from labor costs, we have good reason to ask to what extent underlying injustices – rules and background conditions for which no one current market actor is likely responsible – have distorted the relevant market in some way. Because of these distortions and of other factors affecting particular transactions, a justly set price for a good or service may not be straightforwardly identical with the cost of the labor required to produce it; but the more price and labor cost diverge in any transaction, the more we may reasonably wonder whether there is injustice involved – not so much in the setting of the price itself by the individual traders, but in the underlying legal, cultural, social, and political conditions that shape the price.[27]

C   *The just price*

While it is often the object of criticism today, the notion of the just price, deeply rooted in the natural law tradition, continues to be relevant. It is inconsistent with the demands of practical reasonableness to deprive a trading partner of power in a commercial transaction or to accept unfair terms in one's bargain with her. More broadly, while individual traders do not usually act unfairly simply in virtue of failing to adjust asked and offered prices to levels that might be set in an ideal market, the divergence of price from labor cost often points to the likelihood of injustice in the background conditions that shape market relationships. Thus, we may continue reasonably to speak about justice in pricing in two, complementary ways. We may reasonably identify the process leading to an individual commercial agreement, or the terms of the agreement, as just or

---

[27] Many thanks to Kevin Carson for helping me to see the continuing relevance of the mediaeval notion of just price in this way; *see* KEVIN CARSON, STUDIES IN MUTUALIST POLITICAL ECONOMY 67–103 (2007).

unjust. And we may reasonably speak of prices as pointers to background justice or injustice responsible for market conditions.

III   The public trust threshold

Wealth beyond one's public trust threshold must either be given away (individually or through one communal process or another) or invested in ways that yield benefit to other persons or shared projects (not necessarily *needy* in the narrow sense).[28] The criteria of justice in distribution help to determine the location of the public trust threshold. In Section A, I consider how one's public trust threshold might be specified. In Section B, I critically examine the idea that one's public trust threshold might be determined by one's vocation. In Section C, I note some ways of reasonably employing resources in excess of the public trust threshold. I summarize my account of the public trust threshold in Section D.

A   Specifying the public trust threshold

Resources in excess of the public trust threshold are ones (*i*) which are not needed to fulfill specific duties that flow from the criteria of distributive justice, whether to friends, trading partners, or people in need,[29] and (*ii*) which, in accordance with the requirements of practical reasonableness, it is unreasonable to use to further one's own participation in the various aspects of well being.[30]

The principles of practical reasonableness do not yield results with the precision of those a consequentialist calculus could generate, if such a calculus were actually possible. All one can do is ask whether a given choice or set of choices can be seen to involve participation in genuine aspects of well being and whether, if so, the extent of one's participation is inconsistent with the demands of the Golden Rule, the Efficiency Principle, and the other requirements of practical reasonableness.

[28] For the NCNLTs' own judgments about what does and does not fall below this threshold, *see* Gary Chartier, *Consumption, Development Aid, and Natural Law*, 13 WASHINGTON & LEE J. C. R. & SOC. JUST. 205, 224–29 (2007). It is difficult to avoid a sense of arbitrariness here.

[29] *Cf.* FINNIS, AQUINAS, *supra* note 8, at 193–94 (footnotes omitted).

[30] *Cf.* GRISEZ, QUESTIONS, *supra* note 2, at 436–39; GRISEZ, LIVING, *supra* note 9, at 801. This need not mean evaluating each expenditure individually. Rather, it may be reasonable to consider a package of consumption decisions, taken as a whole. Thus, one may fairly trade off some expenditures against others; *see* GRISEZ, QUESTIONS, *supra* note 2, at 427–28.

Thus, for instance, commitments and attachments honored in virtue of the Integrity Principle can help to determine when it is reasonable to spend resources on oneself, on particular other persons, or on causes that might not otherwise have claims on one's loyalty. Someone who has agreed to be a fundraiser for a development NGO might be under a special obligation to avoid creating the fear that donations to the NGO were being wasted on lavish dinners. And a commitment to being a musician might (quite apart from any kind of work agreement) entail the purchase of a high-quality instrument.

Clearly, then, just where the public trust threshold falls for a particular person at a given time "is not rigidly fixed but somewhat elastic";[31] though the relevant decisions can genuinely be in accordance with reason, "reason's 'mean' here is a zone with vague boundaries rather than a point ...."[32] However, it is clear that the pursuit of "religious, moral, and cultural goods"[33] can justify consumption choices, and that resources used to acquire "everything to be used in living a morally good life, ... [including] such things as a good education for ... children, decent recreation, and appropriate gifts to relatives and friends"[34] fall below the public trust threshold.

B   The potential relevance of personal vocation

The principles of practical reasonableness, together with facts about our circumstances and characteristics, seem to offer a complete specification of the moral life, and so of our distributive responsibilities. But Grisez suggests that the expenditures it is appropriate for each person to make are in fact those "necessary for survival or ... suitable for fulfilling responsibilities pertaining to one's *personal vocation*,"[35] and he clearly doubts that a "standard of living higher than that set by *the limit of an individual's personal vocation* or a community's mission"[36] is justified.

---

[31] GRISEZ, LIVING, *supra* note 9, at 806; *cf.* FINNIS, AQUINAS, *supra* note 8, at 193.

[32] FINNIS, AQUINAS, *supra* note 8, at 194.

[33] GRISEZ, QUESTIONS, *supra* note 2, at 436; *cf.* GRISEZ, LIVING, *supra* note 9, at 801.

[34] GRISEZ, QUESTIONS, *supra* note 2, at 808; *cf.* FINNIS, AQUINAS, *supra* note 8, at 191–93.

[35] GRISEZ, LIVING, *supra* note 9, at 804 (my italics). Grisez's notion of vocation is developed at greater length in GERMAIN GRISEZ & RUSSELL SHAW, PERSONAL VOCATION: GOD CALLS EVERYONE BY NAME (2003).

[36] GRISEZ, LIVING, *supra* note 9, 806 (my italics).

To say that a person has a vocation is to say that she has a task or opportunity that is distinctively hers.[37] Central to the idea that a person has a vocation is the notion that a given choice *fits* her in a way that others do not, that it is right for her in a non-trivial way, so that to ignore it would be to lose something important. A vocation need not extend to one's entire life – it might be more focused – but it certainly *could* be comprehensive, and it is with comprehensive vocations that Grisez seems to be especially concerned.

Certainly, if one's vocation were relatively specific, and reasonable consumption choices were understood to be only those suitable for fulfillment of one's vocation, this might channel one's consumption choices in quite particular ways, readily justifying some while ruling out others that might otherwise seem to be appropriate. Showing that a consumption decision is consistent with the general requirements of practical reason is one thing; justifying every such decision as suitable for the fulfillment of one's vocation is quite another. It is not clear, however, that personal vocations can do the work Grisez seems to want them to do. Central to the idea of vocation as he articulates it is a notion of optimization that is not obviously consistent with natural law theory.

Natural law theory is incompatible with theistic voluntarism.[38] While Grisez and the other principal natural law theorists are theists, their conception of human welfare and of practical reasonableness makes right action a matter of participation in authentic aspects of well being through rational action. Either a given action is consistent with the requirements of practical reasonableness or it is not. And if an action is otherwise consistent with the requirements of practical reasonableness, then it is unclear what sort of reason a divine vocation might be thought to give one for not performing it.

Grisez attempts to respond to this challenge by maintaining that

> [n]ot all possibilities are equally good. As a loving Father, God prefers that we choose the best. If we always did that, we would make the best use of our abilities, take advantage of the greatest opportunities, and benefit others and ourselves as richly as possible. And, as with other good choices, we also would meet the most serious threats and challenges and care for others and ourselves as effectively as we could.[39]

---

[37] *See, e.g.*, LAWRENCE A. BLUM, MORAL PERCEPTION AND PARTICULARITY 104–10, 118–19 (1992); ROBERT MERRIHEW ADAMS, FINITE AND INFINITE GOODS: A FRAMEWORK FOR ETHICS 299–303 (1999); KEITH WARD, ETHICS AND CHRISTIANITY 142–47 (1970).

[38] *See, e.g.*, FINNIS, LAW, *supra* note 1, at 342–43, 406–7, 410.

[39] GRISEZ & SHAW, VOCATION, *supra* note 35, at 10.

God "will guide each of us personally to *what is best* for us and everyone else."[40]

It seems at least difficult to square with natural law theory the notion that there is, in general, a "best possibility" in a given situation. For the natural law rejection of consequentialism depends in part precisely on the recognition that the notion of a best possible state of affairs is incoherent. And even if, as in Grisez's formulation, the focus is on the selection of a best possible action from among many morally good options, the same kinds of objections seem applicable. For reasonable actions will pursue and realize diverse, incommensurable goods in varied ways that do not obviously admit of rank-ordering. Certainly, it is not obvious how a conception of vocation as the choice of the best can be affirmed in tandem with the reminder that "the glory of God may ... be manifested in *any* of the many aspects of human flourishing" and that "love of God may ... thus take, and be expressed in, any of the inexhaustibly many life-plans which conform to the requirements" of practical reason.[41]

Grisez makes clear that no one does wrong by ignoring her personal vocation.[42] If this is the case, then, it seems as if someone who identifies her public trust threshold in accordance with the requirements of practical reason but not with regard to her vocation does not do wrong. But, if *this* is the case, it is unclear why one ought to be overly concerned whether one's standard of living is consistent with one's vocation. If following one's vocation is not a requirement of practical reasonableness, then conforming one's standard of living to one's vocation cannot be a requirement of practical reasonableness, either. An obvious response on Grisez's part would be that a failure to conform to one's vocation is a failure to realize the best possibility for one's life. But, given the array of incommensurable goods we confront when we make choices, I cannot see that there is normally any such possibility.

There is good reason to be thoroughly critical of the "secret, often unconscious legalism" of consequentialism, of "its assumption that there is a uniquely correct moral answer (or specifiable set of correct moral answers) to all genuine moral problems."[43] A natural law view contrasts starkly with consequentialism in virtue of its recognition that there is very often no single best option. It seems most unlikely that an overall life-plan, the central elements of which are chosen in accordance with the principles of practical reasonableness, could

---

[40] *Id.* at 11 (my italics).   [41] FINNIS, LAW, *supra* note 1, at 113.
[42] GRISEZ & SHAW, VOCATION, *supra* note 35, at 10.
[43] JOHN FINNIS, FUNDAMENTALS OF ETHICS 93 (1983).

be said to be better or worse than another such life-plan, given the incommensurability of the basic aspects of well being: the impossibility of objectively rank-ordering options makes the notion of personal vocation as a call to realize the best option problematic. It will be difficult, then, to invoke vocations to specify the range of one's reasonable consumption choices.

C   Targeting resources beyond the public trust threshold

For a particular use of resources in excess of the public trust threshold to be justified, this use must further more than one's own well being. But there will be multiple ways in which these resources can be employed to aid others or support valued projects (Subsection 1). The requirement that one make reasonable use of resources beyond the public trust threshold is not the same as the special duty of moderate beneficence (Subsection 2). And if providing employment is one way of fulfilling one's responsibilities with regard to wealth beyond the public trust threshold, it seems as if there will be times when providing employment indirectly through consumption could be a way of fulfilling these responsibilities (Subsection 3).

1   The diversity of ways in which one can use resources beyond the threshold

One can fulfill the duty to make appropriate use of resources beyond the public trust threshold by providing "grants or loans for hospitals, schools, cultural centres, orphanages, etc., or directly for the relief of the poor." But one can also do so by "investing … in [the] production of more goods for later distribution and consumption; [or] by providing gainful employment to people looking for work,"[44] (especially?) given that "wage labourers are presumptively among the poor to whom distribution of … [resources in excess of the public trust threshold] is owed in justice."[45] Profit-sharing and contributions to communal wealth transfer schemes can also be ways of performing this duty.[46]

---

[44] FINNIS, Law, *supra* note 1, at 173. The assumption, here, is of course that the investment *does* somehow help other individuals or support communal projects. *Cf.* GRISEZ, QUESTIONS, *supra* note 2, at 502–7.
[45] FINNIS, AQUINAS, *supra* note 8, at 194 n.44.
[46] *Cf.* FINNIS, Law, *supra* note 1, at 170.

2 Distinguishing the requirement to make reasonable use of resources beyond the threshold from the requirement of moderate beneficence

Moderate beneficence is a requirement of justice in distribution: reason will require that one aid some people just in virtue of their vulnerability when one can easily do so. But this requirement of moderate beneficence is distinct from the duty to use resources in excess of the public trust threshold to help other people or support communal projects. The requirement of moderate beneficence is a special responsibility to particular people – not everyone qualifies as a vulnerable person one could easily help – which is comparable in this sense to the responsibilities generated by commitments and special relationships. By contrast, the duty to make good use of resources beyond the public trust threshold will typically obtain only after special responsibilities have been met. This duty also differs from the responsibility to meet immediate needs because it can be fulfilled by providing a wide range of benefits to other people or valuable projects, and not just through the direct or indirect relief of poverty.[47]

Suppose, for instance, that someone considers employing people in a given venture as a way of making responsible use of resources in excess of her public trust threshold. She will certainly need to consider other ventures she might support instead. And she will need to ask about other groups of potential workers she might employ if she decided to pursue other projects, and whether she might have good reason to help them by providing them with employment. There will often be less reason, all other things being equal, to provide employment to people already in comfortable economic circumstances if one is doing so to fulfill one's duty to make good use of resources beyond one's public trust threshold.[48] At the same time, of course, there is no reason to promote just one kind of good. It is potentially possible to help a variety of others and serve a variety of projects while behaving in a manner that is consistent with the requirements of practical reason.[49]

---

[47] *Id.* at 173.

[48] Even then, however, particular intelligible aspects of well being might be at stake in ways that would make it fair for one to use resources in excess of the public trust threshold in this way.

[49] *Cf.* GRISEZ, QUESTIONS, *supra* note 2, at 438. Grisez does not seem to want to argue that all credible and deserving NGOs merit our support before all credible and deserving colleges, all other things being equal. The case he discusses involves specific features that raise real, even if not decisive, doubts about donating to the college.

3   Consumption as a means of employing resources beyond the threshold

Under some circumstances, consumption might provide one way of usefully employing resources in excess of the public trust threshold.

Keynes argued "that whenever you save five shillings, you put a man out of work for a day. Your saving that five shillings adds to unemployment to the extent of one man for one day – and so on in proportion. On the other hand, whenever you buy goods you increase employment . . . ."[50] It is not clear that Keynes is right that saving fosters unemployment: after all, saved resources are either invested or placed with an entity (a bank, say, or a mutual fund) that will invest them, and the investment will ultimately contribute to the creation or maintenance of jobs – and perhaps, insofar as it creates wealth, to a greater number of jobs, or to better-paying jobs. Perhaps, however, the overlap between personal consumption and beneficence could justify the consumption of some resources that might otherwise fall beyond the public trust threshold.

The direct provision of employment is one reasonable way to use resources beyond the public trust threshold. But there also may be reason to regard it as appropriate to provide employment indirectly through consumption in some circumstances. Many routine consumption decisions contribute indirectly but significantly to the provision of employment for people, including people with limited resources. Patronizing a restaurant that pays workers fairly, for instance, may well help to ensure that people who need it can secure and maintain satisfactory employment. Other responsibilities may claim resources that one might spend on purchases with the potential to foster needed employment, and the impact of potential purchases on workers' economic well being may be sufficiently limited, in a given case, to make consumption an unreasonably inefficient means of helping others. But it seems as if indirect as well as direct contributions to employment might, in principle, be ways of fulfilling one's duty to make reasonable use of resources beyond the public trust threshold.

It is hard to see why, in principle, promoting employment by purchasing goods and services for consumption might not be a reasonable use of resources beyond the public trust threshold. But there will often be

---

[50] JOHN MAYNARD KEYNES, ESSAYS IN PERSUASION 152 (1963). According to Keynes, "the object of saving is to release labor for employment on producing capital-goods. . . . But if there is a large unemployed surplus already available for such purposes, then the effect of saving is merely to add to this surplus and therefore to increase the number of the unemployed." *Id.* at 151.

more reasonable uses. Whether doing is reasonable will depend on, at least, the degree to which it is actually likely to yield significant benefits and whether one has special or general responsibilities that direct one's resources to other projects or workers.

D   Natural law and justice in consumption

Practical reason requires treating wealth that is not required to meet special obligations and that cannot reasonably be used to further participation in authentic aspects of well being as a public trust. The requirements of practical reasonableness and the criteria of justice in distribution that flow from them specify the threshold beyond which wealth should be treated as a public trust. This threshold is not a precisely fixed point; rather, multiple choices along a continuum of possibilities are compatible with the demands of practical reasonableness. The idea of vocation might be thought to give further specificity to an individual's public trust threshold, but natural law theory does not seem to me to be hospitable to an account of vocation as a product of a divine command – as a call to the best among reasonable options – that could serve as a source of moral constraints on one's consumption choices beyond those imposed by the demands of practical reasonableness. Wealth beyond the public trust threshold should be used to support valuable projects or help people who need assistance – as through investment or the provision of employment.

IV   Justice and distribution

Justice in distribution is a responsibility of each economic actor. Distributive justice is not a matter of shaping the overall state of a community's economy, but of ensuring that each transaction is consistent with the demands of reason. What counts as a just transaction depends on the principles of practical reasonableness. Together with the basic aspects of well being and experiential and experimental evidence about human behavior, these principles generate the underlying rationales for a just property regime and a range of criteria for justice in distribution: need, function, commitments and attachments, efficiency, capacity, reward, productivity, risk acceptance, and the avoidance of harm.

The sale and purchase of goods and services is an important mechanism by which justice in distribution can be either served or undermined. Justice requires that buyers and sellers not force terms on each other or take advantage of each others' straitened circumstances. And it condemns background conditions that lead to significant divergences of price from cost, which provide strong evidence that monopolistic power and other kinds of exploitation are distorting market relationships.

Some expenditures are required to meet the demands of justice in relation to particular others. Other expenditures reasonably further one's own participation in the various dimensions of flourishing humanness. Wealth which is not required to meet one's distributive responsibilities and which cannot reasonably be used to further participation in authentic aspects of well being falls beyond one's *public trust threshold*. Wealth beyond this threshold should be used to support valuable projects, used to create direct or indirect employment, given directly or indirectly to poor people, invested in beneficial enterprises, or otherwise spent with the well being of one's community or of people in need in mind.

Acknowledging the responsibility to put resources in excess of one's public trust threshold to good use does not depend on the assumption that a failure to support particular communal projects or help specific others makes one automatically responsible for the non-occurrence of any particular benefits one has not brought about or for any harms one might have prevented. This would be just the sort of consequentialist reasoning natural law theory undermines. Practical reason does not require that everyone be an equal object of the agent's active concern, nor does it warrant collapsing the difference between acts and omissions.

The resources we distribute are frequently products of work. People's work lives play centrally important roles in shaping their experiences of and involvement in the world. I turn, in Chapter 3, to an examination of natural law moral norms related to work

3

Foundations: work

Natural law theory offers a positive vision of work's potential: in the workplace, people can develop as persons, hone and express their creativity, and produce goods and services that provide others with new opportunities for participation in the various aspects of well being. Work matters, though it need not devour our lives. Natural law theory also makes clear why workers deserve the respect and protection afforded by due process, and why no worker deserves to be denied employment-related opportunities because of characteristics unrelated to her actual or potential job performance. And natural law theory grounds a powerful case for participatory management and a strong case for the democratic governance of firms by workers.

In Part I, I suggest that work is important, but that natural law theory provides good reason to reject rigorist or maximizing views of responsibility in the workplace. In Part II, I argue that decisions regarding hiring, promotion, reassignment, and termination must be made in ways that afford workers with due process. Failing to provide due process is unfair and often inefficient, violates personal dignity, and ignores the significance of people's needs for stable identities and relationships. In Part III, I maintain that fairness requires nondiscriminatory work practices. I argue in Part IV for the view that the workplace ought to be participatory, that each worker should have a voice at work. I draw on the Golden Rule and the Efficiency Principle, as well as the equal dignity of persons, the value of community, and the principle of subsidiarity. I argue that, while practical reason ordinarily requires that workers have extensive opportunities to participate in decision-making, there is also good reason to opt for a stronger position: that firms ought to be governed democratically by workers. In Part V, I consider the potential relationship between workers and investors in the worker-governed firm. In Part IV, I rebut a number of objections to worker self-government. In Part VI, I offer an overview of my arguments.

I   Responsibility at work

Various stances regarding the extent and quality of one's work are consistent with the requirements of practical reasonableness, though individual commitments may sometimes reduce the range of reasonable options.

At its best, work is a cooperative activity in which valuable products are generated, worthwhile services provided, skills enhanced, relationships deepened.[1] Sometimes, "work ... realizes the capacities of those who do it."[2] And, even when it does not, it provides means for direct participation in some dimensions of well being – as, for instance, friendship – and means for the instrumental realization of others: work is a source of income that can be used to enable workers to participate in various aspects of well being, and the goods and services they produce can help others to do so as well.

Nonetheless, many of the activities in which people engage in even justly governed workplaces do not involve sustained participation in basic aspects of well being by the workers themselves.[3] When work offers opportunities for direct participation in the various basic aspects of well being, it can be an important part of a human life. But when it does not, there may often be little reason to celebrate it or to treat it as important beyond its capacity to provide income. Leisure will frequently provide more opportunities for participation in various dimensions of well being than will work; and, except when it is a matter of fulfilling specific responsibilities to others, there is no reason to regard work *as such* as a duty, and certainly none to work just as much as do others in one's community.

Even if all work were inherently valuable, though, not everyone could or should regard it as unreasonable to avoid performing *excellent* work. In general, the Golden Rule's demand of fairness requires not that workers "try to do their *best*,"[4] but, rather, that they perform *good-enough* work,[5] work that is reasonably regarded as consistent with their responsibilities to their firms and co-workers. Absent some special – and probably

---

[1] Grisez defines work as "any human activity – paid or unpaid, in the home or outside it, manual or intellectual – chosen and carried out at least partly for the sake of some good result beyond the activity itself." 2 GERMAIN G. GRISEZ, THE WAY OF THE LORD JESUS: LIVING A CHRISTIAN LIFE 754–55 (1994). I treat Grisez's observations here as if they concerned paid work specifically. While his definition of work includes a variety of activities other than paid work, nothing he says implies that any of his general comments do not apply, or apply with less force, to work in the marketplace.

[2] *Id.* at 759.

[3] *But cf. id.* at 757. Grisez links work with play, suggesting that both be seen as instances of skillful performance.

[4] *Id.* at 759 (my italics).   [5] *Cf.* BRUNO BETTELHEIM, A GOOD ENOUGH PARENT (1995).

unreasonable – commitment, there is no more reason (at least over the long term) to maximize some particular good associated with work than to make maximizing any other good one's goal.

One persistent objection to the maximizing logic of consequentialism is that it seems to require either that we be constantly busy or that our rest and recreation be justified only when they equip us more effectively to do good. The same vice attaches to the valorization of work. Puritan busyness is unattractive, and urging it on others is inhumane, whether its goal is constant excellence or simply the avoidance of idleness. The lives of workers extend well beyond their work, and a worker who refuses to let her work dominate her life characteristically acts reasonably, as long as she takes reasonable account of the burdens of others in her workplace.

This means, among other things, that, even in a position in which her responsibilities are defined with respect to the time she spends on the job, a worker does not necessarily act unreasonably just because she is not always working actively.[6] The necessarily incomplete character of long-term work contracts means that there is some indeterminacy in what her contract requires, and it will not ordinarily be reasonable to interpret a relatively vague agreement as requiring constant effort. And it is hardly consistent with the Golden Rule for some people to impose on others terms they would prefer not to accept themselves. Someone who goes home at 4:00 while expecting others to work another three hours (and for salaries lower than hers!) surely has little basis for objecting if they disregard her wishes.[7]

Certainly, fairness will not ordinarily require that a worker exceed the standards of diligence already set in her workplace. Implicit acceptance of these standards within a firm gives content to the terms of the necessarily incomplete work agreement. And workers cannot reasonably expect that others work harder than they do themselves, so there is a presumption that one does not owe one's co-workers more effort than they invest.[8]

---

[6] *But cf.* GRISEZ, LIVING, *supra* note 1, at 759.

[7] These observations concern the reasonableness of apportioning effort to work-related tasks in a just workplace – the focus of this chapter. But further issues arise in an undemocratic work environment. While fairness may well involve fulfilling the terms of her contract, the justice of those terms, and her duty to comply with them, may be limited if they were arrived at in an unequal bargaining environment. And promissory obligations to an investor-governed firm will obviously be further reduced in the context of an on-the-job work action – a slowdown, say, or a sit-down strike – that is otherwise consistent with the requirements of practical reasonableness. Thanks to Kevin Carson for encouraging me to think more clearly about this set of issues.

[8] Again, since this chapter concerns ideal theory, the focus of the text is on justly governed workplaces; there will be further reason not to exert excessive effort in an

Practical reason limits one's self-investment in work. It also offers good reason to foreswear a fastidious avoidance of unimportant error. Each kind of work has a different standard of quality. There is, for instance, relatively little room for error in neurosurgery, and extreme precision is exceptionally important here – a mistake can have grave consequences. But errors in many fields are not serious; to suppose otherwise is not a call to excellence but a recipe for neurosis. While it is unreasonable – a reflection of either irrationality or malice – to *seek* error, a field-specific tolerance for error seems entirely reasonable. How much error will be tolerable will be a function of the various requirements of practical reason. Clearly, one should not, for instance, tolerate a level of error in the manufacture of a product which one would resent were one a customer using the product (per the Golden Rule). At the same time, one should not pursue error reduction at unreasonable cost to efficiency (per the Efficiency Principle).

There may sometimes be reasons for "workers ... [to] strive to meet high standards for their personal performance."[9] But people realize a variety of aspects of well being in their lives, both in connection with work and outside the workplace. There may be some conflict between working and realizing these dimensions of welfare. And there may be both instrumental and intrinsic value to combining work with the pursuit of various aspects of well being not directly related to work (caring for one's children, for instance, or engaging with friends), rather than focusing exclusively on work.

Workers do not necessarily "harm themselves by not trying to do good work."[10] And even if a worker does harm herself by not trying to do good work, the harm need not be the purpose of her action or a chosen means to some other end: it may be a side-effect of her choice, accepted as consistent with the requirements of practical reasonableness. Not realizing a given capacity is not the same thing as purposefully or instrumentally attacking it. Thus, there is nothing unreasonable, as such, about failing to realize a particular capacity. Indeed, reasonable participation in basic aspects of well being involves declining, constantly, to realize a variety of capacities.

Sometimes, fairness to others or specific personal commitments – to others or to oneself – will make truly excellent work not only valuable but

---

investor-governed firm, in order to avoid increasing the pressure on one's co-workers to meet excessive demands. *Cf.* KEVIN A. CARSON, THE ETHICS OF LABOR STRUGGLE: A FREE MARKET PERSPECTIVE (2007).

[9] GRISEZ, LIVING, *supra* note 1, at 759.   [10] *Id.* at 759.

required. But there is no *general* obligation to make work one of the arenas in which one seeks excellence.[11]

II Good cause and due process

The principles of practical reasonableness constrain the ways in which employment decisions can reasonably be made. The Golden Rule requires fairness, precluding decisions not based on the skills of an applicant or performance requirements for a position. The Pauline Principle precludes making employment decisions based on hostility. And the Efficiency Principle rules out decisions that reflect prejudice and so undermine organizational effectiveness (picking a clearly less-qualified candidate for a position at a given organization because she belongs to a favored political group may be harmful not only to other candidates but also to the organization and those it serves). Thus, practical reason obviously requires that someone be denied a job only for reasons related to her fitness for the relevant kind of work. It also requires that workers be dismissed or demoted only for good cause and only after being afforded due process.

According to a classic statement of the contrasting at-will doctrine, firms may terminate workers "at will, be they many or few, for good cause, for no cause or even for cause morally wrong, without being thereby guilty of legal wrong."[12] The heyday of this view is already over.[13] It has been eroded not only by collective bargaining agreements and by legislation but also by the emergence of a tort of wrongful or abusive discharge. The threat of liability for wrongful or abusive discharge has come to provide workers with increasing protection against arbitrary dismissal.[14]

---

[11] The valorization of work has had destructive social consequences; *see* SHARON BEDER, SELLING THE WORK ETHIC: FROM PURITAN PULPIT TO CORPORATE PR (2000); *cf.* JULIET SCHOR, THE OVERWORKED AMERICAN: THE UNEXPECTED DECLINE OF LEISURE (1991).

[12] Payne v. Western and Atlantic Railroad Company, 81 Tenn. 507, 519–20 (1884); *cf. id.* at 518 ("men must be left, without interference to buy and sell where they please, and to discharge or retain employees at will for good cause or for no cause, or even for bad cause. …"). The court notes, without apparent irony, that "[t]he great and rich and powerful are guaranteed the same liberty and privilege as the poor and weak. All may buy and sell when they choose; they may refuse to employ or dismiss whom they choose, without being thereby guilty of a legal wrong, though it may seriously injure and even ruin others." *Id.* at 519. It is difficult not to think of Anatole France's acid observation that "[t]he law, in its majestic equality, forbids the rich as well as the poor to sleep under bridges, to beg in the streets, and to steal bread." ANATOLE FRANCE, THE RED LILY ch. 7 (1894).

[13] *See* Deborah A. Ballam, *Employment At-Will: The Impending Death of a Doctrine*, 37 AM. BUS. L.J. 653 (2000).

[14] *See id.*; and *cf.* Lawrence E. Blades, *Employment-At-Will vs. Individual Freedom: On Limiting the Abusive Exercise of Employer Power*, 67 COLUM. L. REV. 1404 (1967).

Contract doctrine has provided increasing protection against wrongful discharge as well.[15] And other strategies have also limited the at-will doctrine's applicability or pointed toward ways in which it *could* plausibly be limited.[16] But whatever its current legal status, it is inconsistent with the requirements of practical reasonableness. I argue in Section A for the importance of dismissal only for good cause and in Section B for due process protections against arbitrary dismissal. I seek in Section C to rebut challenges to the appropriateness of such protections.

A   *The importance of good cause*

Roughly speaking, we can say that there is good cause for a firm to demote or dismiss a worker only in one of the following cases: (*i*) the worker is demonstrably unable or unwilling to perform economically significant tasks for the firm in her current position at a reasonable standard; *or* (*ii*) it is clear that, if she continues to work at her current position, she is demonstrably likely to engage in unreasonable conduct that will probably cause significant, genuine harm to the firm, to other workers, or to other stakeholders; *or* (*iii*) financial exigency requires the elimination of her current position.

In general, this ought to be clear and noncontroversial. I offer just two clarifications of the meaning of point (*ii*). First, I emphasize that the relevant judgment ought to be *prospective*. That is, it is not enough that

[15] *See* Cortlan H. Maddux, Comment, *Employers Beware! The Emerging Use of Promissory Estoppel as an Exception to Employment at Will*, 49 BAYLOR L. REV. 197 (1997).

[16] *See, e.g.,* Frank J. Cavico, *Tortious Interference with Contract in the At-Will Employment Context*, 79 U. DET. MERCY L. REV. 503 (2002); Susan R. Dana, *South Dakota Employment At Will Doctrine: Twenty Years of Judicial Erosion*, 49 S.D. L. REV. 47 (2003); Dennis P. Duffy, *Intentional Infliction of Emotional Distress and Employment At Will: The Case Against "Tortification" of Labor and Employment Law*, 74 B.U.L. REV. 387 (1994); Henry H. Perritt, Jr., The *Future of Wrongful Dismissal Claims: Where Does Employer Self Interest Lie?*, 58 U. CIN. L. REV. 397 (1989); Marybeth Walsh, *Public Policy Exception to At-Will Employment Rule Extended to Internal Complaints About Criminal Violations: Smith v. Mitre Corp. and Shea v. Emmanuel College*, 39 B.C. L. REV 490 (1998); Michael D. Moberly, *Negligent Investigation: Arizona's Fourth Exception to the Employment-at-Will Rule?*, 27 ARIZ. ST. L.J. 993 (1995); Sandra S. Park, Note, *Working towards Freedom from Abuse: Recognizing a "Public Policy" Exception to Employment-At-Will for Domestic Violence Victims*, 59 N.Y.U. ANN. SURV. AM. L. 121 (2003); Ann M. Carlson, Comment, *States Are Eroding At-Will Employment Doctrines: Will Pennsylvania Join the Crowd?*, 42 DUQ. L. REV. 511 (2004); Susan Sauter, Comment, *The Employee Health and Safety Whistleblower Protection Act and the Conscientious Employee: The Potential for Federal Statutory Enforcement of the Public Policy Exception to Employment at Will*, 59 U. CIN. L. REV. 513 (1990).

a worker has done something bad; what is important is that it is reasonable to think that the worker *will* do something bad if she continues in her current position. Past misconduct may give good evidence that future misconduct is likely; and, if it does, it provides reason for dismissal or reassignment. But to dismiss a worker simply on the basis of past misconduct, without alleging that it is predictive of future misconduct, is punitive, rather than corrective. It does no good for the worker, the firm, or others. It evidently violates the Pauline Principle, and possibly the Golden Rule and the Efficiency Principle as well, because it makes ineffective use of firm resources. Second, I stress that a possible harm that might serve as a predicate for dismissal must be genuine: it is not, for instance, a genuine harm to a customer to be assisted by a retail worker who belongs to an ethnic group she dislikes.

Dismissing or demoting a worker only for good cause seems to be a requirement of fairness. For someone involved in dismissing or demoting another would be not unlikely to react resentfully were she dismissed or demoted without good cause. Because she would resent being dismissed or demoted without good cause herself, she has good reason to favor the dismissal or demotion of others only for good cause.

Dismissing or demoting only for good cause is a matter of fairness not only to the individual worker involved but also to the firm. An unnecessary demotion or dismissal means that the firm will lose some or all of the services of someone able to perform her duties successfully, and will also need to expend resources recruiting, hiring, and training a replacement. Causing a firm to expend resources for this purpose seems likely, too, to be a violation of the Efficiency Principle. Further, dismissing someone on the basis of personal or group-based prejudice seems to be an instance of acting out of hostility and so a violation of the Pauline Principle.

B The importance of due process

Practical reason requires that people benefit from reasonable due process protections when it is proposed to demote or dismiss them. Determining the precise shape of procedural requirements is not the task of legal or moral theory. But I suggest provisionally that procedural safeguards should ensure (*i*) that, before being dismissed or demoted, a worker (*a*) receives all of the relevant information about her performance possessed by her firm, (*b*) can make available relevant evidence of her own, and (*c*) can defend herself before a neutral decision-making body that includes (appropriately defined) workplace peers, and (*ii*) that she be dismissed or demoted only if this body approves.[17]

The provision of due process protections makes it more likely that employment decisions will actually be made for good cause. Thus, failing to ensure that such protections are available will often be inconsistent with the Golden Rule's mandate of fairness. They ensure that standards for demotion and dismissal are defined and enforced fairly. They safeguard individual workers' autonomy, protect their dignity, help to secure their economic well being, and assist them in dealing with the emotional effects of dismissal, while also helping to protect firms' welfare.

1   Ensuring accuracy

Since most people would want judgments about their own circumstances to be accurate, they have good reason to regard the accurate assessment of others' circumstances as important. Due process protections ensure that multiple people's perspectives are brought to bear on an employment decision. This means both that more relevant facts can be brought to light and that particular people's judgments about matters of fact can be checked against others' and actively challenged in ways likely to expose weak arguments and add credibility to strong ones. In addition, conclusions about the implications of agreed-upon facts can be assessed in light of varied perspectives.

2   Ensuring fairness in treatment

Someone involved in dismissing or demoting another would be not unlikely to react resentfully were she dismissed or demoted without having the opportunity to contest charges against her. Similarly, she would be unlikely to regard it as reasonable if any challenge she leveled against charges made against her could be adjudicated by the person or entity that had accepted the charges, and decided on her dismissal or demotion, in the first place. Because she would resent the absence of due process protections herself, she has good reason to regard it as important to afford them to others.

3   Ensuring fairness in the definition and enforcement of standards

When due process is guaranteed, standards for the determination of facts, the evaluation of conduct, the prediction of outcomes, and the

---

[17] Reason surely does not preclude an emergency suspension, pending adjudication of the sort outlined here, when it is credibly alleged that someone might be prone to violence in the workplace.

specification of appropriate responses to projected outcomes can be framed, at least in general terms, in a fair manner before any individual case is reviewed. This means that the standards will not be shaped in a biased manner in order to yield a desired outcome in a particular case, that everyone affected has the opportunity to participate in formulating, debating, and approving them, and that they are widely publicized and understood. And wider publicity and the involvement of multiple people in the review of a dismissal or demotion decision helps to ensure that standards are interpreted and applied in a predictable and reasonable manner.

4 Protecting autonomy

Due process rights safeguard workers' autonomy. By ensuring that a worker has a voice in the decision whether she will be dismissed or demoted, due process rights prevent her from being subjected to someone else's authority. Her perspective receives the consideration it deserves, and she is acknowledged as an independent, valuable decision-maker.

5 Safeguarding dignity

Due process rights safeguard workers' dignity. Arbitrary dismissal conveys the message, to the worker and others, that the worker is not an equal, valued member of a firm but rather a dispensable item of property. Due process protections undermine this message. They make it possible for a dismissed worker to arrange a departure that need not have about it an air of banishment. They also serve, thus, to eliminate the humiliating, unannounced dismissals, complete with security guards and public embarrassment, that have become so disturbingly common in contemporary workplaces.

6 Facilitating economic preparation for potential dislocation

Characteristically, the impact of dismissal on a worker is much more severe than the proportionate impact on the firm that dismisses her. A firm will typically be more readily able to absorb any stresses associated with the loss of the worker than the worker will be able to absorb the stresses associated with the loss of her job. The risk of significant harm to a worker resulting from dismissal makes the provision of due process protections to the worker especially important. Such protections make it much more likely that she will not be subjected to potentially serious harm without good reason, and they give her the opportunity to take personal responsibility for protecting her own well being.

7   Facilitating emotional preparation for potential dislocation

Due process protections offer a worker the opportunity to prepare emotionally for the possible end of her job. By giving a worker time to prepare and present a case in response to the claim that she ought to be dismissed, such protections also provide the worker with the opportunity to deal with the emotional stresses associated with dismissal and, if necessary, to grieve. Thus, due process protections also afford a dismissed worker time to say good-bye to others.

8   Minimizing the risk that firms will lose valuable workers
and that dismissed workers will be resentful

Due process protections serve the well being of firms as well as of individual workers. They reduce the risk that capable workers who contribute to their well being will be dismissed. And they also reduce the risk that workers will leave firms with resentful attitudes that will lead them in various ways to harm the firms.

C   Defenses of the at-will system

While there is a strong positive case for limiting dismissal and demotion to cases in which there is good cause and in which due process has been followed, a number of defenses might still be offered for the at-will system. Defenses of the system are unlikely to involve the claim that a firm does not need good cause to dismiss or demote a worker. Instead, defenses of the at-will system usually center on whether fairness requires that the existence of good cause be demonstrated in the course of procedures like those I have discussed here, and whether the law should have the authority to require that firms offer due process protections.

Arguments for the legal or moral right to employ people at-will might take at least four forms. They might rely on absolute conceptions of property rights (Subsection 1). They might appeal to concerns about efficiency (Subsection 2). They might rely on the judgment that legal standards ruling out arbitrary dismissal or demotion were not actually effective in protecting workers (Subsection 3). And they might analogize between an employment relationship and friendship, maintaining that we ought to be as free to choose those with whom we will work as we are to choose our friends (Subsection 4). None of these arguments is persuasive.

1 Property Rights

When a decision to demote or dismiss a worker is being made by, or under the authority of, a firm owner (whether in a worker-owned firm or in an undemocratic firm owned by one or more investors or entrepreneurs), an owner might maintain that no one could reasonably object to the dismissal of the worker because stopping the dismissal or demotion or requiring compensation for it would violate the property rights of the owner or owners.[18] But there are (at least) two problems with this move. It is irrelevant, and it presupposes an implausible view of property rights.

Dismissal without good cause and due process is unreasonable for multiple reasons. To maintain that behavior is wrong is distinct from maintaining that the best way to remedy the wrong done by the behavior is to use the force of law to restrain the wrong-doer or require her to compensate the wronged person. The argument against employment at-will is an argument directed initially at each person involved in shaping employment decisions at a given firm. The question is what it is reasonable for *her* to do, not, at this point, what it is reasonable for *others* to ask or demand that she do. And stopping a dismissal or forcing compensation for it need not involve the use of legal force. Communal norms, boycotts, strikes, and other non-coercive social mechanisms for enforcing workplace fairness could be used in preference to a community's legal system.

Further, the claim that a just legal system ought to countenance someone's doing absolutely anything she likes with her own property is, on its face, implausible. Property rights are constrained but contingent communal artefacts, and communities have every reason to structure their property rights regimes in ways that ensure a modicum of fair treatment to workers. This is so for several reasons. (*i*) It would be foolish for the members of a community to support norms and rules regarding property that insulated firms against all challenges to demotions and dismissals. (*ii*) While reliability is important, it is not the only factor relevant to the shaping of property rights, so there is no reason why a community could not decide that it would not treat as legitimate property rules that

---

[18] I make two simplifying assumptions here: that an owner is a single person and that it is an owner who is authorized to make employment decisions. I argue for worker self-government and for a sharp separation of ownership and control in most or all firms. In environments in which these arguments are accepted as persuasive, the presuppositions of debates about the at-will doctrine will be different. But employment at-will would still be an issue in worker-governed firms; and my responses to the claims of an imagined sole proprietor would still be relevant in the quite different environment for which I contend here.

conferred protections on unfair conduct that caused significant harms, even if protecting workers sometimes upended settled expectations. Further, once it was clear that a community's legal system *would* protect workers, providing the relevant protections would not interfere with anyone's reasonable expectations, since reasonable expectations would take into account the availability of protection for workers. (*iii*) Since a key function of the establishment and maintenance of a property system by a community is to benefit the community, it is unreasonable for a member of the community not to accept some reasonable limitations on her property rights in the interest of the good of others. Finally, (*iv*), no one has, in general, any reasonable interest in being able to treat others unfairly. (There may, of course, be a reasonable claim not to be interfered with, but this claim is hardly absolute.)

2   Efficiency

A proponent of the right to dismiss workers at-will might maintain that a rule permitting at-will dismissal served efficiency. But this seems questionable on at least two fronts.

There will often be good reason for firms' organizational structures to be as flat as possible.[19] When a firm is hierarchical, conferring on the firm the right to dismiss workers at will may not serve efficiency. It is at least open to question whether those located at or near the tops of organizational hierarchies or sub-hierarchies are characteristically the most aware of what needs to be done in workplaces and of whose performance is the most effective. In a hierarchical organization, a decision regarding a worker's employment status made by someone located at some distance from the worker in the organization's hierarchy may be grounded in less adequate information than that possessed by the worker's peers. And arbitrary dismissals can reduce workers' trust in a firm as well as its credibility with members of the public, which can certainly impact its economic well being. Imposing these costs on the firm is unfair to those who depend on the firm for income, wealth, and economic security. But it is also, therefore, an inefficient use of the firm's resources.

Efficiency is not, in any case, the only relevant consideration. For dismissal without due process attacks workers' dignity and capacity to govern their own lives. The standard of fairness expressed in the Golden Rule militates against dismissal for these reasons, for no employment decision-maker would welcome the assault on her own dignity or the loss

---

[19] *Cf.* Part IV and Part VI, *infra*.

of control over her own life characteristically involved in dismissal without due process.

Fairness to all workers whose continued well being depends on a firm's success means ensuring that time and resources are not devoured by inefficient dismissal processes and that the replacement of dismissed workers can happen expeditiously. But efficiency concerns relevant to workers can be met while ensuring that workers are afforded due process.

3 Ineffectiveness

Jesse Rudy has argued that legal standards precluding arbitrary dismissal and demotion would not afford any real protection to workers. Rudy maintains that rules against arbitrary dismissal have little effect on people's work experiences because social norms and economic incentives discourage firms from dismissing workers arbitrarily.[20]

It is not clear that the strong social norms to which Rudy alludes exist. In any case, personal vendettas and the fact that firms may sometimes regard it as worthwhile to dismiss workers seeking substantive workplace changes increase the likelihood that, even if there are social norms requiring just cause for dismissal, firms may ignore them absent significant external social pressure or the possibility of legal enforcement. If procedures designed to ensure that dismissals are fair are not in place, a manager may honestly believe she is acting in accordance with relevant social norms even though impartial scrutiny might suggest otherwise.

4 Freedom, friendship, and employment

There are some significant analogies between the worker–firm relationship on the one hand and friendship on the other. A defender of employment at-will might maintain that this analogy highlights the importance of a firm's freedom in selecting its workers, just as one is free to select one's friends.[21] One would not want legal or procedural constraints to limit one's choice of friends; so, if the analogy holds, one should not want such constraints to limit one's employment relationships, either.

As I have already emphasized, whether the objections I have offered to employment at-will are persuasive and whether compensation for

---

[20] *See* Jesse Rudy, *What They Don't Know Won't Hurt Them: Defending Employment-At-Will in Light of Findings that Employees Believe They Possess Just Cause Protection,* 23 BERKELEY J. EMP. & LAB. L. 307 (2002).

[21] Thanks to an anonymous reviewer for emphasizing the need to address this point.

arbitrary dismissal ought to be available at law are quite distinct questions. Even if one has good arguments against the imposition of legal sanctions for dismissal or demotion absent good cause and due process, this would not show on its own that this kind of dismissal or demotion was morally appropriate. Someone ought to subject her own actions to moral assessment even if she believes that no one else is entitled to sanction her for a given sort of morally troubling conduct. And she might have good reason to support a process providing for the impartial third-party review of any termination decision even if no legal norm required her to do so.

The analogy between friendships and employment relationships is, in any case, a limited one. The two are almost unavoidably similar in one way: obligations, often tacit, develop over time; interdependence creates responsibility even in the absence of explicit agreement. But *this* resemblance between friendship and employment does not imply that firms need the same kind of unfettered discretion to make decisions about their relationships with workers as do friends about their relationships with each other.

To the extent that friends do want and need discretion in determining the fates of their relationships, this might be for at least two reasons: the inability of anyone not party to a friendship to assess its viability and the inherently intimate, personal character of friendship. Neither of these features characterizes the relationship between firms and workers.

People who are friends typically know much more about their friendship and how it affects the participants than do observers. Someone might judge that she was particularly well situated – for this reason – to determine whether it was appropriate or desirable for her to end a friendship, that a third party would be unlikely to understand an intimate relationship well enough to know what it was reasonable for a participant to do about the relationship. But whether or not this is true where friends are concerned, it hardly seems accurate with respect to the typical workplace relationship. There is no reason why the evidence for and against the proposed termination of a worker, and thus the fairness of the proposed termination, could not be assessed reasonably by impartial participants in a review process. It should be possible to convey the kind of knowledge required for them to evaluate the merits of the proposed termination.

Friends interact, by definition, on an intimate level, and the decision to continue or end a friendship has to do, very often, with subtle qualities of personal interactions between people. By contrast, there is no requirement that people in a work setting interact on an intimate level. The inherently intimate, private, quality of friendship that makes it unreasonable for anyone else to interfere with friends' decisions about ending their relationships seems to be lacking in employment relationships *qua* employment relationships. Thus, people do not need to be friends in order to work together effectively, as long as they can treat each other decently and respectfully.

The limited analogy between friendship and employment relationships does not support the conclusion that firms should be able to dismiss workers at will. The two kinds of relationships share some features. But the characteristics that make a due process guarantee odd or objectionable in the context of friendship are absent from employment relationships.

A firm dismisses a worker reasonably only if it does so for good cause after following due process. Firms' property rights and their understandable need to conduct their affairs flexibly do not exempt them from the requirements of practical reasonableness.

III Nondiscrimination

Discrimination on the basis of characteristics unrelated to a person's actual capacity to perform in a particular position is clearly inconsistent with the Golden Rule.[22] The Golden Rule rules out arbitrary preferences between persons; and, at least for most purposes, making choices about hiring, promotion, and retention or dismissal based on ethnicity, gender, age, or sexual orientation is arbitrary.

The other practical principles constrain discriminatory conduct as well. The Pauline Principle precludes employment decisions expressive of hostility toward a group or person. The Efficiency Principle will count (whether decisively or not) against employing a worker when it is clear that she can achieve work-related objectives less efficiently than another candidate – something that may well occur when prejudice is the basis for a hiring decision. And acting on the basis of prejudice will often be unreasonable simply because it fails to involve attempted participation in any intelligible good at all.

In Section A, I review possible defenses of employment discrimination involving the claim that discrimination by firms is reasonable. In Section B, I consider the claim that, while discriminatory conduct by

---

[22] *See* GRISEZ, LIVING, *supra* note 1, at 383, 862.

firms is itself wrong, it would be wrong or overly costly to allow legal challenges to such conduct. I find neither of these defenses persuasive.

A   Claims that employment discrimination is reasonable

There are at least two defenses of discriminatory conduct as rational.[23] The first holds that facts about group membership provide firms with useful short-hand information about people's preparation for employment. Because the cost of obtaining better information is frequently too high, it is reasonable for firms to use available information when making employment decisions (Subsection 1). The second holds that firms act rationally when they discriminate, if customers, other prospective workers, or others who can impact firms' circumstances will punish firms if they do not discriminate. On this view, the costs associated with ignoring others' prejudices are too high for firms reasonably to disregard (Subsection 2).

1   Prejudice as short-hand

The first rationale does not, of course, provide any justification for discrimination based on inarticulable beliefs in the superiority and inferiority of particular groups. A person who cannot bring to consciousness and subject to reflection her rationale for preferring members of one group to those of another has a preference no more reasonable than a taste for chocolate over vanilla, and no justification for acting on this preference when the welfare of the prospective worker and the firm itself are at stake.

Someone might, of course, maintain that there is good reason to trust instincts that have been developed over time and sifted and winnowed by experience, and that prejudices of various kinds have been tested in this way, even if she can't always specify just what warrants them. If a decision maker has access only to instincts, however, without understanding their (purported) justifications, there will be no realistic way of determining which ones really are the results of experiential winnowing and which ones are products of other factors, perhaps entirely unrelated to experience. It's one thing to act instinctively when one has little or no time to

---

[23] The possibilities I consider here are canvassed, though not necessarily endorsed, in MILTON FRIEDMAN, CAPITALISM AND FREEDOM 108–18 (1962); THOMAS SOWELL, BASIC ECONOMICS: A CITIZEN'S GUIDE TO THE ECONOMY 139 (2001); THOMAS SOWELL, MARKETS AND MINORITIES 19–33 (1981); cf. GARY S. BECKER, THE ECONOMICS OF DISCRIMINATION (1957).

reflect; in this case, one may have no reasonable opportunity to subject an instinctive reaction to critical scrutiny. But it's quite another when one has time to assess one's reactions and reason one's way toward a sensible judgment. In a case of *this* kind, one will have little reason to accept an instinctive response as action-guiding if one cannot identify a rational basis for it after due reflection.

Suppose, however, that a person does consciously endorse some specific, purportedly factual generalization about the members of a particular group – members of this group are dishonest, say, or lazy. Beliefs of this kind about members of marginalized minority groups are, of course, very common. It is so common to believe negative generalizations about members of groups other than one's own that anyone who finds herself endorsing one of these generalizations has good reason to ask whether there is any basis for it in fact. It is reasonable to discount such beliefs if they seem to be rooted in nothing more credible than persistent prejudice.

If someone making an employment-related decision judges that a given generalization withstands scrutiny (say, in the extreme case, that it is supported by credible statistical evidence), however, she is still responsible for attempting to assess the candidate for employment in light of the candidate's own (relevant) characteristics. If *she* would prefer that she be assessed individually rather than as part of an undifferentiated group, then the Golden Rule suggests that she owes a similar assessment to the candidate: people vary widely within groups, and sharing one sort of characteristic with other people is no guarantee at all that one necessarily shares other characteristics with them. The Golden Rule also suggests that she owes this kind of assessment to the firm on behalf of which she is assessing the candidate, since the firm presumably wants an applicant able to perform well, even if that person might belong to one disfavored group or another; it's not fair to the firm to exclude candidates because of irrelevant characteristics.

2 Discrimination as protective

The second rationale holds that it may be reasonable to make a discriminatory employment decision if the prejudices of others are such that one's failure to make the decision would lead *them* to react negatively. If one judges that their reaction is reflective of unreasonable and unfair prejudice, however, then, following the Golden Rule will often mean that one has a particular responsibility to challenge the prejudice – not only as a matter of fairness to the person directly affected but also as a means of educating prejudiced people about the unreasonableness of their prejudices.

B   Claims that legal interference with employment discrimination is unreasonable

While granting that discrimination itself is wrong, some people object to *legal* challenges to discriminatory conduct. Some defenses of the view that firms should be free from legal liability for discrimination maintain that such discrimination is, indeed, wrong, but that legal challenges to employment discrimination are inappropriate because of firms' property rights (Subsection 1). An alternative position maintains that, because discrimination is irrational, it will not prove economically viable, and that, because of the costs associated with interference with the employment market, it will be preferable to deal with discrimination by removing any legal underpinnings that might sustain it and allowing the market actually to eliminate it (Subsection 2). Neither of these objections undermines the reasonableness of legal remedies for employment discrimination.

1   Discrimination and property rights

One view of property rights suggests that communal interference with discriminatory use of one's property – as, for instance, in employment – is unjust, even if the discrimination is itself wrong.[24]

In Texas in the early 1950s, a prospective employer manifested concern about hiring my father, then an accountant. Though they did not raise the issue directly, questions from the executives responsible for making the hiring decision made it clear to him that they were nervous because, as a Seventh-day Adventist, he would be unable to work from sundown on Friday to sundown on Saturday. He assured them that he respected their right to refuse to hire anyone they wanted to. Their property rights, he clearly believed, were absolute. Simple fairness meant declining a job rather than infringing on the economic freedom of others. Thus,

---

[24]   *See, e.g.,* FRIEDMAN, CAPITALISM, *supra* note 23, at 111: " I believe strongly that the color of a man's skin or the religion of his parents is, by itself, no reason to treat him differently; that a man should be judged by what he is and what he does and not by these external characteristics. I deplore what seems to me the prejudice and narrowness of outlook of those whose tastes differ from mine in this respect and I think the less of them for it. But in a society based on free discussion, the appropriate recourse is for me to seek to persuade them that their tastes are bad and that they should change their views and their behavior, not to use coercive power to enforce my tastes and my attitudes on others."

he opposed employment discrimination laws that would have protected him – and that would have protected women and members of ethnic minority groups.

Even a conception of property rights as absolute would provide no justification at all for anyone's discriminatory conduct. This would be so only if, coupled with the claim that interference with others' property rights was always unreasonable, were one of the following stronger claims: (*i*) all *uses* of one's own property are equally *reasonable* or (*ii*) no such use is subject to moral assessment. But neither of these notions is entailed by even the strongest plausible account of property rights.

For, even on an understanding of property rights as absolute, to say that one has a right with respect to a given property interest is simply to say that others may not use force to interfere with this interest. Whether anyone else can interfere legitimately with someone's property rights has no bearing on what it is in fact reasonable for the person herself to do with her own property.[25] Even if there could be no forcible interference by others with a person's use of her own property, the Golden Rule would still apply to the decisions she made regarding that property; to treat someone else in a manner in which she would resent being treated would still be unfair, whatever the extent of her legal property rights.

In any case, however, absolute conceptions of property rights are thoroughly implausible. As I have already suggested, property rights are best understood as limited in virtue of the principles of practical reasonableness and the underlying rationales for a property system. While there are certainly reasons for respecting these rights, there is none for understanding them as unlimited, as offering the freedom to discriminate on the basis of prejudice. Property rights are constrained but contingent, and there would be no reason for any community to define or regard property rights as absolute; indeed, there would clearly be good reason for any community *not* to do so. And without absolute or near-absolute property rights, it would be hard for anyone to claim that interference with her discriminatory employment-related conduct was in principle unreasonable.

2   Market remedies for discrimination

It may well be that, as the second sort of argument maintains, prejudice will not pay over the long term.[26] Firms that discriminate will tend to lose

---

[25] The distinction is very clear to a property absolutist like MURRAY N. ROTHBARD, THE ETHICS OF LIBERTY 23–24 (1982).

[26] *Cf.* BECKER, *supra* note 23.

out to those that do not, since, on prejudicial grounds, the discriminators will prefer less-qualified to more-qualified workers, and the more-
qualified workers will be hired by and improve the performance of the
non-discriminators. And, for similar reasons, regions in which discrimination is enforced by widespread social pressure will fare less well economically than comparable regions in which it is not.

This does not, of course, again, provide any actor with justification for
discriminating. And, in any case, the envisioned model is highly ideal-
ized. A variety of factors – social, cultural, economic, geographic – may
protect discriminators against competitive pressures. A particular firm
may face no immediate costs for discriminating if discrimination in
general is the norm. And a region may enjoy advantages that insulate it
against the ill-effects of discrimination. For instance, while apartheid-era
South Africa would presumably have been more prosperous had all members of its population been educated and employed to their full potential,
the country's remarkable mineral wealth gave it an enormous advantage
over its neighbors. White South Africans were much freer to discriminate than they would have been had neighboring countries – in which
non-white South Africans could have sought, and often did seek, economic well being without discrimination – possessed comparable mineral wealth. Thus, competitive pressures did not force the South African
government to rethink its policies.[27] But these policies were no less wrong
for surviving immediate market stresses.

Suppose, however, that market pressures *would* tend to erode discriminatory conduct. This still leaves open the question whether communities'
legal systems ought to award damages for discriminatory conduct. The
fact that market pressures would tend to undermine discrimination does
not show that lawsuits (and the exertion of communal pressure) would
not be appropriate mechanisms for reducing its incidence. Perhaps there
might be costs associated with the use of such mechanisms not borne by
the discriminators but rather by the community at large. But it would
surely be reasonable for the members of a community to decide that they
were willing to bear these costs. And, in any event, in view of the harms
to the dignity and economic well being of the particular people who are
unjustly injured by being subjected to employment discrimination, there
is still good reason to use the threat of liability (and other communal

---

[27] They did, however, evidently affect the behavior of private firms, which tended to be
more willing to hire black workers than official policy permitted them to be; *see* SOWELL,
ECONOMICS, *supra* note 23, at 142–43.

pressures) to end discriminatory practices before attachment to these practices is decisively undermined by the market.

IV Natural law and workplace democracy

Natural law theory holds that there is "a fundamental equality of human persons … ,"[28] and clearly precludes some kinds of economic arrangements, such as slavery.[29] And practical reason requires fairness in the workplace as in every other aspect of human life. It may not be possible to show that a workplace governance structure must be strictly democratic if it is to be just. However, I suggest in Part IV that natural law theory provides very strong support for wide-ranging involvement by workers in firm decision-making, and for their right to exercise discretion unfettered by micro-management. I argue, further, that it provides significant support for the democratic governance of firms by workers.[30]

In Section A, I suggest that the equal dignity of workers creates a baseline requirement that they be given respectful consideration when their welfare is affected and that they not be treated as mere means to firm productivity. In Section B, I emphasize that, on the natural law view, a firm is a community that is legitimate to the extent that each member is treated as a member, and that this means that workers deserve to be significantly involved in firm decisions. In Section C, I observe that there is, on the natural law view, no such thing as a natural right to govern, and that investors, owners, and their agents cannot therefore assume that

[28] JOHN FINNIS, AQUINAS: MORAL, POLITICAL, and LEGAL THEORY 117 (1998).

[29] See GRISEZ, LIVING, *supra* note 1, at 385–86; *cf.* FINNIS, AQUINAS, *supra* note 28, at 117 n.67, 170, 184–85.

[30] See generally ROBERT A. DAHL, A PREFACE TO ECONOMIC DEMOCRACY (1985); DEMOCRACY AND EFFICIENCY IN THE ECONOMIC ENTERPRISE (Ugo Pagano & Robert Rowthorn eds., 1996); ALAN GEWIRTH, THE COMMUNITY OF RIGHTS 260–61 (1996); W. E. J. MCCARTHY, THE FUTURE OF INDUSTRIAL DEMOCRACY (1988); CHRISTOPHER MCMAHON, AUTHORITY AND DEMOCRACY: A GENERAL THEORY OF GOVERNMENT AND MANAGEMENT (1994); STEPHEN R. MUNZER, A THEORY OF PROPERTY 336–43 (1991); THE ORGANIZATIONAL PRACTICE OF DEMOCRACY (Robert N. Stern & Sharon McCarthy eds., 1986); CAROLE PATEMAN, PARTICIPATION AND DEMOCRATIC THEORY 67–101 (1971); Carole Pateman, *A Contribution to the Political Theory of Organizational Democracy*, 7 ADMIN. & SOCY. 5 (1975). GEORGE A. POTTS, THE DEVELOPMENT OF THE SYSTEM OF REPRESENTATION IN YUGOSLAVIA WITH SPECIAL REFERENCE TO THE PERIOD SINCE 1974 (1996); JOYCE ROTHSCHILD & J. ALLEN WHITT, THE COOPERATIVE WORKPLACE: POTENTIALS AND DILEMMAS OF ORGANIZATIONAL DEMOCRACY AND PARTICIPATION (1986); DARROW SCHECHTER, GRAMSCI AND the THEORY OF INDUSTRIAL DEMOCRACY (1991); HOWARD J. SHERMAN, REINVENTING MARXISM 322, 326, 332 (1995); Carole Pateman, *A Comment on Robbins on Industrial Democracy*, 15 J. INDUST. REL. 333 (1973).

they are entitled to authority over workers in virtue of social location or property rights. In Section D, I argue that the Golden Rule requires that investors, owners, and executives who would themselves prefer not to be subordinated to others and to participate in shaping decisions affecting their lives acknowledge workers' rights not to be subordinated and to participate meaningfully in decision-making. In Section E, I maintain that participatory governance structures provide workers with an important opportunity to safeguard their own well being, which firms ought to respect. In Section F, I argue that, for multiple reasons, worker participation in governance will enhance firm efficiency and productivity. In Section G, I stress that the principle of subsidiarity requires that workers enjoy as much authority over their work lives as they can effectively exercise. In Section H, I contend that workers' involvement in governance is important because it equips them to participate in decision-making in other contexts, and that firms should ensure that such involvement occurs both for the benefit of workers and for the benefit of the various communities in which they participate outside the workplace. I offer an overview of my arguments in Section I, explaining why the considerations I have adduced ground a very strong case for extensive worker participation in firm decision-making and a plausible case for full workplace democracy.

Obviously, democracy is not a panacea for workplace ills. Within workplaces, procedural safeguards provide important protections for individuals. And even workplaces in which workers are treated fairly may behave unreasonably in relation to communities, customers, competitors, or suppliers. But democracy makes, at any rate, a substantial contribution to the empowerment and dignity of workers and their freedom from domination.[31]

A   Equal dignity

Because each worker is an end-in-herself, she deserves to be treated as an inherently valuable person for whose benefit the enterprise at which she works is in part conducted.[32] This, in turn, will surely require that workers be treated respectfully; and employers, even paternalistic ones, who respect workers' dignity will afford them some meaningful opportunities

---

[31] See PATEMAN, PARTICIPATION, supra note 30; cf. GEWIRTH, supra note 30, at 266–88; GRISEZ, LIVING, supra note 1, at 764, 868–69.
[32] See JOHN FINNIS, NATURAL LAW AND NATURAL RIGHTS 169 (1980).

to participate in workplace decisions.[33] For to deny workers opportunities of this kind is to treat them as instruments, as precisely *not* inherently valuable and persons with dignity equal to that of firm decision-makers, and thus to deny them what they are due in justice.

B *The firm as community*

A firm is, from the perspective of practical reasonableness, a cooperative community. It exists for the benefit of all of those engaged in it, not merely of some subset of investors or would-be managers.[34] Employers (in an investor-governed firm) and workers "are manifestly engaged in a kind of common enterprise."[35] Thus, part of respecting the integrity of this community and its status as a genuinely shared, mutual undertaking is declining either to exclude any participant from genuine membership in the community or to treat her as a mere cog in the organizational wheel.[36] The opportunity to participate in decisions is itself an aspect of meaningful, non-instrumental membership in the community that is the firm. Thus, to undermine or deny such opportunities is to disregard the value of that community, of the persons who are its members, and of their cooperative involvement in its activities. (Further, if there is good reason to believe that participatory governance will enhance the firm's overall productivity in ways that will benefit workers or investors,[37] failing to put participatory governance structures in place because doing so will reduce executives' financial well being or power is blatantly inconsistent with regarding the firm as a community: it suggests that some members of the community are privileged, while others are largely irrelevant.)

Because each person is equal in dignity and worth as, among other things, a member of the community that is a given firm, there would seem to be a presumption that each person should have equal authority over firm decision-making. But a defender of paternalism might argue that this presumption is defeasible. For, the paternalist might argue, equal concern for each member of the community requires precisely that some people cede decision-making authority to others who are more capable of making good decisions on behalf of the firm.

---

[33] As Grisez emphasizes; *see* GRISEZ, LIVING, *supra* note 1, at 769–71, 867–68.

[34] *Cf.* FINNIS, AQUINAS, *supra* note 28, at 264 (discussing political community); I paraphrase these remarks here and apply them in a different context.

[35] FINNIS, LAW, *supra* note 32, at 183.   [36] *See* GRISEZ, LIVING, *supra* note 1, at 763–64.

[37] *See* Section F, *infra*.

This argument obviously assumes that ordinary workers are not capable of making good decisions on behalf of a firm. But this assumption must be qualified even to be remotely plausible. (*i*) The paternalist's claim is an empirical one. Nothing about the natures of managers and workers of any sort (if there are such natures) makes it true. (*ii*) Workers differ enormously in their backgrounds and skill levels, so it is clearly not possible to generalize about all workers as a group. (*iii*) Firm size often creates complexities that make arguments for specialized managerial authority more plausible. But there are good economic reasons for replacing large firms with small ones interacting flexibly in the course of relationships structured by contract.[38] In such small firms, the value of managerial specialization would likely be diminished. (*iv*) There is a difference between exercising authority over a firm's strategic direction and the selection of its operational decision-makers, on the one hand, and exercising operational control on the other. Even if the paternalist could show that ordinary workers could not always engage in the latter task because they lacked certain kinds of technical knowledge, this would hardly show that they were incapable of reflecting seriously on big-picture questions with potentially substantial consequences for their futures.

In short: respect for each member of a community as a member who is equal in dignity to the other members helps to ground a presumption that all participants should enjoy equal authority over the firm's decisions. This presumption will only be qualified when workers genuinely lack the needed skills – not only to evaluate technical operational details but also to gauge someone's effectiveness in managing firm operations. (For the fact that a particular worker cannot perform a particular task does not mean that she cannot help to hold someone else accountable for performing it well.) And this is most likely to be the case only when firms are large enough to be – especially when all relevant costs are internalized – inefficient.[39] That firms are normatively communities means that there is good reason for firms to establish governance structures in which all workers are involved as equals, at least in firms of efficient size.

C   *The absence of a natural right to govern*

The basic equality of persons, the Golden Rule, and, arguably, the Efficiency Principle limit any presumption of managerial authority.[40]

---

[38]   *See* Subsections 1 and 2 of Section F, *infra.*   [39]   *See* Section F, *infra.*
[40]   *Cf.* RANDY HODSON, DIGNITY AT WORK (2001); Walther Müller-Jentsch, *Industrial Democracy: From Representative Codetermination to Direct Participation*, 25 INT. J. POL.

Thus, they preclude a variety of bases for denying workers the opportunity to make decisions: no manager is entitled to a position of authority over workers simply because it will enhance her status or enable her
to control a budget or earn more money; no one is entitled to such a
position just in virtue of her class background, social status, or creden-
tials, rather than on the basis of her potential for effective performance.
Giving someone organizational authority on the basis of such irrelevant
characteristics is inconsistent with the Golden Rule both in virtue of
the interests of those who might want and be equipped to fill leadership
positions while lacking irrelevant characteristics, and in virtue of the
interests of those who might benefit from their leadership but are instead
subjected to the authority of someone selected on the basis of inapposite
qualifications. It is also inconsistent with the Efficiency Principle insofar
as it represents an unnecessarily ineffective pathway toward the achievement of the firm's goals. Neither social status nor organizational title
nor anyone's property rights can confer on investors or managers any
"natural right to govern."[41] Such a right, if there were one, would need to
be justified as fair to workers and as responsive to the needs of the firm
as a community.

D   Fairness and freedom from subordination

The Golden Rule precludes imposing a cost, burden, or risk on someone else that the actor would be unwilling to accept in her position.
Many people, if not all, dislike being governed by masters they did not
appoint and expected to follow rules they did not participate in making.[42]
Someone who would dislike being subordinated within a governance
structure in which her preferences would only be considered at the sufferance of others acts unfairly if she requires that others be subordinated in
such a hierarchy or cooperates in requiring that they do so.

Perhaps someone with authority within a firm would genuinely be
unconcerned about being subordinated within an undemocratic hierarchy; perhaps she retains her status and authority only in the sincere,
reflective belief that her doing so is essential to the welfare of the firm

---

ECON. 50 (1995); Michael Whitty, *Co-Management for Workplace Democracy*, 9 J. ORG.
CHANGE MGMT. 7 (1996).

[41] FINNIS, AQUINAS, *supra* note 28, at 264; the reference in the original is to governance in
the political community.

[42] Someone might regard them as unavoidable in the interest of practicality, or as regret-
table consequences of a property system she views as legitimate, and so may not *resent*
them as explicitly unjust. But she might nonetheless be disposed to assent to the view
that, if they were avoidable, she would welcome their absence.

as a community. If so, the Golden Rule itself might not require that she decline to subordinate others (though there might well be good reasons for her to question her own motives and for others to present her with facts suggestive of the inaccuracy of her belief in her own importance). But anyone who does resent subordination will have very good reason to avoid subordinating others. Certainly, the fact that someone objects to giving others power, and zealously guards her own position, is itself evidence that she values status and authority. If she does, her denying them to others would seem to be inconsistent with the Golden Rule.

In short, then, the Golden Rule seems to entail the conclusion that many people with authority in firms should refuse to support the hierarchical subordination of workers. And, of course, this implies not only that executives and investors in currently hierarchical investor-owned firms should devolve power, but also that workers in cooperatives and other worker-governed firms should refuse to create or support undemocratic hierarchies in their firms.

Worker governance is likely to enhance efficiency and productivity. But even if worker governance were shown likely to exert some negative effect on productivity as compared with investor governance, this would not render the fairness of opting for democracy over subordination irrelevant. The worth of fairness is not commensurable either with the additional money that might be generated by some alternate institutional arrangement or with the various aspects of well being in which that money might enable people to participate. Firm decision-makers must still, finally, apply the Golden Rule to ask – even assuming such a trade-off were necessary – what they personally might find acceptable were they to trade roles with other affected persons. It seems quite possible that in many cases this kind of reflection would lead to the conclusion that democracy was rationally preferable to profitability.

E   The protection of workers' well being

Because workers likely understand what makes for their own well being better than do others, participation in firm decision-making can enable them to use their awareness of their needs and preferences to shape policies and strategies that are appropriately responsive to those needs and preferences. Workers' participation in the basic aspects of well being and their interests in individual fair treatment, in satisfactory compensation, and in the survival and flourishing of the firms at which they work are independently valuable and worth protecting. Thus, there is good reason for firms to provide structural opportunities for them to participate in governance as a means of protecting their interests. While it is possible in principle that their participation in governance might not be required to safeguard their welfare, it is surely most likely that it will be protected if they have meaningful opportunities to shape decisions that will affect them. Firm decision-makers would want *their* interests safeguarded, so it will often be unreasonable for them to deny workers the opportunities to protect their own interests afforded by participation in decision-making.

F   *The enhancement of efficiency and productivity*

The Golden Rule and the Efficiency Principle provide strong support for the establishment of participatory management structures because these structures can enhance firm performance. The Golden Rule requires those creating firm decision-making structures to be concerned about the welfare of all stakeholders. Since the improvement of firm performance will benefit multiple stakeholders, and since participatory management structures will enhance performance, the Golden Rule calls for the establishment of such structures. And since participatory structures allow a firm to produce goods and services more efficiently, the Efficiency Principle provides further reason for the creation of such structures.

Extensive corporate bureaucracies and hierarchies are inefficient (Subsection 1), as is corporate central planning (Subsection 2). Small firms related by contract are thus more likely to be efficient than large integrated firms. There is thus good reason for the replacement of large firms by small ones. And – if they are ever valuable – hierarchies become less and less necessary as firm size decreases. But, even in a large firm, participatory structures enhance productivity and efficiency in multiple ways.[43] They

---

[43] *See generally* Jacques Bélanger, The Influence of Employee Involvement on Productivity: A Review of Research (2000); Richard B. Freeman, Morris M. Kleiner, & Cheri Ostroff, *The Anatomy of Employee Involvement and Its Effects on Firms and Workers*, Working Paper 8050, National Bureau of Economic Research (2000); Derek C. Jones & Takao Kato, *The Effects of Employee Involvement on Firm Performance: Evidence from an Econometric Case Study*, William Davidson Institute Working Paper 612 (2003); Yi Ngan, Estimating the Potential Productivity and Real Wage Effects of Employee Involvement (1996); Thomas Ahrens & Christopher Chapman, *Accounting for Flexibility and Efficiency: A Field Study of Management Control Systems in a Restaurant Chain*, 21 Contemp. Acct. Research 271 (2004); Ismail Bakan Yuliani Suseno, Ashly

can reduce supervision and monitoring costs (Subsection 3), increase workers' cooperativeness by enhancing the perceived legitimacy of firm decisions (Subsection 4), encourage the development of the solidarity and flexibility that come with the emergence of trust-based relationships (Subsection 5), allow workers to use their local knowledge effectively on the firm's behalf (Subsection 6), and foster rapid and flexible responses to customer needs (Subsection 7). Worker ownership, in particular, can increase performance by resolving the principal–agent problem (Subsection 8). Considerations relate to workplace efficiency provide a very strong basis for worker participation in governance (Subsection 9).

Pinnington & Arthur Money, *The Influence of Financial Participation and Participation in Decision-Making on Employee Job Attitudes*, 15 INT'L. J. HUM. RESOURCE MGMT. 587 (2004) (pointing to the importance of participation in decision-making as a predictor of job satisfaction); Chris Doucouliagos, *Worker Participation and Productivity in Labor-Managed and Participatory Capitalist Firms: A Meta-Analysis*, 49 IND. & LAB. REL. REV. 58 (1995); Vanessa Urch Druskat & Jane V. Wheeler, *How to Lead a Self-Managing Team*, 45 MIT SLOAN MGMT. REV. 65 (2004) (noting the effectiveness of self-managed teams); Richard B. Freeman & Morris M. Kleiner, *Who Benefits Most from Employee Involvement: Firms or Workers?*, 90 Am. Econ. Rev. 219 (2000); Jeffrey M. Hirsch, *Labor Law Obstacles to the Collective Negotiation and Implementation of Employee Stock Ownership Plans: A Response to Henry Hansmann and Other Survivalists*, 67 FORDHAM L. REV. 957, 971 (1998) (citing Joseph Blasi, Michael Conte, Douglas Kruse, *Employee Stock Ownership and Corporate Performance among Public Companies*, 50 INDUS. & LAB. REL. REV. 60, 62 (1996); Henry Hansmann, *When Does Worker Ownership Work? ESOPs, Law Firms, Codetermination, and Economic Democracy*, 99 YALE L.J. 1749, 1768 (1990)). Mark Huselid & Brian E. Becker, *Methodological Issues in Cross- Sectional and Panel Estimates of the Human Resource–Firm Performance Link*, 35 IND. REL. 400 (1996); Bradley Kirkman & Benson Rosen, *Beyond Self-Management: Antecedents and Consequences of Team Empowerment*, 42 ACAD. MGMT. J. 59 (1999); Casey Ichniowski & Kathryn Shaw, *The Effects of Human Resource Management Systems on Economic Performance*, 45 MGMT. SCI. 704 (1999); Robert McNabb & Keith Whitfield, *The Impact of Financial Participation and Employee Involvement on Financial Performance*, 45 SCOTTISH J. POL. ECON. 171 (1998); Virginie Perotin & Andrew Robinson, *Employee Participation and Equal Opportunities Practices: Productivity Effect and Potential Complementarities*, 38 BRIT. J. IND. REL. 557 (2000) (highlighting a complex interaction between participation and equal-opportunity policies vis-à-vis productivity); George K. Y. Tseo, Hou Gui Sheng, Zhang Peng-Zhu, & Zhang Lihai *Employee Ownership and Profit Sharing as Positive Factors in the Reform of Chinese State-Owned Enterprises*, 25 ECON. & IND. DEMOCRACY 147 (2004) (suggesting that worker ownership and shop-floor-level participation contributed to productivity, but that worker participation in governance exerted a negative effect on productivity); ADBI INSTITUTE, EMPLOYEES IN ASIAN ENTERPRISES: THEIR POTENTIAL ROLE IN CORPORATE GOVERNANCE, http://www.adbi.org/articles/38. Employees.in.Asian.Enterprises/4.2.Employee.Involvement.on.the.Shop-Floor/Page1. php (citing sources including Sandra E. Black and Lisa Lynch, *What's Driving the New Economy: The Benefits of Workplace Innovation*, Working Paper 7479, National Bureau of Economic Research (2000).

1   The global inefficiency of large firms

Hierarchies are inefficient. Relatively flat management structures and opportunities for workers to exercise independent discretion (personally and collectively) not only do not inhibit but actually enhance overall firm performance even when this discretion is relatively limited. Further, if there is any efficiency-based case for managerial hierarchy, it is that large organizations are more effective than smaller ones, all other things being equal, and that hierarchical structures are needed to coordinate activities in such organizations. But this assumption is questionable on multiple grounds.[44]

(*i*) The viability of large organizations is dependent in significant part on low *transportation* costs. But these costs are rising rapidly as fuel becomes scarcer. And these costs are artificially reduced in various ways by past and continuing subsidies in such forms as targeted tax breaks, state subsidies to inefficient infrastructure projects (including the use of eminent domain to provide land for roads), and the vast state expenditures needed to support military protection of powerful countries' access to petroleum. These subsidies artificially reduce the costs of maintaining large organizations dependent on extended distribution networks. There is good reason for firms to be required to internalize transportation costs they have previously externalized; and, if they are, firm size seems likely to drop significantly. The elimination of the relevant subsidies is almost certainly required by both the Golden Rule and the Efficiency Principle. And their elimination will likely contribute to reductions in firm size and to obviating corporate hierarchies.

(*ii*) Today's corporate behemoths are also plausibly regarded as illegitimate products of injustice and inefficiency because they are not generally required to internalize most or all of the *environmental* costs associated with the long-distance transit required in accordance with their business models. Petroleum-based transportation, in particular, almost certainly contributes to climate change and to other environmental costs. If these costs were internalized, incentives to avoid reliance on long-distance transit would be much greater. (No doubt investment in the development of alternatives to petroleum as the prime fuel source for

[44] I am immensely grateful to Kevin Carson for helping me to see the following points. *See* KEVIN A. CARSON, STUDIES IN MUTUALIST POLITICAL ECONOMY (2007); KEVIN A CARSON, ORGANIZATION THEORY: A LIBERTARIAN PERSPECTIVE (2008).

individual transportation would increase dramatically as well.) And, in turn, this would mean that incentives for a firm to grow indefinitely would be significantly reduced and that, instead, there would be significant incentives for firms to focus their activities locally and thus, likely, to remain relatively small. Requiring that firms internalize their costs is, again, almost certainly required by both the Golden Rule and the Efficiency Principle. Doing so will help to make the emergence of smaller firms a relatively natural economic development.

(*iii*) Large corporations often remain large as a result of other kinds of subsidies, including various sorts of tax subsidies offered by the state and cost reductions resulting from the use of eminent domain to benefit influential businesses, as well as legally maintained barriers to market entry that reduce competition and make it more likely that large corporations will be able to remain large despite the inefficiencies associated with excessive size. The elimination of subsidies and monopoly privileges, almost certainly required by both the Golden Rule and the Efficiency Principle, would likely contribute further to reductions in firm size. And the dependence of firms on unfair and inefficient privileges underscores, again, the illegitimacy of the structural features that make the preservation of elaborate hierarchies seem efficient.

(*iv*) It is too quickly assumed that economies of scale are unlimited. In fact, however, beyond a certain size firms (especially hierarchical ones, given the supervision and monitoring costs incurred by such firms) likely grow no more operationally efficient and may, indeed, become more inefficient.

2 The inefficiency of corporate planning

The inefficiency of corporate central planning provides a particularly good example of, and rationale for, the claim that size breeds inefficiency. The attempt to plan centrally for, the production, consumption, and distribution of goods and services leads inevitably to losses in information that create production and distribution irrationalities. Market prices provide irreplaceable information about production and distribution needs. A central authority almost certainly cannot acquire all of the needed information to plan satisfactorily for production and distribution, and the attempt to do so can lead to the highly inefficient expenditure of resources.[45]

---

[45] As Theodore Burczak's socialist analysis acknowledges; *see* THEODORE A. BURCZAK, SOCIALISM AFTER HAYEK (2006).

NATURAL LAW AND WORKPLACE DEMOCRACY 99

This conclusion is characteristically pressed against proponents of state central planning . But it is important to see that nothing about the argument limits its application to planning by the *state*. Large organizations that engage in central planning encounter comparable difficulties: setting prices by means of central command and control structures *within a corporation* generates inefficiencies and constrains the availability of needed goods and services because a large corporation's central planners lack the ability to acquire and integrate important available information about supply and demand, just as state central planners have proven unable to do.[46]

The inefficiencies and irrationalities associated with corporate central planning can be avoided to a significant degree if firms themselves are small. Where the components of a large hierarchical organization must be coordinated using central planning mechanisms, small firms can regulate their relationships flexibly, by contract. They can adjust requirements, make purchasing and staffing decisions, and so forth, in light of ongoing changes in economic conditions, to which they can respond more rapidly and accurately than can a corporate planning structure. The Golden Rule and the Efficiency Principle thus provide good reason for the replacement of large corporations by small firms related by contract. A common argument for creating and preserving corporate hierarchies is that they are needed to manage and coordinate the activities of large organizations. But if there are good reasons to replace large organizations with small firms related by contract, then the rationale for instituting and protecting hierarchies disappears.

3   Reduction in supervision and monitoring costs

Monitoring workers' behavior is costly and ineffective.[47] Replacing supervisory monitoring with worker self-management will tend to reduce the amount of money firms spend to oversee and regulate workers' behavior,[48] and thus enhance productivity. This is obviously an

---

[46] *See generally* Kevin A. Carson, *Economic Calculation in the Corporate Commonwealth*, THE FREEMAN: IDEAS ON LIBERTY, June 2007, at 13; Kevin A. Carson, *Hierarchy or the Market*, THE FREEMAN: IDEAS ON LIBERTY, April 2008, at 10.

[47] *See* Lawrence E. Mitchell, *Trust and Team Production in Post-Capitalist Society*, 24 IOWA J. CORP. L. 869, 883–87 (1999).

[48] *See* Kent Greenfield, *Using Behavioral Economics to Show the Power and Efficiency of Corporate Law as Regulatory Tool*, 35 U.C. DAVIS L. REV. 581, 618 (2002). Greenfield suggests that decreased monitoring costs are also associated with reduced income inequality. *See id.* at 618–22.

advantage for worker-controlled firms,[49] but it also provides a reason for investor-controlled firms to put participatory mechanisms in place.

4   Enhancing workers' perceptions of workplace fairness

The creation of participatory structures could increase productivity by enhancing perceived fairness in the workplace. By doing this, these changes could affect not only worker well being but also firm performance in positive ways. People typically believe institutional arrangements are fair when they experience respect as particular persons, but also when procedures for decision-making are inclusive, responsive, and transparent, when the well being of all those affected by a decision is taken into account, and when people are treated with a reasonable degree of equality. When workers believe a firm's decision-making structures are fair, they are inclined to see the decisions reached by these structures as legitimate. In turn, they will tend to opt more readily for a cooperative relationship with the firm. And this cooperative relationship can enhance firm productivity.[50] This impact on productivity matters for both the firm and the community, and both the Golden Rule and the Efficiency Principle provide good reason to take it seriously.

5   Facilitating understanding, solidarity, and flexibility

By making them decision-makers, participatory structures can equip workers at a given enterprise to understand the enterprise more adequately.[51] Thus, they can understand the positions of other firm actors more clearly, and equip others to understand their positions more completely as well. This kind of increased understanding is likely to promote greater empathy and solidarity throughout the firm, and thus more effective cooperation. In addition, worker involvement in decision-making can ensure that workers have more information about aspects of firm operations in which they may not be directly involved, and are able to use this information to improve processes and products more immediately affected by their activities.

---

[49] *See* Samuel Bowles & Herbert Gintis, *The Democratic Firm: An Agency-Theoretic Evaluation*, *in* MARKETS AND DEMOCRACY: PARTICIPATION, ACCOUNTABILITY, and EFFICIENCY 13 (Samuel Bowles, Herbert Gintis, & Bo Gustafsson eds., 1993).

[50] *Cf.* Greenfield, *supra* note 48, at 613–16 (explicating the work of Tom Tyler), 617, 641–43; John T. Delaney, *Workplace Cooperation: Current Problems, New Approaches*, 17 J. LAB. RES. 45 (1996) (offering qualified support for the view that workplace participation enhances firm performance); Susan Schwochau & John Delaney, *Employee Participation and Assessments of Support for Organizational Policy Change*, 18 J. LAB. RES. 379 (1997).

[51] *Cf.* GRISEZ, LIVING, *supra* note 1, at 868–69.

The implementation of participatory governance procedures can tend to make all firm–worker relationships more like those that bind senior executives and investors in contemporary corporate law doctrine. Firm–worker relationships of this kind foster flexible, sensitive, respectful, trusting, mutually coordinated, efficient behavior, promote solidarity, and reduce conflict, and thus exert a variety of positive direct and indirect influences on firm performance.[52]

6   Mobilizing workers' local knowledge

Participatory structures can also enhance performance by mobilizing workers' specialized knowledge. Workers develop detailed knowledge regarding firm processes and products that those distant from them in hierarchically structured organizations will often lack. Participatory structures allow workers to use this detailed knowledge to improve processes and products without the need to convince unaccountable supervisors, and so to improve productivity.

7   Improving customer service

Replacing supervision with worker discretion can improve customer service, because when workers are free to use their discretion they can solve customers' problems without waiting for authorization from managers if they need to depart from established practices to meet customers' needs. Because they can do so, productivity is likely to be further enhanced, since time within a firm can be used more efficiently and the firm can respond more quickly and flexibly to customers' concerns, and so foster customer satisfaction and loyalty.

8   Worker ownership and the principal–agent problem

From the standpoint of consumers and communities with the potential to benefit from enhanced firm performance, there is good reason to encourage not just worker *control* but also worker *ownership*. That's because of the principal–agent problem that bedevils investor-governed firms. On the conventional legal and theoretical accounts, the employees of such firms, from executives to janitors, are agents of investors. But the well being of these employees is often not served by furthering the

---

[52] *See* Mitchell, *supra* note 47, at 887–912; Greenfield, *supra* note 48, at 622–27 (citing FRANK H. EASTERBROOK & DANIEL R. FISCHEL, THE ECONOMIC STRUCTURE OF CORPORATE LAW 90–93 (1991), and Daniel R. Fischel, *The Corporate Governance Movement*, 35 VAND. L. REV. 1259, 1264 (1982)).

well being of investors, who are not themselves able to ensure that their interests are furthered on a day-to-day basis within a firm. The divergence between the objectives of executives and other employees on the one hand and those of investors on the other can generate a variety of inefficiencies, arguably raising costs and therefore prices above what they would otherwise be.

When workers are owners, by contrast, the principal–agent problem disappears because, in effect, there are no agents, but only principals. While different factors may obviously contribute to the well being of individual workers, what makes for the welfare of workers as a group will likely be more uniform than what makes for the well being of the various constituencies that make a typical corporation today. (And the strategic and tactical differences between workers in completely different divisions of large, contemporary corporations would cease to be of concern if corporate divisions and subdivisions linked by hierarchical structures were replaced by small firms related by contract.) Obviously, this is advantageous for workers – but also for customers, as well as for communities indirectly impacted by firm productivity. Without the principal-agent problem, firm efficiency, and therefore productivity, increase. And the resulting increase in profits can be passed on to consumers and so, indirectly, to their communities (especially if firms are small and locally focused). The Golden Rule and the Efficiency Principle thus provide good reason for investors, executives, and communities to support the creation of worker-owned firms.[53]

9   Efficiency and workplace governance

The Golden Rule provides good reason for firm decision-makers to care about a firm's productivity, for the gain not only of those who gain directly from the firm's profitability but also, at least under some circumstances, of those who purchase the firm's products and services. The Efficiency Principle requires that, given otherwise reasonable objectives, people pursue those objectives efficiently. Those responsible for shaping the community that is a firm are responsible for making the enterprise efficient and productive. To the extent that workers' involvement in decision-making enhances efficiency and productivity, firm decision-makers thus have good reason to give significant opportunities for decision-making to workers.

---

[53] Thanks to Kevin Carson for helping me to see this set of points.

An efficiency-based argument for workplace *democracy* would need to show that a firm democratically governed by workers would be more efficient than a comparable firm governed by investors or their agents, with participation by workers.[54] And there is certainly reason to believe that worker control can increase efficiency. If worker control will enhance efficiency more than mere worker participation in firm governance, then the Efficiency Principle provides reason for a firm's decision makers to give workers democratic control of the firm.

G   Subsidiarity

There is no realistic reason to doubt that workers can manage their own activities and make reasonable decisions. The principle of subsidiarity implies that, when they can do so, it is unjust for a hierarchical corporate authority to deprive them of the opportunity to do so.[55] Given that a firm is a community with shared goals (and is legitimate only insofar as it is), subsidiarity requires that there be no more hierarchy than necessary to achieve the shared goals of the community (and not just, for instance, the *particular* goals of managers or investors).

To the extent that the principles of practical reasonableness are respected, firms are likely to be small. In small firms, there will be, at minimum, limited need for managerial hierarchy. Thus, in such firms, the principle of subsidiarity will tell with particular force against the creation or maintenance of hierarchies, since allowing people to make decisions for themselves if they can do so is a requirement of justice and it's especially likely that they will be able to do so in small firms. The point can be made even stronger. Workers will have more realistic opportunities to make their own decisions in small firms. Giving them opportunities to do this is a consequence of following the principle of subsidiarity. Thus, dissolving large firms and replacing them with small ones, except when efficiency clearly demands otherwise, may not infrequently be a requirement of practical reasonableness, incumbent on firms to fulfill, that flows from the principle of subsidiarity.

But even in larger firms, the capacity of workers to govern themselves will often be evident. Workers are far more capable of making effective operational, tactical, and strategic decisions than managers may

[54] I simplify here by ignoring the principal-agent problem. As I have suggested, this problem provides further support for workplace democracy.
[55] See FINNIS, LAW, *supra* note 32, at 147.

sometimes suppose. And, even when they are not, it does not follow that they are incapable of effectively evaluating the performance of leaders who are accountable to them. When they *can* do so, the principle of subsidiarity suggests that there is good reason to ensure that they are able to do so organizationally.

Whether subsidiarity requires only extensive worker self-management and discretion or actually full workplace democracy will depend primarily on the answers to empirical questions regarding the capacity of workers to make decisions for themselves efficiently and effectively, how worker self-government will impact productivity, and so forth. If workers *can* manage themselves successfully without the involvement of investor-appointed executives or managers, the principle of subsidiarity provides a very strong argument for investors to allow them to do so (when the workers work at investor-owned firms) and for communal norms, rules, and institutions to facilitate workplace democracy.

H   *Effective participation in community life*

Opportunities to participate in decision-making at work can play a crucial role in equipping people to join in decision-making in other contexts.[56] Thus, in virtue of the Golden Rule and the value of community as a basic aspect of welfare, relevant decision makers have a significant reason to ensure that workers have such opportunities.

People whose day-to-day lives are marked by limited opportunities for effective participation in meaningful decision-making at work may fail to develop the capacity for effective involvement in making decisions related to their families, schools, neighborhoods, and worshipping communities and to the other associations to which they belong, and in the shaping of their communities' norms, rules, and institutions. The capacity for this kind of involvement depends on the possession of adequate normative and practical judgment and the capacity to analyze strategy and policy, as well as the leadership and communication skills required to defend positions on controversial issues.

Most adults spend more time in their workplaces than in other non-domestic settings (and too often more time there than at home). It follows that their experiences at work will likely affect their capacities for participation in decision-making more substantially than their experiences elsewhere. The existence of significant opportunities for decision-making

---

[56] *See generally* PATEMAN, PARTICIPATION, *supra* note 30; GEWIRTH, *supra* note 30, at 266–88.

in the workplace therefore provides an exceptionally valuable opportunity for people to acquire the capacity to engage in such decision-making in other contexts.

Intimately related to the *capacity* for self-government is the *will* to participate in communal life. People who do not regard their participation in the shaping of norms, rules, and institutions as likely to make a meaningful difference will be unlikely to involve themselves in decision-making at any level. They will often be politically quiescent. By contrast, those who discover their own efficacy as contributors to the shaping of norms, rules, and institutions through participation in decision-making in the organizations to which they belong will be empowered to engage with communal issues. They will have gained a new sense of their own capacity to effect change, they will have acquired experience as change agents, and they will be more aware of relevant issues. Thus, they will likely find involvement in associational decision-making and in the shaping of communal rules, norms, and institutions a natural outgrowth of their ongoing involvement in workplace governance.[57]

The Golden Rule and the value of community both provide reason for ensuring that people have opportunities for the development of the skills and character traits that meaningful participation in workplace decision-making affords. Providing workers with these opportunities is a matter of fair regard for them: having the relevant skills and traits can make an important difference in a worker's life and it will be easiest for her to acquire them at work. It is also a matter of fairness to the members of the other communities to which workers belong. More wide-ranging and effective participation in the lives of those communities by workers is likely to enhance the quality of decisions made regarding those communities.

Owners, investors, and executives are not, per se, responsible for actively ensuring the maximum effective functioning of all of the various communities to which workers belong. But to the extent that giving workers the chance to govern themselves democratically – rather than just to participate in firm decision-making along with investors, investor-accountable managers, and perhaps others – seems likely to enhance in significant ways the lives of these other communities and workers' well being within them, investors will have further reason to afford workers the opportunity to govern investor-owned firms democratically.

---

[57] *Cf.* PATEMAN, PARTICIPATION, *supra* note 30, at 19 (noting that collective bargaining is the engine leading to self-government and discovery of the capacity to effect change).

I   Practical reason and workplace democracy

There is a very strong case to be made, from the perspective of natural
law theory, for participatory governance structures, in which workers
have meaningful opportunities to voice their convictions and influence
decisions. Providing support for, at minimum, extensive participation
by workers in decision-making are factors including workers' equal dignity and their status as members of the community that is the firm; the
lack of any natural right to govern on the part of investors, executives,
or managers; the unfairness of subordination; the value of participatory
structures in securing protection for workers' well being; the efficiency of
worker self-management and the positive impact of participatory structures on productivity; the principle of subsidiarity's requirement that
workers be able to govern themselves when they are capable of doing so;
and the positive impact of workplace participation on participation by
workers in other communities. Failing to afford substantial opportunities for participation would be inconsistent with the demands of practical reason.

Multiple governance forms that provide for participation by workers
will doubtless be reasonable. But it seems clear that, at minimum, participatory structures must be sufficient to allow workers to safeguard their
reasonable participation, through their involvement in the life of the firm,
in the basic aspects of well being. They must provide for minimal supervision and monitoring and allow for significant worker discretion. They
must be as flat as possible. And they must give workers real opportunities
to learn to develop policy and strategy. In addition, the implementation
of the principles of practical reasonableness through the creation and
maintenance of participatory structures that fulfill these criteria must
be accompanied by the withdrawal of the artificial life support that often
keeps firms large. When doing so would not be inconsistent with the
requirements of practical reasonableness, communal norms, rules, and
institutions can encourage or require firms to create and maintain appropriate participatory structures.

To varying degrees, the considerations adduced in support of the participatory workplace also count strongly in favor of the democratic workplace. Clearly, for instance, to the extent that a hierarchical structure is
not required for the flourishing of the community that is a given firm, the
principle of subsidiarity calls for the replacement of managerial oversight
with worker self-management. It also calls for workplace democracy to
the extent that workers can govern firms effectively. Since there is good

reason to believe that they can, there is good reason to believe that the principle of subsidiarity requires workplace democracy. Similarly, managers who would prefer not to be subordinated to others in undemocratic hierarchies will have good reason not to subordinate, or support the subordination of, workers in such hierarchies. And if worker governance can increase efficiency, the Golden Rule and the Efficiency Principle give investors, managers, and communities reason to favor it.

Empirical considerations will obviously be very important. *Will workers be able to govern themselves effectively, to foster efficiency, to maintain or enhance firm productivity?* If they can, the paternalist argument against the presumption of equal authority will be blunted, a subsidiarity argument for full workplace democracy will appear very strong indeed, and, obviously, there will be a strong direct argument for worker democracy based on efficiency and productivity. *Will worker democracy, rather than just workplace participation, make a substantial difference in the lives not only of workers but also of the communities to which they belong outside the workplace?* If so, investors have a further reason to foster it. *Do investors and executives like being subordinated to others?* If not, then it is presumptively unfair of them to subordinate workers. *Will worker ownership increase efficiency and productivity by resolving the principal–agent problem?* If so, communities have good reason to encourage worker ownership. At least potentially, multiple considerations provide good reason for investors and investor-accountable executives to transfer control of workplaces to workers, and for communities to encourage the creation of democratic workplaces.[58]

V   Workers and investors in the worker-governed firm

The judgment that worker self-government is appropriate or necessary has no particular implications regarding the appropriate sources of capital for worker-governed firms.

Absent monopolistic restrictions on banking and the issuing of currency, free banking arrangements of various kinds might dramatically reduce the cost of borrowing money and make start-up and operating capital much more readily available, and thus make it easier for small, worker-governed firms to come into being. There are certainly good reasons to eliminate these restrictions. But worker-governed

[58] *But cf.* Louis Putterman, *After the Employment Relation: Problems on the Road to Enterprise Democracy, in* MARKETS AND DEMOCRACY, *supra* note 49, at 129, 145–46.

firms could certainly draw on more traditional sources of investment as well. A democratically organized, worker-governed firm could hire money or capital goods from investors who could in turn be entitled either to fixed returns or to suitable shares of a worker-governed firm's profits.[59]

Presuming that workers held a residual claim on the firm's assets, they would qualify as the firm's owners. But even if investors held such a claim by contract, workers would still be responsible for the *governance* of the firm.[60] Ownership is a *bundle of rights*,[61] the elements of which can be disaggregated; a genuine right to an income stream from a firm's activities need not entail a further right to direct the activities of the firm's workers.

The relationship between investors and workers in a democratically governed firm would simply be a radicalized version of the relationship between investors and executives that has been a persistent feature of modern corporate life. This relationship is marked by a separation between ownership and control.[62] Independent executives have acted less as investors' agents than as partners in ongoing contractual relationships. Investors have frequently treated firms as "black boxes," focusing on bottom-line performance measures rather than internal operating conditions.[63] In the not-so-distant past, it was not uncommon for all investors in a firm, apart from its founder, to be issued stock without voting rights;[64] in effect, on the model for which I am arguing, all investors would be treated no differently from these stockholders. The separation between investors and firm decision-makers in a democratically governed firm need not be seen, therefore, as representing an incomprehensibly radical departure from current arrangements – except, of course, that investors' contractual relationships would link them directly with workers.

[59] *Cf.* Burczak, *supra* note 45, at 102; David Ellerman, Property and Contract in Economics (1988); David L. Prychitko, Markets, Planning and Democracy 84–85, 88 n.20 (2002).

[60] Thanks to Kevin Carson for helping me to think about this model.

[61] This view is widely accepted; it is, however, roundly criticized in James E. Penner, The Idea of Property in Law (1997).

[62] The case that such a separation was in the offing was made, famously, in Adolph Berle & Gardiner Means, The Modern Corporation and Private Property (1932).

[63] *Cf.* Zubin Jelveh, *How a Computer Knows What Many Managers Don't*, New York Times, July 9, 2006, at 32; Martin J. Pring, Breaking the Black Box (2002).

[64] *See* Armen A. Alchian & Harold Demsetz, *Production, Information Costs, and Economic Organization*, 62 Am. Econ. Rev. 777, 789 n.14 (1972); thanks to Kevin Carson for this reference.

VI Objections to workplace democracy

Objections to democratic governance by workers are diverse. I consider several objections here.[65] In Section A, I discuss Henry Hansmann and Reinier Kraakman's argument that investor dominance maximizes social wealth and avoids the paralysis that would purportedly result if workers governed firms. Germain Grisez maintains that owners of capital have inherent authority over workers; I ask in Section B whether Grisez's arguments tell against workplace democracy. Stephen Bainbridge offers a raft of objections to participatory and democratic management schemes, maintaining that there is no necessary link between participation and performance, that participatory schemes rarely involve genuine opportunities for involvement in decision-making, that such schemes are largely exercises in window-dressing, that hierarchies are valuable, that arguments for participation rooted in the supposed value of self-fulfillment are objectionable, and that forcing firms to implement participatory management schemes violates sphere sovereignty. I consider, and attempt to rebut, these arguments in Section C. Finally, in Section D, I assess Friedrich Hayek's suggestions that workers should not govern firms because their objectives purportedly diverge from those of consumers, and that workers who assume managerial responsibilities will soon cease to be workers in anything but name.

A Hansmann and Kraakman: investor dominance maximizes social benefit and prevents paralysis

Henry Hansmann and Reinier Kraakman argue that legal and social norms around the world are rightly converging on support for a model in accordance with which corporate governance structures should be concerned solely with "long-term shareholder value."[66] They are careful to point out that they do not regard the welfare of shareholders as the only morally relevant factor; they wish to argue only that managers should be primarily *accountable* to shareholders, and that this will, in fact, benefit all of society.[67]

Determining whether the current model of corporate governance does, in fact, maximize societal wealth is obviously a non-trivial operation. But

---

[65] Certainly not all. An extensive debate has emerged regarding the economics of worker self-managed firms. For a discussion, *see* PRYCHITKO, *supra* note 59, at 78–88.

[66] Henry Hansmann & Reinier Kraakman, *The End of History for Corporate Law*, 89 GEO. L.J. 439 (2001).

[67] *Id.* at 441.

even if it could be determined that investor governance of firms did clearly have this effect, it would not follow that firms ought to be investor-governed. For the work of particular persons for corporations, just like their activities generally, is not ordered solely to the maximization of societal wealth. Wealth is not an intrinsic good, but rather a means of participating in the diverse aspects of well being, which do not admit of maximization. Certainly, therefore, the well being of an entire community is not identical with its monetizable wealth; maximizing wealth is not the same as maximizing well being (which is a formal category that does not admit of maximization). In addition, if the theoretical and empirical argument supporting the view that worker participation, and likely worker governance, can enhance a firm's efficiency and productivity is correct, then it seems likely that worker governance *can* exert a net positive impact even on wealth narrowly conceived.

Firms are cooperative enterprises that certainly have responsibilities to consumers and communities; they cannot and should not be operated *simply* for the benefit of investors *or* workers. They ought to benefit the wider communities to which they belong; and, obviously, they must be profitable – both because if they are not they will not be able to continue in operation and because their profitability provides some (hardly conclusive) evidence that they are providing products and services genuinely important to other people. But the moral considerations that count in favor of participation, and quite possibly democracy, in the workplace – fairness, subsidiarity, community, dignity – are independently valuable and cannot be trumped by appeals to communal wealth. Workplace democracy is not warranted solely by its efficiency; rather, there is independent justificatory value in the capacity of workplace democracy to give people meaningful control over their own lives, to enable them to engage in self-government, to help them avoid subjection to unaccountable and potentially arbitrary authority.

Hansmann and Kraakman argue that "meaningful direct worker voting participation in corporate affairs tends to produce inefficient decisions, paralysis, or weak boards, and that these costs are likely to exceed any potential benefits that worker participation might bring."[68] This argument is unpersuasive, at least as regards full-blown worker self-government.

If a firm's executives and managers are responsible to the firm's workers, they will have good reason not to exhibit weakness and paralysis.[69]

---

[68] *Id.* at 445.

[69] *Cf.* MILTON FRIEDMAN & ROSE D. FRIEDMAN, TWO LUCKY PEOPLE: MEMOIRS 424 (1998).

The workers' long-term livelihood depends on the firm's profitability: their salaries will be payable only if the firm is viable. The firm will be viable only if it secures capital. And the firm will be able to attract capital from investors only if it is well managed and if investors are treated fairly. Investors will not support firms that squander resources, however they are organized. Workers will therefore have (further) good reason to foster effective and responsive decision-making.

Obviously, workers will be disinclined to support dramatic job cuts even if making such cuts might be the approach the managers of an investor-governed firm might tend to recommend. But, if anything, investor-governed firms have arguably been much too quick to dismiss ordinary workers in response to financial stresses, and their practice ought not necessarily to be seen as emulable. And where workforce reductions are unavoidable, workers will have two reasons to implement them. (*i*) In a genuinely difficult financial situation, workers will be aware that the survival of the firm itself, or of entire divisions of the firm, may be at stake. If cuts in staffing are essential to the survival of a viable firm, workers who care about firm survival will make those cuts. And, indeed, they are more likely than managers to make decisions about workforce reductions in recognition of which positions are most dispensable, and to avoid retaining padded organizational bureaucracies while increasing the pressure on reduced numbers of ordinary workers. (*ii*) Workers will be perfectly aware of the financial importance of attracting investment on an ongoing basis, and this will help to prompt them to make cuts if the cuts are genuinely necessary.

Hansmann and Kraakman seem to assume that workers as a group have significantly more diverse goals than stockholders as a group and that workers' diverse preferences will lead to paralyzed corporate decision-making. But it is not clear that this claim is borne out by the available evidence.[70] The instrumental value of worker self-government may be especially evident in firms with homogeneous worker groups, but it does not follow that workplace democracy cannot be effective elsewhere. And even purportedly homogeneous groups (as of stockholders) are often more diverse than might initially be supposed.[71] There may be some efficiency costs associated with participatory models. But there are also significant efficiency gains, for multiple reasons. In addition, the kinds of costs which Hansmann and Kraakman maintain are endemic to

[70] *See* Hirsch, *supra* note 43, at 979 (critiquing an earlier article by Hansmann).
[71] *See id.*

worker-governed firms are already evident in other governance schemes,[72] so it's not clear at how much of a disadvantage worker-managed firms actually are here.

B   Grisez: owners of capital rightly exercise authority over workers

Grisez maintains that "[w]orkers should respect the authority of employers and obey them ..." and should seek "to understand and carry out the employer's or supervisor's intentions and plans for the work to be done."[73] He attempts to warrant the authority of firms with an account of work as a shared activity. He writes:

> The value of the work is divided and shared. The employer's share and proper good is the work's result: the thing produced or service rendered. The employee's share is self-realization in the work and just compensation for it. Since the work must be ordered to its result, which is the employer's proper good, he or she has authority to choose the result to be sought. Moreover, if employers are capable of it, they have the right to choose among the morally acceptable and technically feasible means available for bringing about the result they seek, and to direct the employee in using those means.[74]

Even when workplace authority is *legitimately* exercised, it may *still* be excessive. And someone may attempt to use it in a manner contrary to the good of the community that is the firm. Thus, while it is not a source of organizational effectiveness to second-guess every choice by firm decision-makers, each such choice must still be consistent with the requirements of practical reasonableness and may, in principle, be evaluated and resisted as inconsistent with those requirements. And it will often be useful for even legitimate authority to be checked by the input of those other than the decision maker.

But it is not clear, in any case, that the exercise of authority by investors over workers *is* reasonable. It seems most reasonable to say that the proper good of the investor or other owner is the share of the proceeds of an enterprise to which she is entitled by agreement with the firm. (She may also be entitled, depending on her contractual relationships with the firm, to appropriate shares of its capital assets if it ceases operations.) The investor does choose the result to be sought by the firm *in the sense* that she decides in what enterprise to invest; she chooses what good she will seek by investing. She may, of course, exercise further influence by

---

[72] *See id.* at 980.   [73] GRISEZ, LIVING, *supra* note 1, at 759–60.   [74] *Id.* at 763.

declining to invest further, by selling her stock, and so forth. But the fact that she may do this does not entitle her to determine who the firm will employ, promote, and dismiss; what strategic direction the firm will take; or what tactical measures it will undertake in fulfillment of its strategy. There is nothing about the ownership of a portion of the profit stream from a firm that entitles the investor to exercise this kind of control, and exercising it is, in any event, unreasonable in light of the considerations I have adduced in support of workplace participation and democracy.

For there is no natural right to rule. Following the Golden Rule will, at least, often mean not subjecting workers to nonconsensual authority. Subsidiarity precludes the exercise of authority over workers that they are capable of exercising themselves. Providing opportunities for democratic participation by workers in workplace decision-making is importantly beneficial to the other communities to which they belong. Support for many structural features of the economy that prop up large firms that may not lend themselves as readily as small ones to worker self-government is inconsistent with the Golden Rule and the Efficiency Principle. And extensive participation, and probably workplace democracy, can enhance efficiency and productivity.

In short, multiple considerations weigh against owners' assumption of the kind of authority to which Grisez refers. Decision makers in firms that are not worker-governed have good reason to cede much or all decision-making authority to workers, not to insist that it belongs to owners. As long as workers *can* reasonably direct their own affairs, it is unreasonable, if they are not themselves owners, for the owners of assets they use in their work to attempt to govern their workplace.

C   Bainbridge: participation is ineffective, hierarchies are valuable, and sphere sovereignty deserves respect

Stephen Bainbridge has challenged arguments for participatory management on several grounds.[75] He rejects the claim that participatory structures necessarily enhance corporate performance[76] or protect workers. He argues that workers in purportedly participation-friendly environments do not, in fact, characteristically regard themselves as having substantial

---

[75] *See* Stephen Bainbridge, *Corporate Decisionmaking and the Moral Rights of Employees: Participatory Management and Natural Law*, 43 VILL. L. REV. 741 (1998).

[76] *See* Stephen M. Bainbridge, *Participatory Management within a Theory of the Firm*, 21 IOWA J. CORP. L. 657, 676–81 (1996).

opportunities to influence corporate decisions,[77] so that implementing participatory mechanisms will not achieve its intended purpose. He objects to anti-hierarchical arguments for workplace democracy on the grounds that corporate hierarchies benefit all concerned. And he maintains that mandating participation schemes violates sphere sovereignty – the integrity of individual organizations and aspects of communal life.

1   Participation and efficiency

Whether full-blown worker self-management enhances performance is difficult to know because so few worker-managed firms, relatively speaking, exist. There is empirical evidence, however, that seems clearly to support the view that greater participation by workers in the management of investor-controlled firms does enhance performance. And there are sensible theoretical reasons – the capacity of worker self-management, and even more so worker self-government, to reduce monitoring costs, increase flexibility, inspire greater commitment on the part of workers, and mobilize workers' local knowledge – to suppose that worker governance improves efficiency. In addition, as I have already suggested, workplace democracy is valuable independently of its effect on efficiency (though of course workers themselves might have good reason to complain in a case in which democracy led to underperformance).

2   Participation as unprotective

According to Bainbridge, workplace participation is not needed to restrain the abuse of workers by firms, and may not be especially effective at doing so.[78] Non-participatory mechanisms, especially laws, exist to protect workers, Bainbridge notes.[79] But it is reasonable to ask whether these mechanisms are either as effective as ones in which workers are directly involved or as efficient as processes that do not depend for their success on time-consuming and costly litigation.

3   Workers' skepticism about participation

Whether workers in firms with participatory management structures believe they are really capable of shaping corporate decisions is an interesting question. But the answer is irrelevant to the judgment whether democratic institutions would be satisfactory. It would be irrational for workers in genuinely democratic workplaces to regard themselves as

---

[77] See Bainbridge, Decisionmaking, supra note 75, at 807.   [78] See id. at 817–25.
[79] See id. at 826–27.

excluded from opportunities for decision-making if their votes really determined who would play relevant leadership roles and which policy changes would be adopted. Surely, then, the right response to the claim that participatory mechanisms don't deliver on their promise is to make them more effective, not to abandon them.

Bainbridge argues, in effect, that workers' skepticism is justified because current participation programs are actually control mechanisms. He recognizes that his opponents might agree "that present forms of employee involvement are ... flawed" while suggesting "that some ideal form exists that would be more effective in promoting human development." But this sort of approach "smacks of the 'if only people were different' fallacy. Sound public policy must be based on how people actually behave, not how we hope they would behave in an ideal world."[80] But the claim is not that human *nature* needs changing, but that the institutional environment within which participation takes place needs to be altered.

Bainbridge also doubts whether workers actually *want* opportunities for participation in large numbers.[81] Perhaps some workers really do prefer hierarchical work forms. But at least some of the benefits these workers find in such forms of organization are available in worker-managed firms. It is not clear, further, that the desires of the workers to whom Bainbridge refers reflect the conditions in genuinely participatory, much less fully democratic, firms; perhaps the real point is that workers don't want sham participatory schemes of the sort he suggests many workers believe really obtain in their workplaces. And there is, in fact, substantial desire for opportunities for participation among many workers.[82]

4   The putative value of hierarchy

Hierarchy, says Bainbridge, is useful because it facilitates monitoring of workers' behavior and because it promotes the dissemination of information.[83] If participation means an end to hierarchy, then, he suggests, we ought not to regard participation as an attractive ideal.

Participatory and democratic workplaces can accomplish much of what hierarchies accomplish more efficiently and less oppressively. And, since, firm size increases the value of hierarchical governance, and since the

---

[80] *Id.* at 771–72 (footnote omitted).   [81] *See id.* at 758–76.

[82] *See* RICHARD B. FREEMAN & JOEL ROGERS, WHAT WORKERS WANT (2d ed. 2006); *cf.* Marley S. Weiss, *Innovations in Collective Bargaining: NUMMI – Driven to Excellence*, 13 HOFSTRA LAB. L.J. 433, 458–59 (1996).

[83] *See* Bainbridge, *Decisionmaking, supra* note 75, at 805; Bainbridge, *Management, supra* note 76, at 661–73.

efficient firm is likely to be much smaller if it fairly internalizes all of its costs, the optimally sized firm will have at most a limited need for hierarchical structure.[84] If, however, despite the efficiencies associated with worker governance and the limitations on size associated with full cost internalization, a hierarchical structure is needed in a democratic firm, the firm's democratic character need pose no barrier to its creation of such a structure.[85]

While hierarchies can constrain freedom, reduce flexibility, and stifle initiative, democracy is not incompatible with functional hierarchies, though it seems likely that the hierarchical organization of a democratic workplace would be flatter than the organization of a non-democratic workplace. Practical reason provides multiple justifications for worker governance; but participatory management and workplace democracy are not incompatible with representative institutions, given that such institutions are needed. Participatory and democratic workplaces can be as hierarchical as efficiency requires while being as non-hierarchical as fairness, efficiency, and regard for community, and thus also subsidiarity, demand.

5   Mandatory participation schemes violate sphere sovereignty

Bainbridge is troubled about the reach of communal interference into firms' affairs and the use of law to settle all disputes.[86] He suggests that the principle of "sphere sovereignty" should preclude "the use of the state's monopoly on the use of coercive force to impose workplace democracy."[87] Such an imposition is an attack, says Bainbridge, on human freedom.[88]

The arguments for workplace democracy (and, secondarily, for workplace participation) I've advanced have been primarily designed to show that practical reason requires owners, investors, and executives to cede significant power to workers. Neither the relative integrity of the individual firm nor the purported integrity of the economic sphere gives

---

[84] See CARSON, THEORY, *supra* note 44, at 105–288. Carson explores the relevant literature in painstaking detail to show that the seeming advantages conferred on many corporations by size are artificial, and that, absent market-distorting factors of various kinds, the small, worker-managed and worker-owned firm would typically be more productive than any alternative.

[85] A worker-selected management could help, for instance, to ensure mutual accountability in a firm large enough to need designated managers; *cf.* Masahiko Aoki, *The Motivational Role of an External Agent in the Informationally-Participatory Firm, in* MARKETS AND DEMOCRACY, *supra* note 49, at 231, 245.

[86] *See* Bainbridge, *Decisionmaking, supra* note 75, at 811.   [87] *Id.* at 810.

[88] *See id.* at 810–11.

an owner, investor, or executive license to ignore what practical reason requires personally of her.

Property rules are, of course, contingent and conventional. Within the confines of practical reason (and so with respect for the multiple, overlapping rationales for property), communities are free to endorse a range of property conventions, including ones that limit the authority of owners and investors over firms. Communal norms, rules, and institutions ought to encourage owners, investors, and executives to do what practical reason requires. But this is a matter principally of expecting them to perform duties they already have, not of creating new duties out of whole cloth (though communal norms, rules, and institutions might sometimes justly give specificity to the demands of practical reason when multiple options are just but one or a limited number must be selected). Even if it could be shown that communal rules and institutions could not justly require an owner, investor, or executive to do what practical reason requires with respect to participatory or democratic workplace governance (I cannot see that it could ever be demonstrated that communal *norms* could not justly do so), this would not change the duties she actually had to her firm, its workers, and the communities affected by her actions.

Contrary to what Bainbridge seems to assume, communal influence on owners, investors, and executives need not involve the actual or threatened use of force by the legal system. If a community becomes convinced that a given firm or group of firms should be structured participatorily or democratically, community members will have ways of ensuring this sort of norm is followed without the use of violence or the threat of force. Concerted community action can make change happen. So, too, surely can collective action by workers. Further, as the extensive literature on law and anarchy should make clear, laws and courts could and would be among the institutions of a stateless society.[89] Even, therefore, if the action of a court were needed to enforce a legal norm requiring workplace democracy, this would not require the activity – or, indeed, the existence – of the state.[90] Thus, Bainbridge's worry about the interference of the state seems unfounded.[91]

---

[89] *See* ANARCHY AND THE LAW: THE POLITICAL ECONOMY OF CHOICE (Edward P. Stringham ed., 2007); LAW AND ANARCHISM (Thom Holterman & Henc van Maarseveen eds., 1984); MICHAEL TAYLOR, COMMUNITY, ANARCHY, AND LIBERTY (1982).

[90] *Cf.* ROTHBARD, *supra* note 25, at 85–95 (discussing the operation of criminal courts in a stateless society).

[91] It is tempting to ask in this connection why state-made laws that currently protect workers and which Bainbridge says he supports do not, in Bainbridge's view, violate sphere

Bainbridge's appeal to sphere sovereignty is rendered more attractive by his appeal to the rights of persons to organize their lives voluntarily.[92] But I confess I am puzzled by the implied assumption that the forms in which workers associate with most investor-controlled firms are especially voluntary. The decision-making structure of the investor-controlled corporation in which the average worker currently finds herself is presented to her on a take-it-or-leave-it basis. Such a corporation has far more power than she does, and while she may have some choice among firms, she will have little choice about whether to accept or reject the potentially subordinative structure of the firm in which she works if most firms are investor-controlled. Defending current workplace governance structures by appealing to their voluntary nature seems unrealistic.

Bainbridge has offered a range of provocative criticisms of participatory and democratic workplace governance structures. It is not clear that they tell decisively against the creation of such structures. Worker governance can be efficient and can lead to greater efficiency. It ought to be able to protect workers more effectively and efficiently than legal regulation. The value of hierarchy is overrated, especially in small firms of the kind to which full cost internalization would likely lead. Workers may be skeptical about sham participation schemes, but are most unlikely to be skeptical about authentic ones, much less about fully democratic workplace structures. And sphere sovereignty provides no reason for owners, investors, and managers to deny workers opportunities for substantial participation in governance or, arguably, for full workplace democracy.

D   Hayek: workers' and consumers' objectives are at odds, and worker-managers cease to be workers

Friedrich Hayek offers two arguments against industrial democracy: "A plant or industry cannot be conducted in the interest of some permanent distinct body of workers if it is at the same time to serve the interests of the consumers. Moreover, effective participation in the direction of an enterprise is a full-time job, and anybody so engaged soon ceases to have the outlook of an employee. ..."[93]

---

sovereignty, and why, if they do not, laws that ensured opportunities for workplace participation or democracy would do so.

[92] *See* Bainbridge, *Decisionmaking, supra* note 75, at 810.

[93] F. A. HAYEK, THE CONSTITUTION OF LIBERTY 277 (1960).

It is hard to find either argument convincing. Certainly, the first argument surely counts as much against the current model of firm governance as it does against industrial democracy. For investor-governed firms admittedly serve the purposes of at least one group other than consumers – investors. Hayek might just as well criticize investor-governed firms by saying, "A plant or industry cannot be conducted in the interest of some permanent distinct body of investors if it is at the same time to serve the interests of the consumers."

The official theory is, of course, that investors ensure that their firms will serve consumers because, if they did not, other firms would be able to undercut theirs. And no doubt investor-governed firms are disciplined by the demands of competitive markets to the limited extent that they are not protected by monopolistic privileges or circumstantial accidents. But it is unclear why the same impetus to consumer service would not drive worker-governed firms. The desire for profitability (and so higher compensation) and continued investment (with potential consequences for compensation and employment) will encourage workers to be responsive to the needs of consumers. Clearly, self-employed people who deal directly with consumers can be responsive to consumer demand. So can partnerships. Worker-governed firms, especially small ones, seem perfectly capable of responding to consumers in the same way as individuals and partnerships. (Indeed, the current professional partnership may provide the best model for the worker-governed firm.) So worker governance ought not to be criticized because it ensures that firms will not be concerned only with the welfare of consumers.

Hayek's second argument might be thought of as posing a dilemma: either a manager in a worker-governed firm will only manage on a part-time basis, otherwise participating in non-managerial work, in which case she or he will not be an effective manager, or she or he will serve on a full-time basis, in which case she or he will tend to adopt the perspective of an owner and to ignore workers' concerns. Larger worker-governed firms might often need full-time managers (though there would presumably *be* fewer large firms absent the various direct and indirect subsidies to corporate size that are currently available). And it is doubtless the case that a manager will be inclined to adopt a firm-wide, long-term perspective on her firm's activities. But this need not mean that a manager who is democratically accountable to workers will be inclined to disregard their well being. And there is certainly no reason to think that a worker-accountable manager would be any *less* responsive to workers' needs than managers are at present.

Considering Hayek's argument might also prompt one to wonder whether workers have good reason not to want to be caught up in the additional work involved in the task of self-management.[94] Obviously, the highly participatory management of a large firm could be time-consuming. But fairness hardly requires that every worker in every firm participate actively in firm-wide decision-making whether she wants to do so or not. What matters is (*i*) that workers have the discretion to shape their own immediate work environments and the production and distribution processes for which they are responsible, as well as the long-term strategic direction of their firm and (*ii*) that, if workers as a group do not make firm-wide decisions, firm-wide decision-makers are selected by and accountable to workers. Workers who were concerned that democratic self-government imposed high participation costs on them could clearly preserve democracy while reducing the costs of participation by opting for more representative and less participatory democratic structures.

VII   Justice at work

Work is important, but not all-important: good-enough work is quite consistent with the requirements of practical reasonableness in many cases. But the work environment can't be good if workers can be dismissed at will; practical reasonableness – fairness and efficiency alike – demands, at least in most cases, the opportunity to make use of a broad-based system of due process. Employment discrimination subordinates and excludes members of disfavored groups while often depriving a firm that declines to hire them, that dismisses them or that fails to place them at appropriate levels, of the full use of valuable skills. Thus, it, too, is inconsistent with the requirements of practical reasonableness.

There is little question that natural law theory provides good reason for the establishment of participatory workplace governance. Workers' equal dignity, the character of the firm as a community of which workers are full members, the complete absence of a natural right to govern, the requirement that decision-makers who don't want to be subordinates not subordinate others, the value of participatory structures as mechanisms for worker self-protection, the positive impact of worker discretion and authority on efficiency and productivity, the principle of subsidiarity's

---

[94] Thanks to an anonymous reviewer for pressing me on the need to address this issue.

mandate that workers have as much authority as they can employ effectively, and the value of participation as a means of developing the capacity for decision-making outside the workplace – all militate strongly in favor of extensive worker participation in firm decision-making.

Provided workers can govern themselves effectively and maintain or enhance productivity levels, these considerations will also weigh strongly, if not as strongly, in favor of workplace *democracy*. The arguments may not be airtight: while democracy at work is clearly compatible with, and strongly supported by, natural law theory, perhaps some other model of workplace governance might be as well. But the cumulative weight of the arguments gives good reason, I think, for proponents of natural law theory to support workplace democracy.

Investors might play various roles in relation to democratically governed firms. Different arrangements are possible: investors might be the residual owners of a firm, but without voting rights as long as the firm was in operation; or the workers might be a firm's residual owners, hiring capital from investors at agreed-upon rates. In any event, such a firm would likely exhibit multiple performance advantages over the large, hierarchical, investor-governed corporation. Not surprisingly, these advantages are not universally recognized. But objections from a wide range of quarters seem to underestimate the capacities of workers to govern themselves and the value of their doing so.

Like respect for the diverse, overlapping rationales for property and for the norms of justice in distribution, extensive participation in management and, quite possibly, democratic worker governance are requirements of ideal theory. Such requirements must often be implemented under less than ideal circumstances. In the remaining chapters of this book, I will focus on the remedial application of the principles I've developed in the first three chapters, beginning, as in the portion of the book devoted to ideal theory, with property.

I want to focus, in particular, on the remedial reassignment of title to property. It seems to many people (rightly, I think) that a developer's claiming a private residence for the putative purpose of fostering communal economic benefit is repugnant. But consider the reassignment to former tenant farmers of land formerly held by them as tenants. Many people inclined to object to reassignment of title to the developer might view this kind of reassignment as entirely warranted. Or take another example: there are multiple settings in which a group of workers who do not have legal title to their worksites might argue that they should be able to buy their workplaces or that title to these workplaces should be reassigned to them. Are there contexts in which such claims might be credible? In Chapter 4, building on what I have argued about property, and also about justice in distribution, I will explore the question of reassigning title to tenant farmers, other workers, and developers in response to economic injustice and insecurity.

4

Remedies: property

Different communities may well enforce different rules regarding the acquisition and transfer of property. But practical reason requires that every community's norms and rules provide for remedies of some kind for significant losses rooted in injustice. And it provides good reason for the recognition of some claims to property grounded in identity-constitutive relationships and for communities to reform property relations by reassigning titles in ways that acknowledge people's sweat equity and prevent wasteful inefficiencies.

In this chapter, I want to consider what remedies might be available in accordance with natural law for inequities related to rights in land and capital assets – among the kinds of property most important in determining people's economic conditions. I develop some general principles in Part I. In Part II, I elaborate several alternative bases for claims that peasants might make to agricultural land held by large landowners and for claims that workers might make to their workplaces. In Part III, I argue for the justice of reassigning title in some agricultural land to peasants. In Part IV, I argue that some workers have some basis for claiming property rights in their workplaces. In Part V, I maintain that it is unreasonable to reassign title to residential property from individual owners to developers for the purpose of, arguably, promoting a community's prosperity. I review my arguments in Part VI.

I   Principles for property reform

I will use the generic label *property reform* to refer to the reassignment of title to property as a way of correcting past injustice, ending ongoing injustice, or honoring people's investment in and attachment to property currently treated as belonging to others (especially when it has been abandoned, left uncultivated, or unjustly acquired or maintained). Reassignment might involve uncompensated transfer of title or court-ordered sale at market rates. In Section A, I explain what I take to be the underlying logic of property reform. In Section B, I examine the implications for property reform of the various overlapping rationales for property rights. In Section C, I briefly consider the application of the principles of practical reasonableness to judgments about the appropriateness of reassigning title in light of the significance of the rationales for property.

A   The logic of property reform

A community's decision to recognize some property rights while extinguishing others can sometimes be reasonable, given the nature of property rights. Property rights are limited (Subsection 1). Property reform can sometimes be a way of rectifying injustice (Subsection 2). And it can sometimes foster efficiency and productivity (Subsection 3), protect people's identity-constitutive relationships with some kinds of property (Subsection 4), compensate people for their work (Subsection 5), and help to undermine subordination (Subsection 6).

1   Property rights as limited

Property is in significant part a public trust. A community's property system is, if it is just, designed to benefit the community's members, and property-owners' rights are enjoyed for the benefit of the community as well as for their own benefit. The multiple, overlapping rationales for a property system provide good reason for the maintenance of a robust set of separate property rights. However, practical reason does not confer absolute privileges on any right-holder any more than it requires just one property rights regime. And it obviously cannot exempt a property-owner from responsibility to take appropriate account of the needs and reasonable claims of others.

No person, it must be emphasized, is a servant of a universal satisfaction system, responsible for maximizing aggregate utility (even if this notion were, as it is not, coherent). Thus, it is not reasonable to juggle even non-absolute rights – like property rights – simply in search of some imagined net communal benefit. But each property owner is responsible for contributing to the well being of her community and to the welfare of those inside and outside it,[1] especially, though not exclusively, (*i*) those with whom she enjoys various special relationships, whether personal or professional and (*ii*) those who require immediate assistance, are especially vulnerable to her actions, and whom she can easily assist.

---

[1] *See* John Finnis, Natural Law and Natural Rights 172–73, 177, 195 (1980); Onora O'Neill, Towards Justice and Virtue: A Constructive Account of Practical Reasoning 189–206 (1996).

Wealth transfers may sometimes be the most effective means for people to contribute to the well being of others. But there will clearly be times when someone can argue plausibly that title to property currently vested in someone else ought to be reassigned to her to remedy a past injustice or to recognize a claim she has acquired to the property as a result of a relationship with it that has not involved the transfer of title. When this is the case, it will at least be possible to consider whether title to the property in question should be reassigned.

2   Property reform and remedies for injustice

A just system of property rights will make appropriate provision for correcting significant injustice in the acquisition and transfer of property. In particular, the Golden Rule demands that people who have caused harms to others, or, often, the successors in interest to those who have caused harms, should take primary responsibility for compensating those who have been harmed, rather than expecting others to shoulder this responsibility.

Property has frequently been acquired by unjust and perhaps violent means.[2] When an accurate chain of ownership can be identified and when appropriate successors in interest can be clearly identified, it may be appropriate to return the property to those who would be entitled to hold it had the community's own property laws not been violated. Sometimes, of course, the injustice in question may have occurred too remotely for those deserving of compensation to be identified with any confidence. And a community's property rules may sometimes impose limits on challenges to good-faith property holdings even in light of injustice. However, even when such rules are just, a community may not deny compensation to the victims of clear injustice or their successors in interest. Those responsible for the injustice (or sometimes *their* successors in interest), if they can be identified, and perhaps the community as a whole if they cannot, are responsible for providing fair compensation to those who have been dispossessed or to *their* successors in interest who have been harmed by their dispossession.[3] Compensating descendants of

---

[2] *Cf.* Joseph Stromberg, *English Enclosures and Soviet Collectivization: Two Instances of an Anti-Peasant Mode of Development*, AGORIST Q., Fall 1995, at 31.

[3] It does not seem to me that compensation ought only to be available when we can clearly trace a chain of title, nor do I believe it would be consistent with natural law theory to limit the reassignment of title to property exclusively to cases in which the property can be shown to have been unjustly acquired. This is so because a community's property rules might justly provide that someone who has justly acquired property might forfeit it if she allows it to lie fallow, and because those rules might also stipulate that someone could

dispossessed people is a matter both of respect for the violated property rights that would be theirs had their ancestors' property not been expropriated and of reasonable concern to ensure their own economic, social, and political independence.

The justice of redress, whether by return of unjustly acquired property or by monetary compensation, does not turn, per se, on the severity of the loss occasioned by dispossession as measured in contemporary markets. Obviously, there may be some advantage to treating a title as presumptively valid after a certain period during which it has been free from challenge. But time-based limits on challenges to title will often be unreasonable when there are significant differences in power and status between the dispossessor and the dispossessed, especially when dispossession is the work of an entrenched ruling class with the ability to limit effective access to the courts or other avenues of redress. Certainly, there will be more reason to ignore standards designed to quiet title when large-scale injustices are involved.

Nor is the extent to which people are currently aware of or sensitive to the wrongness of the violation particularly relevant.[4] What matters is simply whether it is possible to identify someone presently living who is either a victim of the wrongdoing or clearly a victim's successor in interest, and whether the impact of the wrongdoing on the victim or successor can be reasonably ascertained.

3   Property reform and productivity

Title reassignments may be needed to ensure that land is put to productive use. Someone who owns a productive asset, like land, is responsible for using it productively, and a community is entirely within its rights in structuring its property rules in such a way that, if a landowner declines to develop her property, it may under some circumstances be homesteaded and so employed profitably by someone else.[5] (Obviously,

---

lose title to others for other reasons, such as the unjust use of her property. However, I believe there is much to be said for accounts of land reform as specifically designed to return stolen property. *See, e.g.*, MURRAY N. ROTHBARD, THE ETHICS OF LIBERTY 51–76 (1982); Roy A. Childs, Jr., *Land Reform and the Entitlement Theory of Justice, in* LIBERTY AGAINST POWER: ESSAYS BY ROY A. CHILDS, JR. 185–208 (Joan Kennedy Taylor ed., 1994).

[4] Thus, I differ at least somewhat on this point with MARGARET RADIN, REINTERPRETING PROPERTY 153 (1993).

[5] *Cf.* FINNIS, LAW, *supra* note 1, at 172. A case in which land is deliberately withheld from conventional cultivation as, say, a nature preserve, but in which its owner actively cares for it, should presumably count as an instance of cultivation for this purpose.

communities' rules regarding such matters will vary, and the importance of respecting expectations and other relevant factors will often make it unreasonable for someone to seek to claim underdeveloped property in a community in which property rules are not structured to further productive use.[6])

4   Property reform and identity

In some cases, it will be reasonable to protect or reassign title to a piece of property on the basis that it is identity-constitutive for the claimant or the current owner, or on the basis that it is *not* identity-constitutive for the current owner.

5   Property reform and sweat equity

It will sometimes make sense for a community's legal system to contain provision for assigning title to a piece of property to someone in recognition of her investment of her time, energy, and labor in cultivating the property. The Golden Rule requires that people's work and their contribution to a property's value receive reasonable acknowledgment from a community's legal system.

6   Property reform and subordination

The reassignment of title may also be appropriate when concentrated land ownership, whatever its roots, has led to the creation of a subjugated client class of tenant farmers. In accordance with some communities' legal systems, the sweat equity acquired by these farmers may be sufficient to justify transferring ownership of their parcels to them from absentee owners. And in others, the fact that they or their ancestors have been denied ownership rights in their own land by corrupt legal systems in favor of the current putative owners may justify reassignment of title as a means of returning what has been wrongfully taken from them. But even when neither legally recognizing the value of sweat equity nor compensatorily reassigning title is an option, the disempowering consequences of the creation of a large tenant class might be sufficient in some cases to warrant the reassignment of title to land to those who work on it.

Some decisions to reassign title may be consistent with the demands of practical reasonableness. Depending on the interests affected, and the way in which the relevant community chooses to weight them, however,

---

[6] I continue to learn a great deal from multiple discussions of these matters by Kevin Carson; *see* KEVIN A. CARSON, STUDIES IN MUTUALIST POLITICAL ECONOMY (2007); KEVIN A. CARSON, ORGANIZATION THEORY: A LIBERTARIAN PERSPECTIVE 411–19 (2008).

the burden of justification may sometimes be relatively high. No calculus will resolve the question whether a given instance of title reassignment is appropriate or not. But a consideration of the various rationales underlying reasonable property systems, in light of the principles of practical reasonableness, will provide meaningful guidance to courts and other decision-makers.

B   Property reform and the rationales for property

Communities' property systems may take different forms. Thus, in principle, communities are free within limits to define property systems that include reasonable provision for the reassignment of title, provided the legal principles they enforce reflect due regard for the requirements of practical reasonableness and all of the overlapping, mutually reinforcing rationales for property.

1   The general implications of the property rationales

The property rationales might have diverse implications for the aptness of title reassignment for the purpose of property reform. The autonomy rationale could count strongly for or against reassignment, depending on how the rationales were weighed. The need to compensate someone for cultivating or developing a piece of property or rendering it useful will often be relevant, at least when transfer of title is a suitable way of rewarding her for the valuable work involved in doing so. Generosity probably isn't, by contrast, especially relevant. The relationship between the property's future productivity and its ownership surely does matter. The reliability rationale will usually provide good reason for a community's legal system not to reassign title, though it will count less strongly against doing so if a legal system makes clear in advance that it will allow for some possible reassignments. Stewardship will tend to count in favor of giving ownership to a piece of property to whoever is most likely to take good care of it. The identity justification will count *against* the reassignment of title to property that is identity-constitutive for its *current* owner, and *for* the reassignment of title to property that is identity-constitutive for the *prospective* owner (doubly so if it is not identity-constitutive for its current owner).

2   Particular implications of the identity rationale

Reassigning title will be particularly hard to justify when it deprives an owner of a non-fungible piece of property. But of course it is not reasonable to expect that much real property is non-fungible. Many residences will be, but certainly not *all* will be. And presumably many – probably most – commercial facilities *will* fail to qualify as personal property of the relevant sort.

A community's legal system might undermine identity-based challenges to the reassignment of title. The members of a community might agree, for instance, that, whenever another person could demonstrate in court that she could make better use of someone's property, the owner would be required to sell the property to her at a fair market price. A legal regime of this kind could, indeed, make it harder for someone to claim rights in a piece of property in light of its putatively identity-constitutive role in her life, since it would provide good reason for people not to become attached to pieces of property, which courts might order them to sell at any time.

However, it seems clear that, even when this sort of regime is theoretically in place, people *will* grow attached to particular properties if they retain these properties over time. Further, respect for other rationales underlying a reasonable property system – for instance, reliability and autonomy – will tend to militate against the creation of a legal regime that provides people with relatively little security. And it must at least be asked whether a system that encourages people to sit light to their attachments is in principle a desirable one, or whether important values are not served by encouraging people to set down deep roots in particular places – or at least not discouraging them from doing so. A reasonable property system will acknowledge identity-based claims to property; and it will not avoid doing so just to minimize identity-based challenges to title reassignment.

Perhaps the best argument against conferring rights to people in particular pieces of property on the basis that those pieces of property are identity-constitutive for them is simply that doing so could create enormous confusion and uncertainty. If any identity-constituting attachment can ground a property right, detailed historical and sociological and psychological enquiry might be necessary to resolve almost every property dispute. People could claim attachments in order to trump all sorts of competing property claims.

There is no reason in principle why the question of identity-constituting attachment could not be treated as a question of fact subject to jury resolution, just like any number of other questions about people's attitudes. But reasonable limitations on identity-based property claims are surely needed to foster predictability and stability. It might be reasonable to delimit those of which the law could take cognizance and specify clearly the facts to be proven in order to establish an identity-based interest in a piece of property. It might also be presumed that some relationships, as to residential property occupied for a specified length of time, *are* identity-constitutive and that others, as to commercial property leased to others, are not. In any event, whatever limits are put in place should not rule out at least many claims like those I suggest below might be made by tenant farmers and workers.

C   The significance of the practical principles

How these rationales should be taken into account will ultimately be a function of the application of the principles of practical reasonableness.

1   The Golden Rule

The Golden Rule will require compensation for injustice and for people's contributions to making property productive. And it will require that people honor others' interests in property when they would expect similar interests of their own to be honored. For instance: if someone is arguing that she (or a group of which she is a member) ought to have the right to buy what is putatively someone else's property at a fair market price, she ought to ask whether she would be willing to accept compelling the sale in question as legitimate if *her* property were at stake, and if her relationship with that property were the same as that of her opponents in the case concerned with the claim.

2   The Pauline Principle

The Pauline Principle will rule out reassigning (or resisting the reassignment) of title out of hostility – out of a desire to punish, retaliate, humiliate, or frustrate.

3   The Efficiency Principle

The Efficiency Principle is a requirement of efficiency as a norm of *personal* choice; it does not require or permit someone to promote some imagined overall utility in each of her actions. But efficiency will play a role in one's deliberations, of course, when one is contributing – as a community member, as a judge, or, sometimes, as a litigant – to the development of the *rules* of a property system. Thus, this principle will rule out unreasonable compensation for property when title is transferred as a matter of property reform. But it will also count against seeking any title transfer that is likely to be wasteful or seeking or resisting such a transfer in a wasteful manner.

4   The Integrity Principle

In virtue of the Integrity Principle, someone might seek vigorously to retain property in the face of a proposed reassignment because of her attachment to the property. It might also lead someone else to pursue a reassignment claim vigorously, either because of her own attachment to the property or because of her commitment to the well being of a person or group she expects to benefit from the reassignment.

Within the limits set by the principles of practical reasonableness, communities' legal systems may rightly assign different priorities or weights to the different rationales underlying a just property system. The resolution of questions regarding a particular proposed reassignment of title to property will obviously depend on these priorities, as also on the sensitive application, within the terms of these priorities, of the principles of practical reasonableness and the relevant community's norms and rules.

II   Alternative bases for peasants' and workers' claims

In many places in the world, land is concentrated in the hands of a limited number of families. Some of this land is worked by peasants who do not own it and often receive minimal compensation for their work, while other land is simply allowed to remain uncultivated. Peasants could reasonably claim title to the land on which they work, and they or others might make defensible claims to title in empty land kept uncultivated. Workers might also seek title to the property on which *they* work, as also to worksites which have been abandoned or to which no one has legitimate title.[7]

Peasants might claim title to land on agricultural estates and workers might claim title to their workplaces on various bases. Tenant farmers might simply want the freedom to buy the land on which they work, as a group of workers might simply want the freedom to buy their

---

[7] A similar issue might arise in a worker-owned firm, if one group of workers in a multi-site firm wanted to acquire their workplace. I don't pursue the issue here, but the analysis is likely to be similar (though not identical, since identity interests may weigh differently when absentee investor-owners aren't involved) to the one I offer in the text.

workplace, whether at market (we can call this *priority market purchase*) or below-market rates (we might label this *sweat equity purchase*); I consider this possibility in Section A. I note in Section B that peasants might maintain that they are entitled to the land on which they work, and a group of workers might maintain that they are entitled to their workplace, because they have put underutilized property to productive use (call this *moderate homesteading*). Or peasants or workers might argue that what amounts to a homesteading claim on their part should be considered because of their sweat equity in property to which they maintain the putative owners are not entitled at all (we can call this *radical homesteading*); I examine this kind of claim in Section C.

A   Nonstandard purchases

Whether or not they would otherwise be entitled to buy at all, a group of tenant farmers or workers might sometimes argue for priority purchaser status in virtue of their sweat equity and their identity-constitutive relationship with the land on which they work or the firm at which they are employed. That is, they might ask for the right to buy at a fair market price a property the owner does not wish to sell, or they might ask for the right – when the property *is* already on the market – to buy at a fair market price before other buyers' offers are considered. Their claims might be rooted especially in the identity and compensation rationales for property.

Farmers and workers might also argue for the right to buy at a below-market price with allowances made for their sweat equity – perhaps even that the extent of their sweat equity was such that they should receive title without further investment. The availability of this option might be especially important to workers if the firm at which they work will likely close if it is sold to another purchaser.

Giving farmers or workers priority purchaser status would be a matter of protecting them against economic or identity-related losses associated with the sale of property important to them to someone other than the current putative owner, assuming, typically, that this might lead to evictions for tenant farmers or job losses for workers. Whether farmers' or workers' sweat equity could ever entitle them to buy at below-market rates would obviously depend on whether there were a satisfactory method of accounting for sweat equity and whether, if so, the farmers' or workers' compensation could be judged not to have fully captured the value of that equity.

B   Homesteading abandoned property

Perhaps in some cases peasants might begin to work at their own risk on empty or abandoned land, just as workers might begin work at their own risk at an abandoned worksite – say, a manufacturing plant (at which they might, but might not, have worked previously).[8] After a certain amount of time, they might maintain that both their sweat equity and the evident fact that the property had been abandoned entitled them to homesteaders' rights in the property.

C   Homesteading property to which the putative owner purportedly lacks legitimate title

Most aggressively, tenant farmers or workers might ask that title to property be assigned to them without purchase because – in virtue of the role of injustice in its acquisition and continued possession by the current putative owner – the property should be treated as unowned and their work on the property therefore treated *as if* it amounted to the homesteading of abandoned or unowned property. In Subsection 1, I explain what this sort of radical homesteading claim might amount to. In Subsection 2, I offer an example of a radical homesteading claim in a setting in which those making the claim lack any sort of prior entitlement to the property they are claiming. In Subsection 3, I suggest some reasons why a community's legal system might be inclined to deny validity to property titles grounded in injustice. In Subsection 4, I offer some general observations about radical homesteading claims.

1   The meaning of radical homesteading

Farmers or workers making a radical homesteading claim might maintain that (*i*) the relevant property had been misappropriated, perhaps through violence, fraud, or the abuse of monopolistic privileges; (*ii*) it was not realistically possible to identify the rightful owner or owners; (*iii*) the current putative owner was not entitled to the property *either* because (*a*) it was itself the illegitimate acquirer of the property and should not be compensated or incentivized, *or* (*b*) its title was illegitimate because grounded in a previous occupier's unjust acquisition, *or* (*c*) it maintained

---

[8] Perhaps, for instance, a group of workers might enter, occupy, and work at a factory at which they were previously employed by investors who have now abandoned the factory; *cf.* THE LAVACA COLLECTIVE, SIN PATRÓN: STORIES FROM ARGENTINA'S WORKER-RUN FACTORIES (2007).

its occupancy of the property to a significant extent by means of ongoing force, fraud, or monopolistic privilege; and (*iv*) the extent of the farmers' or workers' continued presence on the property and of their sweat equity entitled them to homestead the property.

Radical homesteading claims will be possible for farmers and workers in communities with various kinds of rules regarding the acquisition of property. Whatever a community's rules of acquisition, it will be possible that a firm's roots lie in violations of those rules. Justice does not *demand* that title to property that has been unjustly acquired be regarded as invalid, though it does require that those wronged be compensated fairly. But a community's legal system could at least sometimes invalidate titles to unjustly acquired agricultural, commercial, or industrial property. And it could at least sometimes award those titles to farmers and workers.

2   Potential settings for radical homesteading claims

Validating radical homesteading claims will be an especially natural step to take with respect to agricultural land when peasants or their ancestors were themselves deprived of title to the land on which they currently work. Here, reassignment of title will often be a straightforward matter of compensating them for past injustice. But radical homesteading will also be reasonable in cases in which those seeking to qualify as homesteaders have no particular claims to the property they seek to homestead that predate their beginning to work on it for the current putative owner.

Suppose, for instance, that a dictator has extorted money at gunpoint from the members of a community relatively even-handedly (cronies aside), and has used money thus extorted to start a business with fellow oligarchs. After the dictator's overthrow, workers at the business sue to obtain title to the business. The workers might reasonably claim that the dictator had no right to the money used to start the business and that the actual owners of the business were not entitled to the money because it was not the dictator's to give. They might further argue that, as enthusiastic collaborators in his tyrannical rule, the business owners were effectively complicit in the dictator's extortion. Thus, the workers might argue, the business was not the rightful owner of the property. If no one else whose prior claim justified return of the property could be identified, they might maintain, their sustained investment of labor in the business might reasonably be thought to give them sweat equity, and their acquisition of this sweat equity over time ought to give them rights comparable to those of homesteaders. Thus they might conclude that they were entitled to own their workplace just as homesteaders on unowned or abandoned land would be.[9]

3 The invalidation of unjustly acquired titles

Consider the imaginary example I just elaborated. Now, assume that (*i*) homesteading claims are legitimate in a community's legal system, (*ii*) the facts would support a homesteading claim if the property were unowned, and (*iii*) practical reason does not require compensating the victims of the dictator's extortion by selling the firm and giving the proceeds to them. The question still remains whether a community's legal system can or should regard titles acquired through massive injustice as invalid.

It is not clear that practical reason would require a community to invalidate them. But there are, at any rate, good reasons why it might do so. (*i*) The unjust acquirer of a piece of property is not entitled to anything like what would otherwise be a full compensation for investing in it since, *ex hypothesi*, she did not pay a fair price for the property. (*ii*) Allowing the unjust acquirer's title to be regularized runs the risk of encouraging unjust acquisition in the future, and those who might be victims of such acquisition could reasonably resent a practice that made their victimization more likely. (*iii*) It is not obvious that anyone could reasonably expect to be able to retain unjustly acquired property.

4 The disposition of radical homesteading claims

General considerations like these cannot obviate a fact-sensitive analysis of the details of a particular case. However, they do, I think, suggest why radical homesteading claims might sometimes be credible, whether or not finally successful. There is no point in trying to imagine the shapes of all of the cases in which this might be so. They will need to be resolved in fact-sensitive ways in light of the requirements of practical reasonableness.

III   Property rights for peasants in the land they work

Peasants might reasonably be entitled to land which is putatively the property of large landowners. In Section A, I will indicate why, depending

---

[9] *Cf.* Kevin Carson, *The Subsidy of History*, THE FREEMAN: IDEAS ON LIBERTY, June 2008, at 33.

on how they are weighted and prioritized, the property rationales seem to provide strong support for reassigning title to the peasants. I briefly note the significance of the principles of practical reasonableness in Section B.

A   The relevance of the property rationales

The overlapping rationales for a system of separate property rights will provide significant guidance regarding the appropriateness of tenant farmers' claims to the land on which they work. All of the rationales for property rights may count in a particular case either for or against the reassignment of title, apart from the reliability rationale, which will tend to weigh against any reassignment of title. The impact of autonomy on a decision whether to reassign title to property will rightly depend, of course, on whose autonomy is in view (Subsection 1). Certainly the compensation rationale will provide very good reason for taking tenant farmers' sweat equity seriously (Subsection 2). Reassignment may impede or foster generosity (Subsection 3). Productivity (Subsection 4) is likely to be a mixed bag, though this rationale probably provides more support than not for reassignment. Reliability will almost certainly provide support for retention of title by landowners (Subsection 5). Reassignment may, though it need not, foster stewardship (Subsection 6), while identity seems very likely to weigh in favor of assignment of title to tenant farmers (Subsection 7).

1   Autonomy

A landowner may sometimes use her ownership interests to reduce farmers' autonomy. Thus, reassigning title from landowners to tenant farmers can sometimes be an effective and appropriate way of securing the farmers' autonomy and protecting them against subordination to the landowner. At the same time, obviously, reassigning title can significantly reduce the landowner's freedom to achieve her purposes, and so diminish her autonomy. Relatively speaking, however, it will often be more likely that the landowner's autonomy will continue largely unabated if title is transferred to peasants, while the peasants' autonomy may be dramatically limited as long as they do not own the land on which they work. A reliable property system will not reassign title on a piece-meal basis in order to maximize autonomy, but the autonomy-enhancing character of a title transfer reasonable on other grounds will provide justification for the transfer that is internal to the logic of property.

2   Compensation

Tenant farmers have often acquired sweat equity in the land they farm. And they may reasonably be regarded as having been undercompensated to the extent that (*i*) they have been forced to work at gunpoint or (*ii*) the threat of violence and the abuse of legal political power have created monopolistic advantages for the landowner in the local labor market or (*iii*) they have not been compensated at all because they have been work- ing at their own risk on apparently abandoned land, their labor has been obtained in significant part at exploitative rates. They have been under- compensated. While different kinds of compensation may be appropri- ate, provision to them of the land on which they work *may* be appropriate compensation for their labor. They might be thought to have property rights in virtue of their work, much like the slaves to whom it was pro- posed that the plantation land on which they had worked be given in the wake of the American Civil War.[10]

The compensation rationale will be even more relevant if the property has been acquired as a result of unjust expropriation, as it frequently will have been. "Nowhere and at no time has the large scale ownership of land come into being through the working of economic forces in the market. It is the result of military and political effort. Founded by violence, it has been upheld by violence and by that alone."[11] Colonial powers or their rep- resentatives have often, though not always, played key roles in this kind of violence. "The foundation of apartheid" in South Africa, for instance, "was a system of racial zoning that reserved eighty-seven percent of the land for ownership and occupation by whites, who … [constituted] approximately thirteen percent of the population."[12] The fact that such a system obtains raises serious questions about the validity of land titles acquired under a legal regime of which it was or is a pervasive feature. If a landowner's title is illegitimate, there will be reason to treat her land as essentially unoc- cupied and to treat the tenant farmers as homesteaders whose labor on the land should be rewarded through transfer of title to them.

The Golden Rule requires remedies for past wrongs, but sometimes a community's legal system might make remedies available that did not

---

[10] *Cf.* CLAUDE F. OUBRE, FORTY ACRES AND a MULE: THE FREEDMEN'S BUREAU AND BLACK LAND OWNERSHIP (1978). Thanks to Murray Rothbard for calling post-Civil War land reform efforts, and the phrase "forty acres and a mule," to my attention.

[11] LUDWIG VON MISES, SOCIALISM: AN ECONOMIC AND SOCIOLOGICAL ANALYSIS 375 (1951).

[12] Catherine M. Coles, Comment, *Land Reform for Post-Apartheid South Africa*, 20 B.C. ENVTL. AFF. L. REV. 699, 701 (1993).

involve disturbing existing land titles. And there will obviously be reasons for respecting settled expectations under some circumstances. But if a title reassignment is likely to make a substantial contribution to remedying an injustice, the existence of a defect in title to property resulting from the unjust acquisition of the property will surely serve to strengthen the case for the justifiability of reassignment. It will also likely warrant a reduction in the compensation an owner could reasonably claim to deserve – indeed, if the owner is also the expropriator or the expropriator's heir, presumably there should be no compensation at all for the land itself (though not necessarily for improvements).[13]

The compensation rationale will often provide good reason to transfer title from landowners to tenant farmers. Of course, landowners will also have invested personal effort and capital in maintaining their estates and rendering them productive. The compensation rationale will thus provide some support for claims on both sides.

3   Generosity

To some degree, acknowledging the significance of generosity as a rationale for property will provide a reason for non-interference with landowners' titles, to the extent that they may wish to transmit estates by gift or will. At the same time, recognizing the importance of generosity does not require anything like absolute regard for whatever owners wish to do with their property; and, in addition, reassigning title to peasants will obviously make it possible for *them* to be generous in ways that they otherwise could not be.

4   Productivity

Reassigning titles to peasants will be unlikely to have negative consequences for overall productivity. When tenant farmers become owners, they will likely work more productively than they did as tenants – certainly, at any rate, they are unlikely to work *less* diligently. At the same time, of course, large landowners may reduce investments in their land because they fear the reassignment of title to tenant farmers.

To the extent that the maintenance of a large agricultural estate requires significant supervision costs, breaking the estate up and allowing individual farmers to police themselves seems likely to conduce to efficiency – and so, at least potentially, to productivity. Certainly, farmers

---

[13] *Cf.* Timothy Milton Hanstead, *Philippine Land Reform: The Just Compensation Issue*, 63 WASH. L. REV. 417 (1988).

are perfectly capable of cultivating their land efficiently without over-sight, and, to the extent that economies of scale are relevant, farmers can pool resources and meet common needs without the aid of an aristocratic Leviathan.

5   Reliability

The reliability rationale clearly counts against reassignment of title. But no owner has a reasonable interest in being able to avoid fulfilling her responsibilities to others. While these responsibilities may ordinarily be fulfillable through contributions to common funds, it will sometimes be the case that they can be fulfilled only through the reassignment of title. This will be especially true if (*i*) an owner's title is vitiated by past injust-ice or (*ii*) the owner has abandoned the land or sought actively to prevent cultivation.

6   Stewardship

If someone knows that title to her agricultural estate might be reas-signed to tenant farmers, she might care less effectively for the land. However, reassignment will vest responsibility for a particular piece of property in a particular former tenant farmer who will be specific-ally charged with the care of a manageable, identifiable farm. Thus, the concern with the focused care for particular assets which the steward-ship rationale reflects may in some cases be served more effectively after reassignment of title than before. Stewardship will obviously count with particular force in favor of peasants when they seek title to land the owner has apparently abandoned but which they have cultivated, both because they have demonstrated care for the land and because the putative owner has exhibited lack of concern for it that makes her claim to it seem especially hollow.

7   Identity

The identity rationale may often provide an additional positive reason for reassigning title. Those who work the land may have long-standing, inter-generational attachments to the land they till. These identity-constitutive attachments may well enhance *their* claim to the land.

By contrast, for the owner of a vast array of agricultural land, specific pieces of agricultural property need not be identity-constitutive, and therefore need not implicate the identity rationale. This will be especially true for property that the putative owner has failed to develop: undevel-oped land will infrequently play a key role in constituting the owner's identity.[14] Even if land *is* developed, however, it will not follow that it is identity-constitutive. Instead, the owner may have an arms-length relationship with the property if it is held exclusively or primarily for commercial purposes. In this case, there will be little reason to protect title to it against a claim from peasants who are arguably entitled to it for other reasons and for whom it *will* have identity-constitutive significance.[15]

B   *Agricultural land as peasants' property*

The importance of respecting a landowner's *autonomy* does not provide an especially strong reason not to reassign title, and the parallel value of autonomy for affected tenant farmers will often provide a good reason to do so. The *compensation* rationale can often be seen as providing significant support for reassignment. This may be true if peasants or their ancestors failed to receive compensation for land taken by force or fraud, if they deserve to be compensated for having improved or cultivated land to which the putative owner is not really entitled, or if their labor has been undercompensated or (as when some homesteading claims are in view) uncompensated.

The *generosity* rationale will likely make little difference in disputes over the claims of landowners and tenant farmers. The *productivity* rationale may count in a landowner's favor, but it need not, since peasants are likely to work hardest on land that is their own and because large-scale agricultural (and other) production tends not to be efficient. The *reliability* rationale for property will provide a significant reason not to reassign title, though this will be largely irrelevant when the current putative owner holds title because of the dispossession of former owners. The *stewardship* rationale is likely to count against absentee owners and in favor of tenants who have invested in their land. The *identity* rationale provides little reason not to regard assigning to tenant farmers title to the land on which they work as reasonable, as long as primary residences and other instances of legitimately identity-constitutive property are not affected.

Variation in communal property rules may be reasonable. But practical reasonableness may provide good reason for communal legal systems to ensure that people are fairly compensated, often through the return of

---

[14] An obvious exception here will be land withheld from circulation precisely to conserve it in an undeveloped state – say, as a nature preserve.

[15] For another recent argument that non-owners might enjoy (identity-based?) property rights, see Kristen A. Carpenter, *A Property Rights Approach to Sacred Sites Cases: Asserting a Place for Indians as Nonowners*, 52 UCLA L. REV. 1061 (2005).

stolen property, when they or their predecessors in interest have been dispossessed by violence or fraud. It will appropriately dispose communities to reduce the arbitrary power of landowners over tenant farmers and to address problems related to their persistent marginalization. And it will justify honoring peasants' labor by validating some homesteading claims.

Obviously, a fact-sensitive application of the principles of practical reasonableness will be required to determine which principles a community's courts should enunciate and how they should resolve particular cases. But it seems likely that priority market purchase rights, sweat equity purchase rights, moderate homesteading rights, and radical homesteading rights for peasants might all be acknowledged in property systems that took reasonable account of the multiple rationales for property rights. Especially, but not only, when reassignment was compensatory, it might be reasonable for a court to transfer title to agricultural land held by large landowners to peasants working on the land.

IV Property rights for workers in their workplaces

Reassigning title to their workplace to a group of workers may be especially crucial when the alternative is the closure of a workplace on which workers are dependent in a variety of ways.[16] It can increase workers' security in uncertain times, since they can be assured that they will have access to the immediate resources needed to do their jobs. And the reassignment of title can be an acknowledgment of their investment in and attachment to their workplaces.

In Section A, I note the ways in which the rationales for property apart from identity, particularly *compensation*, might affect workers' claims to their workplaces. In Section B, I contend that the identity rationale for property will often ground significant, even if not always decisive, claims on the part of workers to a workplace slated for closure. In Section C, I conclude that there could be merit to a property claim to their workplace on the part of people who work at an investor-governed firm.

A *The relevance of the property rationales other than identity*

The autonomy rationale might provide support for workers' claims to their workplaces, though it could be thought to provide support for investors'

---

[16] *Cf.* United Steelworkers v. U. S. Steel, 492 F. Supp. 1 (N. D. Ohio 1980); Local 1330, United Steel Workers v. U. S. Steel, 631 F.2d 1264 (6th Cir. 1980).

claims as well. Generosity is likely in most cases to be irrelevant. The reliability rationale, conservative as usual, will provide a significant reason for leaving investors' titles undisturbed. The compensation rationale (Subsection 1) could ground an especially strong property claim for workers. Productivity might provide support for workers' or investors' claims (Subsection 2). Similarly, stewardship might support the interests either of workers or of current precative owners (Subsection 3).

1   Compensation

The compensation rationale will provide a basis for acknowledging workers' sweat equity. The labor of the workers at a given workplace not only creates particular salable products or services but also adds value to the enterprise for which they work. Subsequent investors and purchasers of products may be attracted to the workplace's products in part because of the quality of what the workers produce and the way in which they produce it. To the extent that they have not been fully compensated for their work, then it seems as if they ought to enjoy at least a limited additional claim to their worksite, a claim proportionate to the contribution their own uncompensated work has made to its value. The compensation rationale for property will provide reason, of course, to recognize investors' contributions, as well. The relevance of a compensation-based claim will depend, therefore, on whether workers or investors have been undercompensated for their contributions to a firm's development.

2   Productivity

Whether transferring ownership from investors to workers will lead to a net increase in productivity clearly depends in large part on whether worker self-ownership will enhance productivity in general. Certainly, the incentives for worker performance, the reduction in monitoring costs, and the elimination of the principal–agent problem effected by worker ownership might all help to increase the productive use of property reassigned to workers. On the other hand, worries about possible reassignment might lead investors to limit their expenditures on a given worksite in ways that diminished productivity.

3   Stewardship

The knowledge on the part of a group of workers that they could obtain title to their workplace could well ensure that they took better care of it. And certainly, were they to acquire it, they would have a particularly strong incentive to maintain it. At the same time, an investor obviously might care less for a facility if she expected that title to the facility was likely to be reassigned to those who worked at it.

B Identity-based claims and worker rights

Identity-related claims will offer significant support for people's claims to property rights in their workplaces.[17] They may also help to strengthen claims grounded in other property rationales (like homesteading claims, which will frequently be compensation-based).

I suggest in Subsection 1 that workplaces can play identity-constitutive roles in people's lives that are distinguishable from their contributions to people's economic well being. I note in Subsection 2 that, by contrast, it is much less likely that investors will have reasonable identity-based claims to facilities they own under current law. In Subsection 3, I suggest two possible responses to attempts by investors to block identity-based claims to workplaces.

1 Workplace closings and psychic death

Workplaces contribute to shaping people's identities. This seems particularly obvious when those workplaces are threatened. The psychic debilitation that can result from a workplace closure may plausibly be interpreted as partly a result of economic loss and insecurity. But I do not believe that an economic analysis captures all of the harms that result from a workplace closure. "It's like a death in the family," according to one worker at a Utah semiconductor plant slated for closure.[18] What died in Flint and Ypsilanti, Michigan, when General Motors closed up shop or in Ohio when US Steel departed – leading to "an economic tragedy of major proportion to Youngstown and Ohio's Mahoning Valley"[19] – was not merely thousands of jobs; it was a way of life.

> Youngstown in 1976 … was a place in which the American Dream seemed to have come true for many working-class families. … Often three generations of a family worked in the same mill and lived close

---

[17] *See* Joseph William Singer, *The Reliance Interest in Property*, 40 STAN. L. REV. 611 (1988). It should be clear to any reader of Singer's article how much I have learned from him. His arguments provide support for a variety of non-monetary remedies in workplace closing cases, including a notice requirement, a right of first refusal for workers interested in buying workplaces slated for closure, and the right for affected community groups to purchase such workplaces. He grounds the reliance interest for which he argues in, for instance, non-promissory relational obligations reflective of reasonable expectations.

[18] LOUISE MOSER ILLES, SIZING DOWN: CHRONICLE OF A PLANT CLOSING 6 (1996).

[19] *Local 1330*, 631 F.2d at 1265.

> to each other in the same neighborhood. Graduation from high school
> was the occasion for a party, hosted by proud parents for relatives and
> friends. Communities united behind their football and basketball
> teams. Roller rinks and bowling leagues flourished. So did theatrical
> groups. The A & P was open twenty-four hours a day for the convenience
> of all three shifts, and the hardware store sold building and plumbing
> supplies on Sunday. It was a way of life that did not exist before the
> 1930s.[20]
>
> [T]he pain caused by the shutdowns ... was not only a question of
> money. Steelworkers in Youngstown tended to stay at particular mills
> over long periods of time because of the fringe benefits which came with
> seniority. This meant that they might work with certain other men and
> women for twenty, thirty, or even forty years. Such long-time associates
> became a second family.

Not surprisingly, shutdowns meant the death of many such "families."[21]

Manufacturing jobs can be boring, repetitive, and physically debili-
tating. But in places like Michigan and Ohio those jobs formed part of
the fabric of a community that helped to bond people with each other,
give them a history, tell them who they were. General Motors workers
in Flint could recall the famous sit-down strike as a key element of their
heritage. They could see each other on a daily basis at work, share in
social events made possible by their combined presence, live in homes
their parents and grandparents had inhabited. They could experience
community on the job with people they had known since elementary
school. They could participate together in the life of a city that was what
it was because of their ongoing lives there. Who they were at work, at
home, at worship, at play were all shaped to a profound degree by the
company's presence.

Narratives of people's responses to workplace closures emphasize the
degree to which a workplace can sometimes help to constitute the identity of its workers. Thus, they can help to highlight important aspects of
the bases of the claims that groups of workers might make to workplaces
that help to determine who they are.

---

[20] STAUGHTON LYND, THE FIGHT AGAINST SHUTDOWNS: YOUNGSTOWN'S STEEL MILL
CLOSINGS 6 (1982).

[21] *Id.* at 77. In support of his claim regarding the contribution of shared work to the creation of community among blue-collar workers, Lynd cites WILLIAM KORNBLUM, BLUE
COLLAR COMMUNITY 36–67 (1974). On the social costs associated with plant closings
in Youngstown, *see generally* TERRY F. BUSS & F. STEVENS REDBURN, SHUTDOWN AT
YOUNGSTOWN: PUBLIC POLICY FOR MASS UNEMPLOYMENT (1983). *Cf.* ILLES, *supra* note
18, at 13–14.

2 Workplace property claims as typically fungible for investors

Just as an object's personal character helps to warrant a stronger claim to it on the part of someone whose identity it helps to constitute, its *lack* of such a character for someone may reasonably be thought to reduce the strength of the claim she might make to it.[22] While relationships with some businesses may, indeed, be identity-constitutive for some people, investors' rights in large, multi-site corporations are far less likely to be identity-based. To the extent that they are not, the claims of others to workplaces operated by such businesses merit more serious consideration than they otherwise might.

3 Anticipatory repudiation of identity-based claims[23]

Perhaps an investor-governed firm might seek proactively to blunt the force of an identity-based claim to a workplace by workers. It might seek to do so by demanding that workers contractually relinquish identity-based claims. Even in the case of such an explicit denial, however, there might be good reason to take such claims seriously. Such claims reflect actual relationships that may persist despite announcements and contracts. And power relationships may raise significant questions about the legitimacy of an agreement waiving identity-based rights in a workplace.

An identity-based claim depends on the role a workplace has come to play in people's lives, the relationships it has served to foster, the sense of selfhood to which it has contributed. To the extent that it has created social bonds and became an integral part of people's lives, a workplace might well play an identity-constituting role for people in a given community, even if workers were to abandon identity-based claims to a firm's assets contractually. And if it did play such a role, identity-based claims might well be possible even in a case of anticipatory repudiation.

It might be reasonable to question whether, if workers have repudiated identity-based claims in a contract, the contract should be upheld. The influence that is exercised by investors and firm executives and the corresponding absence of genuine alternatives available to workers and communities could provide good reason for a court to call the

[22] *See, e.g.,* RADIN, *supra* note 4, at 68–69 ("Shopping center property is not likely to be bound up with the personhood of the shopping center owner, while public speech, especially if considered political, is likely to be tied to the personhood of the speaker. ...") (footnote omitted).

[23] Subsection 3 reflects the beneficial influence of Steve Munzer's thoughtful reading of my work.

validity of such an agreement into question, or for a community's legal system to deny validity to all such agreements.

In any event, while the contractual abandonment of identity-based claims on the part of workers might be relevant in some sorts of non-standard purchase cases, they would not be especially relevant to moderate or radical homesteading claims by workers. Sometimes, workers bringing homesteading claims will have no contractual relationships with firms claiming the property to which the workers are seeking title. Sometimes, even when workers have agreed to a contract relinquishing homesteading claims, a firm will have abandoned the property referred to in the contract and so, at some point, their right to enforce the contract. And, when (as in connection with some radical homesteading claims) a firm can be shown to have acquired and maintained title to a piece of property unjustly, there will be good reason for a court to proceed on the assumption that the firm could not legitimately negotiate regarding the property in the first place.

C   Workplaces as workers' property

A court's decision to assign title to a workplace to those who work there or to allow them priority purchase rights may sometimes be a reasonable instance of property reform, just like a decision to assign title to a plot of land to the tenant farmer who works it. To the extent that it is, it will be a way of acknowledging the degree to which transferring title to workers makes sense in light of the rationales underlying a just property system, as the various interests highlighted by these rationales are reasonably weighted and assessed within a given community's legal system. It will be especially important that a particular workplace has come to be constitutive of workers' identities and they have acquired uncompensated sweat equity in it, though other kinds of claims may be significant as well.

This hardly means that workers will always be entitled to buy or homestead their workplaces. The rationales that justify a property regime may weigh in favor of investors instead. But, for a range of reasons, a just property regime will be one, at minimum, that takes workers' interests in their workplaces significantly into account.

V   Residential property rights and urban renewal

It is possible to accept the legitimacy of title transfers to tenant farmers and other workers without opening the floodgates to a range of abusive dispossessions. In Section A, I consider a controversial contemporary instance of reassigning title from homeowners to private developers. I outline in Section B my argument that the rationales for property provide little justification for granting developers title to residential properties for the purpose of economic development. In Section C, I explain why I believe it will make sense in most or all reasonable legal systems to reject the reassignment of title to developers even while accepting as legitimate some reassignments to tenant farmers and other workers.

A   Assigning title to private developers

A recent United States Supreme Court case, *Kelo v. City of New London*,[24] illustrates the problems created when the compulsory transfer of title from a homeowner to a developer receives legal sanction.

Kelo began after a private development corporation created by the city of New London, Connecticut, planned a project in the vicinity of an anticipated industrial research facility. It was able to purchase most of the property needed for the project. But owners of fifteen parcels – ten residences and five investment properties[25] – refused to sell to the corporation, which then sought to acquire their properties compulsorily. The Supreme Court upheld the compulsory purchase of the property for the immediate benefit of private developers. Given the economic impact of the projected development, the compulsory acquisition of property to facilitate it could, the Court said, be justified. In a powerfully populist jeremiad, Justice Clarence Thomas dissented:

> So-called "urban renewal" programs provide some compensation for the properties they take, but no compensation is possible for the subjective value of these lands to the individuals displaced and the indignity inflicted by uprooting them from their homes. ... [E]xtending the concept of public purpose to encompass any economically beneficial goal guarantees that these losses will fall disproportionately on poor communities. Those communities are not only systematically less likely to put their lands to the highest and best social use, but are also the least politically powerful. If ever there were justification for intrusive judicial review of constitutional provisions that protect "discrete and insular minorities," surely that principle would apply with great force to the powerless groups and individuals the Public Use Clause protects.[26]

---

[24] Kelo v. City of New London, 545 U.S. 469 (2005).   [25] *Id.* at 475.
[26] *Id.* at 521–22 (Thomas, J., dissenting) (citation omitted).

A satisfactory account of property rights can provide a principled basis for rejecting the reassignment of title to people's homes to facilitate redevelopment projects. At the same time, such an account can provide reason for acknowledging that the reassignment of title from landlords to tenant farmers or from investors to workers might sometimes be appropriate.[27]

B   Urban renewal and residential property

Given the rationales for separate property rights and the principles of practical reasonableness, developers will have little justification for maintaining that they should receive titles to personal residences simply so that they can, purportedly, exert a positive affect on communal well being. The autonomy, compensation, and generosity rationales all seem generally, if not exclusively, to weigh in favor of leaving homeowners' titles undisturbed (Subsections 1–3), though the productivity rationale might count more strongly in favor of some reassignments to developers (Subsection 4). The reliability rationale will ordinarily pose a very high barrier to such reassignments (Subsection 5), and the stewardship rationale will tend to count against them as well (Subsection 6). The identity rationale will ground a particularly strong argument against reassignment (Subsection 7).

1   Autonomy

The autonomy rationale will provide little or no positive reason *for* the reassignment of title from residential owners to developers. And reassignment will clearly exert a negative impact on the autonomy of the homeowners. They may be unable to find alternative housing in a location of their choice, and losing their homes could exert a negative effect on their psyches that might impair their capacity to exercise autonomous judgment. It is also important to consider the impact of disrupting poor people's residence patterns. Residential concentration can offer greater communal influence, which will be reduced by their dispersion.[28] By limiting their ability to exert this kind of influence, depriving them of their property – and so, unavoidably, dispersing them to other neighbourhoods – may further reduce their autonomy. So the

---

[27] *Cf.* RADIN, *supra* note 4, at 66.

[28] *Cf.* Brief for Amici Curiæ National Association for the Advancement of Colored People et al. at 15, *Kelo* 545 U.S. 469 (No. 04–108).

autonomy rationale may count against court – ordered sale purchase for the purpose of fostering redevelopment in this way as well.

2   Compensation

Certainly, a developer's own investment in any particular homeowner's property is likely to be nonexistent, so there is no basis for compensating her for any investment by conferring title to the property on her. If the homeowners have inherited their homes, there will often be little reason to treat the compensation rationale as weighing in *their* favor, either, of course, unless they have made improvements to the homes for which a fair market price paid by the developer would not appropriately compensate them.

3   Generosity

The generosity rationale is probably not particularly relevant. If anything, it will count toward the homeowners' rights insofar as retaining their property enables them to solidify and honor particular relationships, particularly with their children, by passing on their property.

4   Productivity

The productivity rationale seems to weigh against the homeowners, since, *ex hypothesi*, commercial development might be thought to put their land to more productive use than they would. At the same time, of course, the homeowner violates no duty by failing to maximize the economic benefit derived from her property.

5   Reliability

Obviously, the reliability rationale will largely tilt in favor of homeowners: the transfer of titles to their homes to developers in the purported interest of communal productivity does not seem to be a state of affairs they could reasonably predict or take into account in their planning, given how contingent communal economic circumstances must unavoidably be.

6   Stewardship

Stewardship clearly would not be served if homeowners believed that they held their property on sufferance, though one possible stewardship argument against a homeowner's retention of title might be available if it appeared that she had thoroughly neglected the upkeep of her property.

7   Identity

The identity justification provides good reason for furnishing substantial protection to property that helps to constitute people's identities, and so good reason not to reassign title to this property.[29] Indeed, it is doubtless the identity rationale which counts most clearly in favor of homeowners faced with forced developer buyouts. Consider those affected by *Kelo*: "Wilhelmina Dery, for example, lives in a house on Walbach Street that has been in her family for over 100 years. She was born in the house in 1918; her husband, ... Charles Descend, moved into the house when they married in 1946. Their son lives next door with his family in the house he received as a wedding gift. ..."[30] Both people's attachments to their own homes and the community they have been able to create in the neighborhood threatened by the developer implicate the identity rationale and tell strongly against reassignment.

Identity-based property claims reflect ties not only to specific pieces of land but also to communities where landowners reside.[31] The right to remain in a home in which one has lived for years – in which one's family may have lived for generations – is a right to remain rooted in a community. Allowing courts to order the sale of residential property to developers will lead to the compulsory dissolution of many communities. People will often be unable to re-establish these communities if they are forced to sell their property: sales to developers will often dramatically increase housing prices and make it impossible for people to find housing near their former residences. Thus, they will be forced to disperse. While the law should obviously not impede their doing so if that's what they want to do, it should recognize the value of maintaining stable communities, and avoid uprooting these communities where possible.[32] The negative impact

---

[29] Margaret Radin's discussion of (what I am calling) the identity rationale includes an explicit rejection of the legitimacy of the reassignment of title from homeowners to developers, even at market rates; *see* RADIN, *supra* note 4, at 141.

[30] *Kelo*, 545 U.S. Lexis at 494–95.

[31] *Cf.* NAACP, *supra* note 28, at 4, 14. It will not do to propose the reassignment of title to all of the parcels in a neighborhood, only then to review claims about these parcels in isolation, in each case treating the fate of the rest of the neighborhood as given. One cannot, for instance, maintain in a case like this that since the neighborhood is set for redevelopment, the community can have no interest in the persistence of a business, since the community itself will cease to exist.

[32] Similarly, a group of long-term tenants may have an independent claim, rooted in their identities, in the continued existence of an apartment building in which they or their families have lived on an extended basis. Their identity-based link with the community should clearly be recognized when a developer is asking for compulsory transfer of title to the building or complex in which they live. The condemnation and destruction of the

of reassigning title to residential property to developers on communities and people's connections with those communities counts strongly against reassignment.[33]

The identity rationale will likely count strongly against the reassignment of title to residential property to developers, as will the reliability, stewardship, and autonomy rationales. The compensation rationale may weigh in favor of homeowners threatened with expropriation; the generosity rationale will likely be irrelevant. The only rationale that might be thought to count in favor of reassignment would be productivity. The application of the principles of practical reasonableness by the participants in a given case, and with a focus on the particulars of that case, will obviously be crucial. But it is difficult to believe that parties honestly applying the Golden Rule would ordinarily judge that the reassignment of title from homeowners to developers was appropriate.

C   Distinguishing reasonable and unreasonable instances of property reform

It is relatively easy to distinguish claims by developers to residential properties from more readily justifiable transfers of title to tenant farmers and other workers. The grounds for the distinction include the relative merits of homeowners' titles (Subsection 1), the compensatory significance of transfers to tenant farmers and, perhaps, workers (Subsection 2), the importance of the ties of tenant farmers and other workers to the property

---

building that contains their homes could, in principle, be very disruptive to them. The autonomy of such tenants could also clearly be compromised by the reassignment of title to the property in which they live. They will not be compensated should they be evicted from their apartment building. And in some markets, they may be unable to find alternative, comparably located housing. They will therefore have good reason to object to reassignment, and they should.

[33] In *Poletown*, disturbingly similar to *Kelo*, Detroit asserted the right to take the homes of the residents of a city neighborhood for the benefit of General Motors. *See* Poletown Neighborhood Council v. City of Detroit, 410 Mich. 616 (1981). The identity-based claim is plausibly recognized in the *Poletown* dissent. Reassignment of title in a case like this can bring about "great social dislocation" and "can entail, as it did in this case, intangible losses, such as severance of personal attachments to one's domicile and neighborhood and the destruction of an organic community of a most unique and irreplaceable character." *Poletown*, 410 Mich. at 682–83 (Ryan, J., dissenting). *Poletown* has recently been overruled by the Michigan Supreme Court in County of Wayne v. Hathcock, 684 N.W.2d. 765 (2004). *Cf.* Ilya Somin, *Overcoming* Poletown: City of Wayne v. Hathcock, *Economic Development Takings, and the Future of Public Use*, 2004 MICH. ST. L. REV. 1005 (2004).

on which they work (Subsection 3), and the capacity of title transfers to tenant farmers and other workers to reduce subordination (Subsection 4) and poverty (Subsection 5).

1   The status of titles

Landowners whose properties are transferred to tenant farmers may have acquired their property as a result of violence and exploitation – whether their own or someone else's. This will often *vitiate the legitimacy* of their titles – particularly, though not exclusively, if they are themselves responsible for the violence and exploitation. Whether it does so will depend partly on communities' property rules, but, as I have already suggested, there are good reasons for such rules to avoid honoring unjustly acquired titles. Residential homeowners' titles may sometimes be similarly compromised, but it is less likely that they have been. And it is even more unlikely that the homeowners themselves have been responsible for or purposefully complicit in the unjust eviction of others from their land.

2   Desert

Landowners will often *owe compensation* to peasants in virtue of the forcible seizure or some other kind of exploitation of their property or their ancestors'. Assigning title to the peasants in particular can undo at least some of the harm brought about by past injustice. And, of course, it will at least often be more reasonable that those who have benefited from the injustice be responsible for this compensation rather than that they ask others to accept, or at least share, such responsibility. By contrast, in most urban redevelopment projects, homeowners owe no compensation for anything to the developers who wish to evict them from their homes.

3   Honoring particular ties to affected properties

Tenant farmers and other workers to whom title might be reassigned will ordinarily be working on the property to which they seek title, and they will thus have a quite specific claim to it because of their ties with it. By contrast, there is likely nothing that gives a private developer a *particular* claim to land she might seek to claim in order, arguably, to enhance its productive value. (To be sure, the importance of such ties *will* count against the reassignment of title to a traditional family *residence* to developers, but also to peasants.)

4   Minimizing subordination

Assigning title to tenant farmers or other workers serves to reduce potentially oppressive power. Owning a large company or a large amount of
land can allow a person or entity to exercise substantial power over
not only land, and presumably wealth, but also social power – power
to which the owner would not wish to be subject were roles reversed.
Assigning title to tenant farmers and other workers can serve to disperse social power more widely and reduce the subordination of those
with little or no property. But residential homeowners rarely exercise
oppressive power over others in virtue of their homeownership – and
even more rarely over developers. And while there are doubtless cases
in which homeowners have exercised unjust power over some neighbors, reassigning title to their property to developers in connection with
urban redevelopment projects will be most unlikely to benefit these
neighbors.

5   Reducing poverty

One way in which property owners can justly fulfill their duties to share
resources beyond their public trust thresholds is by transferring title to
tenant farmers or workers. Transferring title to tenant farmers or other
workers may sometimes be a way of empowering the excluded and vulnerable and of helping to offer them economic security. It can also make
it less likely that they will need to be clients of the wealthy. By contrast,
reassigning title from a residential homeowner to a developer will likely
serve simply (at best) to confer a marginal benefit on a community at significant cost to the homeowner. It seems more troubling to impose the
burden created by reassignment of title on someone for the purpose of
maximizing communal wealth – a goal that could in principle license any
reassignment of title at any time – than it would to do so for the purpose
of remedying poverty. And the distributional impact of court-ordered
title transfer as a means of fostering urban redevelopment is often likely
to increase the subordination and exclusion of poor people: they will
often *lose* resources, while rich people will gain them.

Several morally significant factors distinguish reassigning title to
property to developers from reassigning title to tenant farmers and other
workers. They help to show why just property rules will frequently rule
out transfers of title from homeowners to developers as a means of promoting communal prosperity. The Golden Rule and the other norms
of practical reasonableness suggest that the community benefits from

redevelopment schemes are unlikely to justify property reform designed simply or primarily to foster putative economic benefits.

VI   Property rights and remediation

A community's legal system, taking reasonable account of the nature and value of separate property and the principles of practical reasonableness, will have good reason to give effect to priority purchase, moderate homesteading, and radical homesteading claims by tenant farmers and other workers. Practical reasonableness would place some significant limits on the reassignment of title to people's homes, but relatively few on the reassignment of title to fungible agricultural or commercial property. It would, however, almost surely preclude court-ordered transfers of title from homeowners to developers, designed, at best, to enhance economic well being at the cost of identity-disrupting losses to particular persons.

Remedial questions arise repeatedly in conjunction not only with the assignment of title to land but also with the distribution of money and services. Communities' norms might rightly call on people to share wealth with other members and support communal projects. It might be reasonable, for instance, for people to share the costs of providing health care and basic income support within their community. People will also often be responsible for sharing resources with economically disadvantaged people in other communities. I consider remedial issues related to distribution in Chapter 5.

5

Remedies: distribution

Remedial questions regarding justice in distribution arise in connection with rectifying injustice, responding to disaster and accident, addressing the problem of economic insecurity, and avoiding distributive choices that cause unjust harms.

Poverty and economic insecurity result primarily from violence, fraud, exploitation, and structural inequities – monopolies, subsidies, patents, tariffs, cartelizing licensing requirements, and artificial limitations on the availability of capital – that often reinforce the effect of prior wrongs. The long-term resolution of these problems will therefore depend much more on eliminating present injustices, shunning harmful distributive choices, and compensating people directly or indirectly victimized by past injustices, than on wealth transfers. Such transfers may sometimes, however, be useful or necessary in response to disaster, accident, and economic insecurity.

In Part I, I explain why many criticisms of the belief that people have remedial responsibilities to share wealth with others do not count against an understanding of these responsibilities grounded in natural law theory. In Part II, I emphasize that natural law theory leaves open a range of ways in which the effects of past or continuing injustice in distribution can be remedied and economic security fostered. In Part III, I suggest briefly that, as a way of fostering shared economic security, the members of a community might reasonably seek to ensure that each of them had access to adequate health care. In Part IV, I sketch an argument for the view that there might be good reason for the members of a community to provide basic income grants to each other. In Part V, I outline a natural law defense of a duty on the part of many members of industrialized communities to assist economically disadvantaged people outside their own communities.[1] In Part VI, I develop a natural law account of the duty to participate in a boycott as a remedial requirement of justice in distribution. I sum up my conclusions in Part VII.

---

[1] *Cf.* Liam Murphy, Moral Demands in Non-Ideal Theory (2000); Martha C. Nussbaum, Frontiers of Justice: Disability, Nationality, Species Membership 224–324 (2007).

I   Natural law and redistribution

Justice in distribution is, in an important sense, a *personal* responsibility, though communal norms may facilitate its fulfillment.

A well-functioning communal system of shared support for valuable projects and the welfare of vulnerable people can relieve particular persons of the responsibility of assessing and organizing strategies for social improvement. A community's norms, rules, and institutions can coordinate people's fulfillment of their responsibilities to strangers more effectively than they likely can do themselves and can render it more likely that the more generous are not overburdened by the irresponsibility of free riders.

In Part I, I consider five potential criticisms of the claim that people have redistributive duties.[2] In Section A, I examine the claim that redistributive norms could interfere unjustly with people's property rights and their freedom to transfer property and money in accordance with free contracts. In Section B, I assess the objection that the redistributive norms encourage the treatment of each particular person as a means to universal well being rather than as an end in herself. In Section C, I consider the assertion that norms calling for redistribution fail to respect the essentially *historical* character of justice by focusing on end-states rather than transactions. In Section D, I reject the claim that limitations on information make redistributive norms and rules unfeasible. In Section E, I maintain that such norms and rules need not subject people to anyone's arbitrary dictates or render personal planning impossible.

A   *Interference with property and contract rights*

One objection to redistributive norms might be that expecting people to fulfill their redistributive duties interferes with free transactions between persons and violates their property rights. But the claim that a community's facilitation of people's fulfillment of their redistributive duties interferes unreasonably with personal property rights and with people's freedom to contract assumes either that no one has any duties to share with others or to support worthwhile projects, or else that, even

---

[2] One might think of these criticisms as articulated with particular vigor by Friedrich Hayek, Murray Rothbard, and Robert Nozick. For examples, *see* 2 FRIEDRICH A. HAYEK, LAW, LEGISLATION AND LIBERTY: THE MIRAGE OF SOCIAL JUSTICE 62–106 (1976); ROBERT NOZICK, ANARCHY, STATE, and UTOPIA 149–231 (1974). It will be clear that I have drawn on Nozick and Hayek here, but I will not hold either of these complex and thoughtful authors responsible for the precise formulations I employ.

though people have such duties, it is unreasonable for anyone else to expect that they be fulfilled or to foster their fulfillment.[3] But natural law maintains that people do have such duties. Thus, communal norms that call for people to share wealth remedially can be understood as asking that they to fulfill open-textured, but pre-existing, duties to others[4] (and not, for instance, as mandating that they seek any particular end-state or attempt to impose a pattern on the overall distribution of wealth).

Natural law theory denies that people have *absolute* property rights: property rights flow from and so are limited by the principles of practical reasonableness (in tandem with the basic aspects of well being and general truths about how human persons and communities function). Thus, it need not in principle be any violation of their rights for communities to sustain norms that call for them to perform their redistributive duties and which facilitate their fulfillment of these duties.[5]

Similarly, natural law theory denies that all contracts are fair, both because the bargaining situations that lead to some contracts are unfair and because the actual terms to which people agree may sometimes be unreasonable. Thus, a legal system's denial of validity to some contract terms and a community's refusal to treat the results of a particular contractual exchange as necessarily reasonable and enforceable need not automatically violate the requirements of justice. Further, just because someone has justly obtained a piece of property or some money in a contractual exchange, it does not follow that she has no obligations in justice to use some of her resources to care for people in need or support communal projects – obligations in virtue of which she may need to part with money or property she has justly acquired.

B   *Treating the individual as a means*

Another objection amounts to the claim that supporting redistributive norms means treating the particular person as a means to an imagined overall good. But affirming a duty to help others and to support communal projects doesn't involve regarding anyone as simply a servant of the general good as long as each person retains a significant zone of control over her

---

[3] *See* JOHN FINNIS, NATURAL LAW AND NATURAL RIGHTS 187 (1980).

[4] Thanks to an anonymous reviewer for emphasizing the need to make this point more clearly.

[5] *Cf.* LUKE TIMOTHY JOHNSON, SHARING POSSESSIONS: MANDATE AND SYMBOL OF FAITH 136–37 (1981) (describing the systematic collection and distribution of alms in, especially, Diaspora Judaism).

own existence within which positive duty does not intrude. And the principles of practical reasonableness provide the material needed to construct an account of justice in distribution (and of other aspects of justice) that clearly leaves space for individual autonomy.[6]

C   Pursuing end-states rather than respecting the integrity of transactions

A related objection is the claim that supporting redistributive norms and rules means supporting the imposition of a particular distributive pattern on a community's economy, and that, because it is most unlikely that any finite set of individual transactions will result in the desired pattern, such norms and rules must ignore the essential role of history in explaining the justice of a given state of affairs. What matters, on this view, is *how* a state of affairs came about, and not just what sort of state of affairs it is. But the point of redistributive duties as natural law theory understands them is *not* an end-state, some overall distribution of wealth, and the justice of a given state of affairs need not be determined without reference to the choices leading to that state. Natural law theory maintains, rather, that some *transactions* must be redistributive, in virtue of the duty to help others and support communal projects. This duty requires us to do many things that will count as redistributive, but it does not involve any responsibility to achieve some patterned end-state for a community's economy purportedly viewed as a whole or to participate in reordering the allotment of resources on the macroeconomic level.

D   Limitations on information

A further objection also seems to assume that the fulfillment of redistributive duties must involve the attempt to achieve a macro-level outcome. This objection holds that redistribution is problematic because it presupposes falsely that anyone could acquire and deploy enough information to make it possible for her to impose an intended pattern on the economy as a whole. But accepting the natural law view of redistributive duties does not commit anyone to the impossible task of managing the overwhelmingly complex spontaneous order of a community's economic

---

[6] *Cf.* JOHN FINNIS, AQUINAS: MORAL, POLITICAL, and LEGAL THEORY 239–42 (1998) (arguing that Aquinas's account of the law's reach understands it as limited, and comparing it with Mill's).

life. It is possible for people to identify behavior inconsistent with their distributive responsibilities and for communal a norms and institutions to facilitate the remediation of this behavior without anyone's supposing that she could bring about any overall distributional pattern, even if it were (as natural law theory's rejection of consequentialism suggests it is not) desirable to do so.

E   Redistribution as a source of arbitrariness and unpredictability

A further objection is that redistributive requirements cannot be expressed in general, impersonal rules offering reliable, predictable guidance for human action and leaving clear scope for personal decision. For the critic, it follows that the attempt to fulfill such requirements will involve intrusive interference with individual choices. This kind of interference, it is alleged, will inhibit effective personal and organizational planning, with dire consequences for a community's economy. It will also interfere dramatically with personal autonomy. But redistributive norms can leave people free to plan. This is because they need not involve the attempted assessment of the justice of end-states. They can instead help to shape how people behave in generically specifiable situations and provide general guidance for their support for valuable projects and people in need. Thus, these standards can be general, impersonal, and reliable in ways that need not leave anyone subject to someone else's arbitrary whims or unable to plan effectively.

Critics seem often to think of redistribution as conceivable only as the work of a rational planner integrating all available information and directing the whole economy toward an end-state. In different ways, this image of redistribution underlies all of the attacks on redistributive rules and norms I have considered in Part I. But this image is not the image implicit in natural law theory's account of redistribution. Redistribution as understood by natural law theory is something people owe to other people and to their communities. Communal norms and rules do not create the responsibility to redistribute wealth; rather, they may, in a manner consistent with the requirements of practical reason, facilitate and coordinate people's fulfillment of this responsibility.

II   Natural law and economic norms, rules, and institutions

Practical reason does not ordinarily require a particular allocation of wealth beyond the public trust threshold. But communal norms and rules may offer valuable coordination and help to prevent "backsliding, arbitrariness, and inequity."[7]

The exact shape of communal efforts designed to provide remedies for injustice, accident, and economic insecurity is not a matter for philosophy to decide; practical reason is consistent with diverse institutional designs. A natural law account of morals, law, and politics is surely hospitable to various sorts of income security and poverty relief systems. But practical reason does not require the implementation of particular norms or rules by a given community; rather, it constrains the available options.

Thus, as regards health care: there might be good reasons, from a natural law standpoint, to judge "that it should be available to people of limited means, insofar as possible, at little or no direct cost," and that, in accordance with the principle of subsidiarity, it "is best provided through voluntary associations formed for that specific purpose," albeit with appropriate communal support.[8] But such judgments of principle leave a great deal of room for differences regarding the implications of the Golden Rule and the Efficiency Principle. Given the actual and likely relevant features of individual, social, and economic life, a community's funding of universal health-care coverage for all of its members, for instance, seems to me to be appealing on natural law grounds, for reasons I seek to spell out below. But someone who understood the relevant circumstances differently, or who made different predictions about human behavior, or who made different judgments about the fairness of allocating particular benefits and burdens might hold different views above appropriate communal norms.

It might, for instance, be quite consistent with natural law theory, taken by itself, to support an approach not grounded in community-wide funding.[9] Depending on the nature of the reasons offered for such an approach, I might agree that it was fully consistent with natural law thinking, while rejecting it because I made different empirical assumptions, or preferred to weigh differently the burdens and benefits of particular options in my own case and so, to be consistent with the Golden Rule, in the cases of others. It need not, *ex hypothesi*, be the case that I differed with the proponent of the alternative approach about the essential implications of natural law theory itself.

---

[7] *Id.* at 195.

[8] 2 GERMAIN G. GRISEZ, THE WAY OF THE LORD JESUS: LIVING A CHRISTIAN LIFE 864 (1994).

[9] *Cf.* DAVID BEITO, FROM MUTUAL AID TO THE WELFARE STATE: FRATERNAL SOCIETIES AND SOCIAL SERVICES, 1890–1967 (2000); KEVIN A. CARSON, ORGANIZATION THEORY: A LIBERTARIAN PERSPECTIVE 594–603 (2008); RICHARD C. CORNUELLE, RECLAIMING THE AMERICAN DREAM (1993).

III   Health care

There is good reason to share the costs of providing health care for the members of a community throughout the community.[10] Among the obvious alternatives to sharing costs are payment by firms and payment by individual consumers' insurers. Both seem to me to be less attractive; I argue against the former in Section A and against the latter in Section B. In Section C, I argue briefly for the communal funding and private delivery of health care.

A   Health care and employment

Coverage linked with employment is problematic for multiple reasons. Obviously, it fails to ensure care for those who are unemployed or self-employed. And it may create significant and unnecessary burdens for many firms. Small firms, in particular, find providing health insurance to workers costly.[11] The costs associated with providing health-care coverage to full-time workers has played a significant role in encouraging investor-controlled firms to rely on part-time workers and putatively independent contractors.[12] Because of rising costs, some firms may demand higher premium payments from workers who participate in their health plans,[13] while others may lay off full-time workers for whom they are required to provide health-care coverage only to rehire them as part-time workers without such coverage.[14]

Firms may face understandable and considerable pressure from workers and community groups to retain workers who might lose their access to health care if they are laid off. This is a further way in which linking health care with employment places a substantial burden on particular firms.[15] And the fact that, in the United States, health-care and retirement

[10] Cf. id. at 864.
[11] Cf. Small Businesses Have Their Views and They Aren't That Bad, 63 CPA J. 11, 12 (1993) (reporting that "[f]orty one percent of businesses surveyed felt providing health benefits is the number one obstacle facing the growth and survival of their companies"). Cf. Charles P. Hall, Jr., and John M. Kuder, Health Benefits and Small Business: What Now and What Next? 6 BENEFITS Q. 14 (1990).
[12] See Anna M. Rappaport, Policy Environment for Health Benefits: Implications for Employer Plans, 43 DePAUL L. REV. 1107, 1109, 1115 (1994).
[13] See Susan Adler Channick, Come the Revolution: Are We Finally Ready for Universal Health Insurance?, 39 CAL. W. L. REV. 303, 304–5 (2003).
[14] See, e.g., Ann Bookman, Flexibility At What Price? The Costs of Part-Time Work for Women Workers, 52 WASH. & LEE L. REV. 799, 805 (1995).
[15] See John J. Kang, Student Paper, Perpetuating Market Misallocations in Health Care through Employer Health Insurance Mandates, 12 AM. J. TAX POL'y 513 (1995) (criticizing the use of firm mandates as inequitable, inefficient, and overly complex).

benefits are often not available to workers who opt for what firms seek to classify as part-time work has been among the most pressing reasons workers have felt unable to choose shorter work weeks, despite increasingly oppressive demands on workers' time.[16] Sharing health-care costs throughout a community seems likely to avoid many of the pressures on workers and firms associated with employer-provided health care.

B   Health care funded by consumer-purchased insurance

Communally funded universal coverage also seems preferable to coverage provided by insurers selected and paid for by individual health-care consumers. Such universal coverage has the potential to reduce transaction costs for individual community members who would otherwise be required to search for and compare a wide range of alternative private insurance options. It can make it easier for people with high-cost pre-existing conditions to obtain health care. It can relieve people of the responsibility for ensuring that they are adequately covered – or covered at all. It can make it more likely that any member of a community can make use of the services of any health-care provider, rather than just the limited number affiliated with a particular health insurance plan. And universal enrollment helps to ensure that public support for the provision of health-care services persists: people are much more likely to favor the continuation of such services if they benefit from them personally, rather than seeing them as simply designed to aid a limited group of poor people.

C   Health care, cost sharing, and freedom

Firms, workers, and community members all stand to gain, therefore, if health-care costs are communally shared. If the cost of caring for people's health were shared across the community, small firms would not be overwhelmed by the need to cover potentially catastrophic health-care expenses.[17] Firms forced to lay off workers could do so knowing they were not denying these workers access to health care. Unemployed and retired

---

[16] Cf. JULIET SCHOR, THE OVERWORKED AMERICAN: THE UNEXPECTED DECLINE OF LEISURE (1991) (examining the significance of working hours).

[17] See Timothy Stoltzfus Jost & Sandra J. Tanenbaum, Selling Cost Containment, 19 AM. J. L. AND MED. 95, 109–12 (1993). Jost and Tanenbaum suggest, plausibly, that malpractice reform is a crucial feature of cost containment. They argue that "the government ought to take on the burden of defending medical malpractice litigation and covering malpractice liability." Id. at 113.

persons would retain access to health care.[18] And workers would feel more free to negotiate for shorter working hours, thus reducing firms' payroll expenses and enabling the workers to avoid being overwhelmed by excessive work-related demands.

Shared funding of health care is perfectly compatible with anyone's being free to purchase additional coverage.[19] It is also quite compatible with the private delivery of health-care services. And, indeed, there are good, whether or not decisive, reasons for the private delivery of communally funded health care. First, private delivery might allow for greater flexibility and permit patients and health-care providers more control over the course of treatment.[20] Second, communal delivery of health care could easily involve the creation of unwieldy, unresponsive bureaucracies. Third, private delivery of communally funded care could foster greater patient choice regarding the nature of health-care services by allowing patients to opt for non-standard therapies and providers.[21] And, fourth, depending on how funding arrangements were structured, choice among private health-care providers could foster competition that could lead to the enhancement of health-care quality while promoting the efficient use of communal health-care funds.[22]

Of course, an effective system of communal support for health care can be effective only if costs are controlled. Among the strategies a reasonable community will likely implement is the refusal to provide legal sanction to occupational and institutional cartels that conspire to

---

[18] Security seems to me among the more obvious of the advantage of the model I elaborate here, an advantages which provides some reason to disagree with JOHN KAY, CULTURE AND PROSPERITY: THE TRUTH ABOUT MARKETS – WHY SOME NATIONS ARE RICH BUT MOST REMAIN POOR 242, 350 (2004).

[19] This is comparable to the approach taken by the proposed United States National Health Insurance Act; cf. Channick, supra note 13, at 321.

[20] Cf. Grisez's appeal to the principle of subsidiarity to argue for private delivery of health care: see GRISEZ, LIVING, supra note 8, at 864.

[21] One approach might be to provide each patient with access to (i) limited-quantity vouchers she could use to fund ordinary health-care costs, bankable to allow planned performance of higher-cost elective procedures, and (ii) high- or no-ceiling funding for major medical expenses. The bankable nature of the vouchers could help to encourage efficient health-care choices. This is my version of a proposal offered by TIM HARFORD, THE UNDERCOVER ECONOMIST: EXPOSING WHY THE RICH ARE RICH, THE POOR ARE POOR – AND WHY YOU CAN NEVER BUY A DECENT USED CAR! (2005).

[22] This might be especially likely if health-care providers were certified by communal institutions rather than being licensed by monopolistic professional groups. Cf. Milton Friedman's discussion of occupational licensure in CAPITALISM AND FREEDOM 137–60 (1962).

drive health-care costs ever higher.[23] A reasonable community will likely also decline to support monopolistic patent that dramatically increase the cost of pharmaceutical products.[24]

IV   Basic income

A basic income is a source of economic security not directly linked to employment – a guaranteed minimum income.[25] A basic income scheme is not a substitute for a fair wage but a supplement to it, offering a level of security, independence, and dignity not available if income support is linked with paid work.[26] Basic income schemes have been widely discussed at least since the 1960s.[27] They have attracted endorsements not

---

[23] *Cf.* CARSON, *supra* note 9, at 596–99.

[24] *Cf.* MICHELE BOLORIN & DAVID K. LEVINE, AGAINST INTELLECTUAL MONOPOLY (2008); STEPHAN KINSELLA, AGAINST INTELLECTUAL PROPERTY (2008).

[25] For an argument that wealth or income transfers remain effective responses to a variety of significant social and economic concerns, organized around comparative analyses of approaches in Germany, the Netherlands, and the United States, see ROBERT E. GOODIN ET AL., THE REAL WORLDS OF WELFARE CAPITALISM (1999).

[26] *Cf.* GRISEZ, LIVING, *supra* note 8, at 767 (arguing for the use of communal funds to make up the difference between fair compensation for individual workers and the needs of families).

[27] *See, e.g.*, ARGUING FOR BASIC INCOME: ETHICAL FOUNDATIONS FOR a RADICAL REFORM (Philippe van Parijs ed., 1992); ANTHONY BARNES ATKINSON, PUBLIC ECONOMICS IN ACTION: THE BASIC INCOME/FLAT TAX PROPOSAL (1995); SAMUEL BRITTAN & STEVEN WEBB, BEYOND THE WELFARE STATE: AN EXAMINATION OF BASIC INCOMES IN a MARKET ECONOMY (1990); VINCENT J. BURKE & VEE BURKE, NIXON'S GOOD DEED: WELFARE REFORM (1974); TONY FITZPATRICK, FREEDOM AND SECURITY: AN INTRODUCTION TO THE BASIC INCOME DEBATE (1999); THE GUARANTEED INCOME: NEXT STEP IN ECONOMIC EVOLUTION? (Robert Theobald ed., 1966); ROBERT HAVEMAN & ROSS FINNIE, STARTING EVEN: AN EQUAL OPPORTUNITY PROGRAM TO COMBAT THE NATION'S NEW POVERTY 154, 156–58 (1988); ADRIAN LITTLE, POST-INDUSTRIAL SOCIALISM: TOWARD a NEW POLITICS OF WELFARE (1998); DANIEL PATRICK MOYNIHAN, THE POLITICS OF a GUARANTEED INCOME: THE NIXON ADMINISTRATION AND THE FAMILY ASSISTANCE PLAN (1973); MICHAEL L. MURRAY, – AND ECONOMIC JUSTICE FOR ALL: WELFARE REFORM FOR THE TWENTY-FIRST CENTURY (1997); HERMIONE PARKER, INSTEAD OF THE DOLE: AN ENQUIRY INTO INTEGRATION OF THE TAX AND BENEFIT SYSTEMS (1990); ROBERT R. SCHUTZ, THE $30,000 SOLUTION (1996); PHILLIPE VAN PARIJS, REAL FREEDOM FOR ALL: WHAT (IF ANYTHING) CAN JUSTIFY CAPITALISM? (1995); WALTER VAN TRIER, EVERY ONE A KING: AN INVESTIGATION INTO THE MEANING AND SIGNIFICANCE OF THE DEBATE ON BASIC INCOMES WITH SPECIAL REFERENCE TO THREE EPISODES FROM THE BRITISH INTER-WAR EXPERIENCE (1995); TONY WALTER, BASIC INCOME: FREEDOM FROM POVERTY, FREEDOM TO WORK (1989); ANDREW J. WINNICK, TOWARD TWO SOCIETIES: THE CHANGING DISTRIBUTION OF INCOME AND WEALTH IN THE U.S. SINCE 1960 217–19 (1989); Carole Pateman, *Another Way Forward: Welfare, Social Reproduction, and a Basic Income, in* WELFARE REFORM AND POLITICAL THEORY 34 (Lawrence M. Mead & Christopher Beem eds., 2005); Carole Pateman, *Democratizing Citizenship: Some*

only from liberals and socialists but also from libertarians like Milton Friedman and Friedrich Hayek.[28] Helping to provide each person in a given community with a basic income guarantee might be an effective way in which the members of the community could meet many of their responsibilities in distributive justice.

I want here briefly to emphasize the capacity of basic income to foster independence (Section A), empower workers (Section B), encourage self-respect (Section C), contribute to people's identification with the fortunes of their communities (Section D), and ensure that people can affect the ways in which their cultures develop (Section E).

A   Basic income and independence

A basic income scheme increases independence and thus allows people to exercise judgment about communal norms, rules, and institutions. Someone who lacks basic resources also lacks the capacity to exercise meaningful direction over her or his own life. But, with a basic income, a person would have greater latitude as she made significant life choices.

The systematic provision of a basic income could help to ensure that a recipient's well being was not contingent on the arbitrary will of someone dispensing assistance, whether a bureaucrat or a powerful benefactor. Dependence on patronage may compromise a person's independent judgment. She is not free to make the choices she would like to make as she contributes to the shaping of communal norms, rules, and institutions. Indeed, her sense of what is actually *possible* may be substantially constrained by her dependence on a patron. The welfare or approval of the patron may be the principal factor influencing her decision making. Indeed, she may simply *identify* with the patron. By contrast, insulated to some extent from economic reprisal, someone with a basic income will

---

Advantages of a Basic Income, 32 POL. & SOC. 89 (2004); Carole Pateman, *Freedom and Democratization: Why Basic Income Is to Be Preferred to Basic Capital, in* THE ETHICS OF STAKEHOLDING 130 (Keith Dowding, Jurgen De Wispelaere & Stuart White eds., 2003). *Cf.* BRUCE A. ACKERMAN & ANNE ALSTOTT, THE STAKEHOLDER SOCIETY (1999) (proposing that a large lump sum should be made available to everyone at an early age).
[28] *See, e.g.,* FRIEDRICH A. HAYEK, THE CONSTITUTION OF LIBERTY 257–59 (1960); 3 FRIEDRICH A. HAYEK, LAW, LEGISLATION, AND LIBERTY: THE POLITICAL ORDER OF A FREE PEOPLE 54–56 (1979); Milton Friedman, *The Alleviation of Poverty, in* INEQUALITY AND POVERTY 189–93 (Edward C. Budd ed., 1967). Friedman acknowledges forthrightly that private charity is likely to be inadequate to address the problem of poverty in mass society. He argues for a negative income tax proposal that would compensate anyone whose income fell below a fixed level by providing her with a percentage of the difference between her income and the poverty line.

have significant freedom to reflect independently on her community's norms, rules, and institutions, and so to choose how she will contribute through her words, her gifts, and her life-plan to its development.

B   Basic income and workplace vulnerability

Related to the general problem of economic dependence on the powerful is the problem of vulnerability in the workplace, especially the investor-governed workplace. If workplace democracy – or, at minimum, extensive participation by workers in decision-making – is a requirement of practical reason, then firm decision-makers must ensure that workers can exercise as much influence as possible and communities must foster active involvement by workers in management. But workplace freedom will tend to give way in the face of institutional pressure if people cannot depend on a bedrock of economic security that will sustain them if unpopular stances cause them to lose their jobs.[29] Basic income gives people the security they need to take positions in their workplaces that might attract negative attention from other workers or, in investor-governed firms, managers. Because having a basic income would probably increase the likelihood of someone's taking such positions, it would thus also increase the likelihood that people would be able to make their workplaces more responsive, fair, and participatory through their active support for justice.

C   Basic income and self-respect

Enjoying the measure of independence made possible by a basic income scheme gives people the opportunity to develop a sense of themselves as competent decision-makers. And because having a basic income would mean having access to basic necessities, people could avoid the stigma associated with visible deprivation, and so elicit positive responses from others – responses unavoidably crucial to their positive self-perceptions. Self-respect contributes to the sense both that one has the capacity for involvement in communal life and that one's contribution has inherent value: if I matter, then my ideas and perspectives matter as well. Thus, basic income would help to contribute not only to people's awareness of their own dignity but also to their capacity to join in shaping the lives of their communities.

---

[29] Firms act wrongly if they discharge workers for expressing unpopular opinions. But that is precisely why basic income is so important as a remedial device: it is likely to be most useful in environments in which institutions are not justly ordered.

D   Basic income and community identification

A basic income can give someone a stake in her community – prompting her to identify her fortunes with its fortunes and equipping her to exercise influence in its markets. The sense of being a stakeholder is a crucial prerequisite to participation in the shaping of communal norms, rules, and institutions. A lack of concern with a group of which one is theoretically a member is likely to predispose one to avoid commitment to communal well being or participation in common life. Poor people may fail actively to participate in the lives of their communities for a whole range of reasons, of course. But to the extent that someone's willingness to do so is affected by the sense that she simply does not belong, basic income can help to encourage active engagement in the process of shaping norms, rules, and institutions by guaranteeing each member a piece of a community's economic pie and thus prompting her to think of the community as her own.

E   Basic income and cultural self-determination

Basic income enables people to make choices about how they will live their lives and so to influence how others will live theirs. A basic income scheme may make it easier for a person to conduct experiments in living, to participate in the process of *cultural* self-determination,[30] to vote through her or his behavior for a wide range of lifestyles and life-plans. Not only can the freedom guaranteed by a basic income scheme encourage healthy social experimentation on the part of particular people; it can also make it easier for variant options to be put on *display* for others in ways that enable them to assess divergent positions as actually embodied in real people's lives. Thus, by giving people greater freedom, a basic income scheme could contribute to their ability to enrich the debate on cultural values by the way they live their lives, thus rendering the process of cultural change more open, responsive, accountable, and inclusive.

V   Poverty relief outside one's own community

Basic income and universal health care schemes can provide important assistance to people within particular communities. But it is not reasonable to be concerned only about the members of one's own community;

---

[30] *Cf.* Kenneth H. Karst, *Local Discourse and the Social Issues*, 12 CARDOZO STUD. LAW & LIT. 1, 27 (2000).

the needs of people in other communities are morally significant, too.[31] There is good reason for people in industrialized communities (ICs) to help to remedy the effects of injustice, disaster, and economic insecurity in less developed communities (LDCs).

It is so clear from the standpoint of natural law theory that our responsibilities extend beyond the borders of our own communities that, while he is perhaps the most politically conservative of the NCNLTs, Robert P. George has, in stark contrast to most conservatives in the United States, maintained that the establishment of global governance institutions is a morally important goal.[32] There may be good reason to be skeptical about the potential legitimacy and usefulness of a global government, just as there is good reason to be skeptical about the legitimacy and usefulness of existing states. And natural law theory gives us good reason to nourish our own communities and to value local loyalties: its sense of the value of connection and sociability and of the interdependence of persons makes it hospitable to the development of thriving communities with distinctive profiles. But there is little question that natural law theory is thoroughly inconsistent with chauvinistic nationalism and insensitive disregard for those outside our communities.

Natural law theory entails no commitment to a naïve view in accordance with which the disparities in communities' material conditions are exclusively or primarily accidental or inevitable. Poverty is frequently the result of exclusion, subordination, and dispossession. Declining to engage in continuing injustice is a bedrock requirement of justice; and if political and economic elites in ICs and LDCs simply met this requirement, deprivation in LDCs – reflective as it is of violent dispossessions, monopolies, and tariffs – would likely be significantly reduced. Thus, the most important responses to global poverty will be the elimination of structural injustices and the compensation of the victims of past injustice. The proposals for property reform canvassed in Chapter 4 provide the groundwork for some kinds of reasonable approaches to securing redress for victims.

The prime responsibility for remedying injustice lies with the direct beneficiaries, but it will not always be possible to identify them, so more

---

[31] See, e.g., PAUL COLLIER, THE BOTTOM BILLION: WHY THE POOREST COUNTRIES ARE FAILING AND WHAT CAN BE DONE ABOUT IT (2007); JEFFREY SACHS, THE END OF POVERTY (2005); but cf. WILLIAM EASTERLY, THE WHITE MAN'S BURDEN: WHY THE WEST'S EFFORTS TO AID THE REST HAVE DONE SO MUCH ILL AND SO LITTLE GOOD (2006).

[32] See ROBERT P. GEORGE, IN DEFENSE OF NATURAL LAW 228–45 (2001) [hereinafter GEORGE]; cf. GRISEZ, LIVING, supra note 8, at 868–69.

broad-based remedies will often be unavoidable. And disaster and economic insecurity warrant responses from those able to provide them
even when no injustice is involved.[33] Thus, assisting LDCs through donation, investment, or both is likely a duty of most ICs, whether or not of
each their individual members.[34]

I examine the remedial responsibility to make distributional choices
that address the problem of poverty in LDCs below. In Section A,
I underscore the ways in which the criteria of distributive justice can
generate specific responsibilities to aid poor people and communities.
(These criteria are obviously relevant within ICs as well, though it may
be easier for people in ICs to help foster economic security in their own
communities simply by supporting schemes already organized for this
purpose than it is to contribute to the well being of people in poor communities in this way.) In Section B, I note that, when these responsibilities have been met and one has made reasonable choices regarding one's
own participation in the various aspects of well being, there may well
be resources left over. One need not necessarily use these resources –
those in excess of the public trust threshold – to assist poor people or
communities, but doing so will certainly be appropriate. In Section C,
I emphasize that, whatever an *individual's* options with regard to the
use of resources in excess of her public trust threshold, it would likely
be unjust for most members of an IC to contribute nothing to the relief
of poverty locally and globally. In Section D, I note that the requirements of distributive justice do not entail the conclusion that people
in general must focus their professional activities or their resources on

[33] Debt relief may be one response to these problems; *see generally* Søren Ambrose, *Social Movements and the Politics of Debt Cancellation*, 6 Chi. J. Int'l L. 267, 272–75 (2005); Eric A. Friedman, *Debt Relief in 1999: Only One Step on a Long Journey*, 3 Yale H.R. & Dev. L.J. 191 (2000); David L. Gregory, *From Pope John Paul II to Bono/U2: International Debt Relief Initiatives "in the Name of Love,"* 19 B.U. Int'l L.J. 257, 258, 268 (2001); Alon Seveg, *Investment: When Countries Go Bust: Proposals for Debtor and Creditor Resolution*, 3 Aspen Rev. Int'l Bus. & Trade L. 25, 68, 77 (2003).

[34] It seems clear that this will rarely mean a responsibility simply to transfer wealth. Targeted assistance can be effective, as Sachs and Collier both suggest; but it often achieves less than we might like (as Easterly reminds us), especially when it does not occur in tandem with changes in politics, culture, and global rules and institutions. Responses to the problem of poverty will often, appropriately, take the form of enterprise development; *cf.* Stuart L. Hart, Capitalism at the Crossroads: The Unlimited Business Opportunities in Solving the World's Most Difficult Problems (2005); C. K. Prahalad, The Fortune at the Bottom of the Pyramid: Eradicating Poverty through Profits (2005); Mohammed Yunus, Creating a World without Poverty: Social Business and the Future of Capitalism (2007).

poverty relief (though, of course, some people may be responsible for doing so in light of their circumstances or commitments). I offer an overview of my arguments in Section E.

A   Particular responsibilities for poverty relief and justice in distribution

The specific criteria of justice in distribution provide several reasons for those with resources to provide assistance to poor people outside their own communities. It is a requirement of justice in distribution that we assist those whom we can easily aid (Subsection 1). Particular commitments and attachments may give us reason to respond to the needs of particular poor people and communities (Subsection 2). Directing resources toward poor communities may sometimes be a requirement of efficiency (Subsection 3). And justice requires that we offer reparations to people when we have harmed them, and perhaps also that we provide at least some compensation to people when we have clearly and directly benefited from injuries they have suffered (Subsection 4).[35] All of these reasons for action are relevant within most or all communities, and to relationships between communities and their proximate neighbors. But they are particularly significant as regards the responsibilities between members of ICs and poorer, more distant neighbors.

1   Need

We ought to help those in need who are particularly vulnerable to us and whom we can easily assist. This requirement points to a special responsibility, just like special responsibilities to friends or co-workers – it is not a duty to provide help anywhere and everywhere. This will often mean caring specifically for members of our own communities whom we encounter. But it might also require prudent responsiveness to the needs of those we encounter when, say, traveling in LDCs. Fulfilling this responsibility might involve rescuing a drowning child, helping someone change a tire, or buying a meal for a hungry person.

---

[35] Finnis observes that "the problem of assessing the extent of one's responsibilities in reason for the welfare of persons in other political communities ... is one of the most difficult of all practical problems; and its resolution, by each of us (for our situations and thus our responsibilities differ), is constantly threatened by the pull of unreasonable self-preference, group bias, and lukewarmness about human good." FINNIS, LAW, *supra* note 3, at 177.

2   Commitments and attachments

Special relational responsibilities arising from our attachments and commitments can also give us particular reasons to donate to or – since targeted investment will often be an effective means of addressing poverty – invest in LDCs. These might include links with a particular LDC – as a result of family ties or past or present work there. They might also include special ties with an NGO seeking to benefit a given LDC or with a responsible firm proposing to invest in the LDC.

3   Efficiency and productivity

Efficiency and productivity may provide good reason to invest in an LDC, if (given that – see Chapter 6 – working conditions are just) doing so will reduce net production costs for the venture one seeks to support.

4   Reward

If one has been *involved* in the dispossession of people in an LDC, one will obviously have particular reason to contribute fairly to compensating them. One will often also have reason to do so if one has benefited directly from their dispossession. We are all caught up in webs of injustice over which we often have little control, and there is no virtue in nurturing a vague sense of having dirty hands. But if there is a reasonably unimpeded connection between one's profit and their injustice, then, even if one is not responsible for the injustice, it will often be appropriate for one to share reasonably in the burden of remedying it.

B   Using resources beyond the public trust threshold for global poverty relief

Apart from these particular responsibilities, donating to or investing in LDCs will be an appropriate use of resources in excess of the public trust threshold. However, practical reason will often leave open a range of destinations for such resources.

1   The nature of the threshold

The criteria of justice in distribution, along with the residual options for one's own reasonable participation in basic aspects of well being that are consistent with the requirements of practical reasonableness, help one to make a reasonable judgment about one's public trust threshold. Wealth exceeds this threshold if it may not reasonably be expended either in fulfillment of specific distributional responsibilities or in furtherance of

one's own participation in basic aspects of well being. It is wealth in excess
of the public threshold that may reasonably be invested in or donated to
LDCs to help relieve global poverty.

2   Discretion in the use of resources beyond the threshold

One may have considerable discretion as regards how to use resources
in excess of the public trust threshold to assist people in need or support valuable projects. It is not the case that one must always focus one's
resources, even those beyond the public trust threshold, on promoting the *subsistence* of others.[36] Indeed, assisting all sorts of people and
associations in participating reasonably in diverse aspects of well being
"contributes in incommensurable ways to the well being and fulfillment
of persons." Thus, the choice to help anyone participate reasonably in
any authentic dimension of welfare "is the willing of at least *some* person's good," and fostering the realization of one kind of (genuine) well
being "is not in and of itself ... [preferable to fostering the realization]
of another."[37] "We must make choices, opting for certain areas of concentration in preference to others, and doing so precisely as our particular contribution to the common life of commitment to ... [the various
aspects of well being] which we share with those with whom we live in
community."[38]

This is why "cultural centers" are appropriate recipients of resources
in excess of the public trust threshold, just as are the poor and charities
serving them. Similarly,

> [e]ven if the money you could donate to ... [a development NGO] would
> save the lives of people who otherwise would die, you will not ... [sup-
> port a college] *at the cost of those lives* by giving the money to the college
> instead. You neither will have willed those people to die – for example,
> by choosing to kill them as a means to some other end – nor judged their
> lives of less worth than the benefits of ... [the gift to the college]. You only
> will have reluctantly accepted their deaths as a side effect of promoting
> the other good. And, provided you can choose that other good fairly, you
> need not be unreasonable in choosing – not as better, but simply as the
> irreplaceable good it is.[39]

---

[36] *See* 3 GERMAIN G. GRISEZ, THE WAY OF THE LORD JESUS: DIFFICULT MORAL QUESTIONS 438 (1997).
[37] *Id.* at 438 (my italics).
[38] GERMAIN GRISEZ & RUSSELL SHAW, BEYOND THE NEW MORALITY: THE RESPONSIBILITIES OF FREEDOM 236 (3rd ed. 1988).
[39] GRISEZ, QUESTIONS, *supra* note 38, at 438 (my italics).

3   Directed discretion.

One will not be *required* in virtue of special relational responsibilities to employ resources beyond the public trust threshold in particular ways. If special responsibilities require that one spend resources in a particular way, then these resources do not – by definition – fall beyond the public trust threshold. That is because resources beyond the public trust threshold are ones which one may not expend in order to benefit oneself or one's dependents or to fulfill specific resposibilities to others. However, particular features of one's identity and one's circumstances may *channel* one's use of these resources toward particular people and projects. Thus, in the example of the person deciding between the college and the NGO, special ties to the college, the fact that a gift might memorialize a dead spouse, the fact that one's children may attend the college, and the fact that one might obtain a seat on the college's board of trustees as a result of the gift – all might give one good reason to give to the college rather than the NGO.[40] Obviously, this very case-specific judgment is not meaningfully generalizable. The point is simply that there can be intelligible reasons for choosing one beneficiary over another even though none would finally be *necessary*.

C   Shared responsibility for global poverty relief

Communities may certainly invest their resources in a range of good causes. However, it will be unreasonable for people not to support norms and rules that call for significant assistance of one kind or another to poor people. Perhaps some particular person might, without committing injustice, choose to devote much or all of her resources in excess of the public trust threshold to cultural enrichment. But the same would not be true of an entire community.

(*i*) Negatively, while personal identities and commitments may channel private resources into purely cultural channels, a *community* has made and could make no commitments, has no identity, consistently channeling its concern away from poor people. (*ii*) Positively, the Golden Rule would seem to rule out as unfair general disregard both for the proximate poor and for neighbors beyond a community's borders. It will condemn as unjust the maintenance of those structures that create and perpetuate poverty. And it will thus provide support for norms, rules, and institutions responsive to the problem of poverty within communities and

[40]   *See id.* at 439.

beyond their borders,[41] including those furthering not only investments but also other wealth transfers of various sorts.

D Poverty relief and universal responsibility

There is good reason for someone with resources to give respectful consideration to the needs of poor people in her own community and in other communities. But this does not mean that "every one of us is responsible for everyone else in every way."[42] If one supposes that "each person counts for one and only one," then, Finnis observes, everyone must be

> morally bound to devote his wealth and energy (which he might otherwise have devoted to the interests of himself, his "dependants", his own local and political communities, etc.[]) to the interests of the most disadvantaged persons whom he can find anywhere in the world, up to the point where his (marginal) sacrifice of wealth and energy would render himself and his "dependants" worse off than those most disadvantaged persons. Any other use of one's wealth and energy is, on this view, simply unjust.[43]

---

[41] *Cf.* GEORGE, *supra* note 32, at 244 n.32.   [42] FINNIS, LAW, *supra* note 3, at 176.

[43] *Id.* at 177. *Cf.* Peter Singer, *Famine, Affluence, and Morality*, 1 PHIL PUB. AFF. 229 (1972). In the first edition of *Practical Ethics*, while declining to offer a general norm for particular donors, he suggested that readers persuaded by his argument *advocate* everyone's payment of a 10 percent tithe for development and relief purposes, with the understanding that the persuaded themselves would give a good deal more. *See* PETER SINGER, PRACTICAL ETHICS (1st ed. 1979). In the second edition, he simply defended a 10 percent minimum for everyone without a large number of dependants, without actively arguing that a higher donation level should, in reality, be expected of most people. *See* PETER SINGER, PRACTICAL ETHICS (2d ed. 1993). In a *New York Times* magazine article, he attempted a different tack, suggesting that everyone adopt a budget equal to one identified as standard by The Conference Board, and give away anything in excess of this amount. *See* Peter Singer, *The Singer Solution to World Poverty*, NEW YORK TIMES, Sept. 5, 1999, at 6:60. Singer's philosophical predilections are consequentialist. His own practice, he has made ruefully clear in multiple interviews, is to give away a mere 20 percent of his income. *See, e.g.,* Debra Galant, *Peter Singer Settles in, and Princeton Looks Deeper; Furor over the Philosopher Fades Though Some Discomfort Lingers*, NEW YORK TIMES, Mar. 5, 2000, at 14NJ:1. Peter Unger has developed the case for a very extensive duty to support global development and poverty relief efforts using intuitionist moral arguments. *See* PETER UNGER, LIVING HIGH AND LETTING DIE: OUR ILLUSION OF INNOCENCE (1996). For alternative views, *see, e.g.,* ROBERT E. GOODIN, PROTECTING THE VULNERABLE: A REANALYSIS OF OUR SOCIAL RESPONSIBILITIES (1985); David Schmidtz, *Islands in a Sea of Obligation: Limits of the Duty to Rescue* 3–7 Independent Institute Working Paper 18 (2000) (available at www.independent.org/pdf/working_papers/18_islands.pdf (last visited Jan. 31, 2006)); Robert Goodin & Phillip Pettit, *The Possibility of Special Duties*, 16 CAN. J. PHIL. 651 (1986); Paul Gomberg, *The Fallacy of Philanthropy*, 32 CAN. J. PHIL. 29 (2002); Robert Hanna, *Must We Be Good Samaritans*, 28 CAN. J. PHIL. 453 (1998); Garrett Hardin, *Lifeboat Ethics, in* ENVIRONMENTAL ETHICS: READINGS IN

This conclusion is doubtful for more than one reason. In many cases, belief in universal liability will be grounded in consequentialist reasoning. To the extent that they depend on consequentialist foundations, arguments for universal responsibility should be rejected because consequentialism is itself incoherent and insupportable. The incommensurability of basic aspects of well being (both the aspects of welfare as *categories* and particular *instances* of these categories), and the resultant non-viability of consequentialist moral reasoning, rule out any argument that anyone has a duty to optimize or maximize some imagined overall good.

In addition, the principle that "each person counts for one and only one" "is not reasonable as a principle for the practical deliberations of anyone."[44] The specific duties of justice in distribution which anyone has reflect her particular responsibilities and commitments, particular relationships, others' vulnerabilities.[45] Thus, Finnis insists, no one can "reasonably give equal 'weight', or equal concern, to the interests of every person anywhere whose interests he could ascertain and affect."[46]

In addition, once one has fulfilled the requirements of justice in distribution, one will still likely have *options*: one will be free within the constraints imposed by practical reasonableness to participate in the diverse aspects of welfare. There is ordinarily space between the expenditure level required to fulfill one's specific distributive obligations on the one hand and the public trust threshold on the other, though how much will, of course, depend on one's circumstances. Thus, George underscores the common-sense conviction

> that one ordinarily has no moral duty to forgo one's ordinary pursuits, including playing golf, to devote oneself to life saving or to joining famine relief projects and other worthy lifesaving endeavors in far off places. Although he may very well have a moral duty to contribute money or goods in kind to the effort, and, perhaps, to pray for its success, a professional golfer who lives in Scotland does not violate the Golden Rule (or any moral norm) when he declines to abandon his career in order to, say, join the relief effort in Bangladesh.[47]

THEORY AND APPLICATION 356 (Louis Pojman ed., 1974); Garrett Hardin, *Living on a Lifeboat*, 24 BIOSCIENCE 561 (1974).

[44] FINNIS, LAW, *supra* note 3, at 177.   [45] *Id.* at 175.   [46] *Id.* at 177.

[47] GEORGE, *supra* note 32, at 98. If one need not devote one's time exclusively to relief efforts, it does not seem plausible that one would need to devote one's resources to such efforts, either. George goes on: "Of course, the absence of a moral duty to abandon golf to go to Bangladesh does not entail the presence of a moral duty *not* to give up the good of playing golf in order to help save famine victims in Bangladesh. It may turn out that a choice either way is not only rationally grounded (and, therefore, not strictly arbitrary) but morally permissible (*i.e.*, not excluded by any moral norm)." *Id.* George observes that

Practical reasonableness requires that we respond to others' emergency needs and that we use resources in excess of the public trust threshold to help others or support communal projects. However, in virtue of the indefensibility of consequentialism, the requirements of distributive justice, and the latitude allowed by practical reason, people may appropriately invest time and resources in a wide range of rational life-plans.

E   Natural law and global justice

Natural law theory provides a helpful framework within which questions about responsibilities for responding to the problem of poverty can be addressed. By elaborating a systematic understanding of justice in the acquisition and distribution of property and the provision of assistance to others, it simultaneously mandates personal and communal assistance (among other appropriate remedies) and cabins personal duties of aid within reasonable limits.

VI   Boycotts

Giving money to others can be a requirement of justice in distribution. So, too, can withholding money. Of course, the Efficiency Principle requires that we avoid spending money on wasteful projects. But avoiding unreasonable harm through our distributive acts is itself a requirement of justice in distribution; the Golden Rule, the Pauline Principle, and the Integrity Principle may all require that we boycott trading partners that engage in harmful activities. Boycotting a trading partner may be a requirement of practical reasonableness because (*i*) (as in rare cases) it is impossible to trade without willing the harm caused by the trading partner or (*ii*) (more commonly) trading might make one an unreasonable facilitator of the harm.[48]

"[d]epending on the circumstances – in particular, on any special duties he might have as a father, husband, colleague, valuable participant in worthy local causes, etc. – we might commend (and even recommend) his going to Bangladesh as a supererogatory act." *Id.* at 101 n.22.

[48] Participating in a boycott may also be valuable as an expression of unhappiness with the practices of a potential trading partner, and perhaps as part of an attempt to call attention to the harm caused by the potential trading partner. But declining to trade in this case will ordinarily be commendable but discretionary; I am concerned in Part VI only with cases in which it would be wrong not to join a boycott, since they are the most clear-cut and arguably the most important.

In Section A, I spell out a natural law account of unreasonable cooperation in the infliction of harm,[49] a model which is obviously relevant to other issues but which lends itself naturally to the moral assessment of boycotts. I note the difference between *purposeful* cooperation with those who cause harm and *substantive* cooperation, which involves facilitating harm as an unintended side-effect of doing something for another purpose.[50] Purposeful cooperation is always wrong; in Section B, I elaborate a casuistical approach to determining when substantive cooperation is reasonable, and so when joining a boycott is and is not required.

A   *Purposive and substantive cooperation in the infliction of harm*

Human actions are caught up in complex webs, and it is easy to find connections between our own actions and others which cause harms. Natural law theory provides a way of taking these consequences into account without obscuring the difference between responsibility for personally chosen action and (often tenuous) causal influences on the actions of others.[51]

One can cooperate both *purposefully* and *substantively* with the infliction of harm.[52] That is, one can *will* (as the goal of one's action or as a means to another goal) that harm be inflicted – whether one "commands, directs, advises, encourages, prescribes, approves, or actively defends" it.[53] Or one can in some way *facilitate* or *contribute to* the (culpable or non-culpable) infliction of harm by someone else without

---

[49] By *harm* I mean *harm to a basic aspect of well being.*

[50] Grisez prefers the expression *cooperation with evil.* I don't use *evil* here in part because I prefer to reserve that term for culpable wrongdoing, and it seems to me that the problem of cooperation here arises whether or not harms I facilitate are brought about purposefully or, indeed, in any sense culpably.

[51] I think it is reasonable to see the kind of casuistry elaborated here as building on the sort of analysis involved in the principle of double effect. *See* David S. Oderberg, Moral Theory: A Non-Consequentialist Approach 88–126 (2000); Warren Quinn, Morality and Action 175–97 (1993); Joseph M. Boyle, *Toward Understanding the Principle of Double Effect*, 90 Ethics 527 (1980); Germain Grisez, *Toward a Consistent Natural-Law Ethics of Killing*, 15 Am. J. Juris. 64–96 (1970). Following the rule of double effect is not itself among the requirements of practical reason; rather, the rule is one – not necessarily flawless – way of summarizing the implications of several such requirements.

[52] *See* Grisez, Questions, *supra* note 38, at 871–97. The NCNLTs prefer "formal" and "material"; I opt not to use these terms because I suspect that those I employ may be more readily comprehensible to some readers.

[53] 1 Germain Grisez, The Way of the Lord Jesus: Christian Moral Principles 301 (1983).

willing in any sense that it occur. Any purposeful cooperation in the infliction of harm clearly violates the Pauline Principle.[54] Substantive cooperation may or may not be reasonable.[55] One can determine whether substantive cooperation is reasonable in a given case by considering several questions.[56]

1. *Consequences.* What are the various side-effects of cooperation likely to be? How widespread, how great, and how likely are the possible harmful side-effects of one's cooperation?[57]
2. *Special obligations.* Do commitments, attachments, or special duties – to particular causes, persons, or projects – give one particular reasons to cooperate or not to cooperate?[58]
3. *Fairness and efficiency.* Is cooperation in this case otherwise consistent with the requirements of practical reasonableness?[59] In particular, does it impose unfair risks of harm? (One evidence of unfairness will be the availability of an alternative way of achieving the non-harmful goal one seeks to reach by cooperating that does *not* result in harm.[60] For the failure to opt for such an alternative suggests either that one actually does want to bring about the harm or that one is carelessly unconcerned about the harm resulting from one's cooperation.)

---

[54] *Id.* at 302.   [55] GRISEZ, QUESTIONS, *supra* note 38, at 873.

[56] I draw freely here on Grisez's analysis, though I do not follow it in all cases. His principal concern is with cooperation in a relatively narrow sense – with, for instance, the acts of accountants and lawyers associated with a criminal conspiracy, *see* GRISEZ, PRINCIPLES, *supra* note 55, at 301; an engineer who maintains a building housing a hospital that performs abortions, of which he disapproves, *see* GRISEZ, LIVING, *supra* note 8, at 441; or someone wondering whether, and if so how, to support a strike, *see id.* at 769. But one can extend his analysis so that it applies as well to more situations in which the putative cooperator is much more tenuously involved. *See id.* at 788–834; GRISEZ, QUESTIONS, *supra* note 38, at 439–626; the closest Grisez comes to addressing the issue in question of boycotts is in connection with an analysis of some questions related to investment (*see id.* at 502–7) and tobacco farming (*see id.* at 600–3), and an aside about a purchasing manager who acquires vegetables from growers who mistreat their workers (*see id.* at 879–81). For a concrete example of the NCNLTs' casuistry of cooperation at work, see Robert P. George, *Reflections on the Ethics of Representing Clients Whose Aims Are Unjust*, 40 S. TEX. L. REV. 55 (1999) (arguing that "[s]ometimes it is possible for lawyers to represent clients whose aims are unjust without willing the injustice of their clients' aims").

[57] *See* GRISEZ, QUESTIONS, *supra* note 38, at 878–84.

[58] *See id.* at 882. Such responsibilities will derive (per the Golden Rule and the Integrity Principle) from one's promises, attachments, and commitments and from one's regard for such particular goods as friendship.

[59] *See id.* at 876.   [60] *Id.*

Thus, for instance, while Grisez judges (whether correctly or not) that, because they can do significant harm, casinos ought to be illegal, he recognizes that his position is quite compatible with the possibility that even some "people of modest means" might be able "rightly [to] gamble in casinos."[61] The wrongness, as Grisez understands it, of the casino does not require that it be *boycotted*. By contrast, "when … workers have a just cause," customers "*should* cooperate in boycotts of products, in just strikes … [,] by respecting picket lines, and so on."[62]

To take another example: Grisez, Finnis, and Boyle regard the payment of taxes as presumptively obligatory. But they also regard the maintenance of a nuclear deterrent as morally wrong. However, in light of the relevant facts, they maintain that "no-one can reasonably judge, in present circumstances, that the withholding of tax payments will in any way affect the amount spent on the nuclear strategic system."[63] Thus, it is not the case that failure to withhold one's taxes makes one responsible for the nuclear deterrent: one is not required to participate in what amounts to a tax boycott of the federal government.[64]

Or consider someone's rational reflection on highway driving. Highway driving can be very hazardous.[65] Choosing to drive might be thought to make one a contributory cause of accidents, at minimum because of one's contribution to overall traffic volume or because of unpredictable ripple effects of minor driving choices. One might still opt to drive, treating the overall volume of traffic on the highway as a given. One might reasonably judge that one's use or non-use of the highway was unlikely to make any but the smallest difference in the risk of serious injury posed to other drivers or to oneself, and that there was therefore no duty to boycott the highway system.

---

[61] *Id.* at 839.

[62] GRISEZ, LIVING, *supra* note 8, at 769 (my italics); he observes that "the responsibilities of investors and customers, as indirect employers, are limited by their knowledge of a business's activities and their power to affect them." Thus, while more direct cooperation with workers may sometimes be appropriate, in other cases, investors and customers "fulfill their responsibilities by being alert to the possibility of injustice to employees and urging management to rectify injustices when they arise." *Cf.* GRISEZ, QUESTIONS, *supra* note 38, at 837–39 (discussing casino gambling).

[63] JOHN M. FINNIS, JOSEPH M. BOYLE, JR. & GERMAIN G. GRISEZ, NUCLEAR DETERRENCE, MORALITY, AND REALISM 352 (1987).

[64] Finnis, Grisez, and Boyle suggest that withholding taxes will actually have *negative* consequences, and judge that doing so covertly is likely to be unreasonable. *Id.* at 352–53.

[65] *See* FINNIS, ETHICS, *supra* note 3, at 91–92.

B Boycotts and cooperation

Trading with an entity that causes harm in one way or another is always unreasonable *to the extent* that one's purpose in trading is to further the harm the entity causes. If one is motivated by hostility to victims of a company's misbehavior, for instance, one might support the company with one's business. Doing so for this purpose would be unreasonable, for the same reason that harming the victims oneself out of hostility would be.

Realistically, however, the question of boycotting a potential trading partner is characteristically faced by someone who clearly does *not* endorse some harmful action in which the trading partner is engaging. By trading, someone ordinarily cooperates substantively with her trading partner. But whether she is required to boycott the trading partner depends on whether, in the case in question, her unintentional facilitation of the harm inflicted by the trading partner is or is not reasonable.

An important factor in assessing the consequences of the potential trader's choice is the *scale* of her potential trading partner's harmful activity. Choices by a reasonably small number of relatively uncoordinated consumers without collective authority will likely have little or no impact on the production levels or techniques of an industry that operates on a global scale,[66] and so are not reasonably regarded as morally significant contributory causes of the harms done by the firm or industry. If an independent, local firm with which an individual consumer does a significant amount of business is involved, however, her decision not to trade with it might sometimes actually prevent it from causing some sorts of harm. Similarly, a decision by a *merchant* who regularly buys from a particular firm or industry to avoid trading with the firm or industry might sometimes prevent some harms. In these cases, depending on the likelihood, magnitude, and extent of the harms, trade with the firm or industry might be unreasonable.

The most important test of the reasonableness of my imposition of the risk of harm resulting from my purchasing decisions will ordinarily be the Golden Rule. I might reasonably imagine a hypothetical case: (*i*) Suppose someone else acted in a way that subjected me to risk of harm. (*ii*) Suppose the kind of harm was as severe, from my perspective, as the sort of harm typically suffered by a victim of the firm or industry I'm considering boycotting. (*iii*) Suppose the risk that I'll suffer this harm is no

---

[66] I explore this issue in detail in *On the Threshold Argument against Consumer Meat Purchases*, 37 J. SOC. PHIL. 235 (2006).

less than the risk that, as a result of my purchase, some victim would suffer what I'd regard as a comparable harm. Would I be willing to regard an act that imposed the relevant sort of risk on *me* as acceptable? If I wouldn't, then my own choice to trade with the industry or firm seems unreasonable; if I would, then my choice may be reasonable.

To revisit an earlier example: the risk that the consumer or those dear to her might be harmed increases marginally when she drives or when others drive, but she may not necessarily regard the act of driving as unjustifiably risk-enhancing. If she is willing to tolerate the level of increased risk associated with a particular driver's decision to enter a freeway, she might also be willing to tolerate a similar level of risk that she could suffer the kind of harm to which a victim of her potential trading partner's misbehavior might be subjected. If so, her decision to do business with the potential trading partner might be reasonable.

At the same time, the ready availability of alternatives to trading with the industry or firm in question that are as attractive and that are reasonably priced will obviously count against a trading decision if there is any chance that it will contribute to harm. (It will be hard to escape the conclusion, if one trades with the industry or firm despite the availability of these alternatives, that one actually wills the harms the firm or industry causes, does not regard them as significant, or is not reasoning competently.) And, of course, in particular instances there might be actual benefits associated with avoiding the trade, which the potential purchaser ought to consider. A thoughtful reflection, in light of the Golden Rule, on the implications of the availability of alternatives might lead the potential purchaser to avoid the trade. Questions about special responsibilities will also be relevant, though in too many ways to take helpfully into account here.

Natural law theory provides a set of useful tools that equip us to respond discerningly to ambiguous situations.[67] It helpfully calls our attention to the difference between, on the one hand, directly harming and, on the other, participating in a social web in which one's actions affect the likelihood that harm will take place.[68] It suggests that employing the products of evil action may be objectionable, but only if one shares the evil purpose

---

[67] For an initial exploration of a natural law view of boycotts, its application, and its similarities to and differences from some other approaches, *see* Gary Chartier, *Consumers, Boycotts, and Non-Human Animals*, 12 BUFF. ENV. L. J. 123 (2005).

[68] All, or almost all, of us participate in such a web; *cf.* MICHAEL ALLEN FOX, DEEP VEGETARIANISM 169–70 (1999).

of the evildoers, if one violates special obligations, or if one's actions will lead unreasonably to subsequent harm.[69]

Declining to join in a boycott is not the same thing as engaging in or endorsing the objectionable activity being boycotted.[70] We are not liable for all of the choices of the industries our purchases may happen to support. We are caught up in ambiguous webs of action and reaction; many of our actions have harmful consequences, and we can't obsess about all of these consequences.[71] At the same time, however, it will be unreasonable to trade with entities that harm, even if we don't will the harms they cause, when satisfactory alternatives are available or when imposing the risk of harm effected by a decision to trade is inconsistent with the Golden Rule.

VII   Remedies for injustice, disaster, and economic insecurity

Practical reason constrains, though it does not determine, what will count as justice in distribution. Justice requires that people support valuable common projects and, as a matter of remedy, projects designed to deal with the consequences of injustice, disaster, and economic insecurity. But they are typically free to do this – often, though not necessarily, in and through communal organizations and movements – in a variety of ways. This is so because the circumstances of people suffering as a result of injustice, catastrophe, or crisis are complex, and theoretical reflection provides no short-cut to the careful assessment of these circumstances. It is also the case because natural law theory does not compel particular distributive patterns or choices.

Practical reason requires that we avoid active injustice – that we avoid evicting people from justly held property; creating or maintaining monopolies; imposing barriers to market entry that limit the occupational options of the poor or their access to credit or their ability to sell their products;[72] or extracting subsidies for the wealthy from poor, working-class, and middle-class people. But it does not require that we

---

[69] Thanks to an anonymous reviewer for underscoring the need to clarify this point.

[70] Cf. CHRISTOPH VON FÜRER-HAIMENDORF, MORALS AND MERIT: A STUDY OF VALUES AND SOCIAL CONTROLS IN SOUTH ASIAN SOCIETIES 187 (1967) (noting the view that the butcher, but not the consumer of meat, is morally culpable). I owe this reference to Stephen Clark.

[71] Cf. RAYMOND G. FREY, RIGHTS, KILLING, AND SUFFERING: MORAL VEGETARIANISM AND APPLIED ETHICS 227–42 (1983).

[72] See Charles W. Johnson, Scratching By: How Government Creates Poverty as We Know It, The FREEMAN: IDEAS ON LIBERTY, Dec. 2007, at 12.

make remedying such injustice our central activity, and it leaves open the ways in which we will remedy the effects of injustice.

Thus, for instance: past and ongoing acts of violent dispossession, and more subtle aggression in such forms as the creation and maintenance of monopolies by law, lie at the root of much poverty. Where specific, culpable aggressors and their victims, or their successors in interest, can be identified, justice provides good reason to expect aggressors to compensate victims. But even when it is not possible to identify aggressors and hold them responsible, it will often be clear that there *are* victims, and we have good reason to seek to see that they are made whole.

How we do this is a matter for prudent judgment. Communally shared funding of health care and basic income schemes and transfers of wealth from ICs to LDCs may be reasonable remedial responses to injustice, accident, and economic insecurity,[73] but they are hardly the only possible options. (There may, for instance, be good reason for people to contribute to communal schemes designed to provide education at all levels to qualified students and to consider supporting pension and disability schemes, and perhaps even universal insurance schemes,[74] but I will not address these possibilities here.) Perhaps other mechanisms will ultimately prove more effective. What is important is that problems resulting from injustice, disaster, accident, and economic insecurity be addressed, not that a particular norm or rule develop or be maintained.

Similarly, in some cases, participation in a boycott will be a requirement of justice in distribution, because failure to participate would amount to purposeful cooperation in the harm caused by a potential trading partner. But in many cases, when a boycott serves as a means of expression or advocacy, it will be one of several options available to those who wish to respond to injustice.

Natural law theory provides a careful response to consequentialist arguments for a duty on the part of many people to shoulder what may seem like a crushing burden of redistribution, especially at the global level. But it also makes clear both that individuals have responsibilities to assist other people or support valuable, shared projects, locally or globally, and that they may rightly be expected to fulfill these responsibilities in virtue

[73] On the difficulties associated with linking "benefits" with employment, see Mary E. O'Connell, *On the Fringe: Rethinking the Link between Wages and Benefits*, 67 TUL. L. REV. 1422 (1993).

[74] Perhaps, for instance, it would make sense to consider many of the kinds of radical risk management tools proposed in ROBERT J. SHILLER, THE NEW FINANCIAL ORDER: RISK IN THE TWENTY-FIRST CENTURY (2003).

of communal norms and rules, though it does not require that they do so in just one way. Transferring wealth directly to poor communities may be a valuable way of helping people to move beyond poverty, whether it results from injustice, imprudence, or disaster. But investments of various kinds may also be effective.

How people structure the transactions that shape workplaces plays a particularly important role in remedying the effects of injustice and accident and reducing the risk of economic insecurity. There is a strong argument on the basis of practical reasonableness for workplace democracy – which can itself serve as a remedy for the injustice of workplace subordination and which can contribute indirectly to reducing the unjust treatment of workers and their economic insecurity. Perhaps sometimes it will not be possible for a workplace to be democratically organized. And perhaps, more frequently, a workplace that *could* be democratically organized is not because of resistance of one kind or another. The combination of collective bargaining and participatory management can be a meaningful second-best option for workers in such workplaces, affording them with at least some meaningful opportunities for involvement in decision-making and helping them to make progress toward democratic workplace governance. In this sense, the institution and protection of collective bargaining and participatory management can be useful remedial developments. While they are incomplete substitutes for workplace democracy, their availability may be a meaningful way-station en route to workplace justice, and they can play a particularly important role in securing justice for sweatshop workers. I want to examine the remedial application of natural law principles of justice at work in Chapter 6.

6

Remedies: work

Justice at work means extensive participation by workers in governance, and frequently, or always, actual democratic governance by workers. But most contemporary work environments are not just: they are not democratic or even participatory; in addition, they often violate workers' dignity and autonomy, minimize their opportunities to participate in decision-making, subject them to unreasonably unsafe working conditions, and underpay them. In some work environments, especially in LDCs, working conditions are particularly dangerous and abusive.

A number of interim measures, while not satisfactory substitutes for workplace democracy, could help to bring contemporary workplaces into greater alignment with the requirements of practical reasonableness. These remedial measures could help to foster justice at work even in environments in which the dominance of investors and managers prevented the establishment of democratic workplace governance and in which background injustices had not been remedied.

I defend collective bargaining as an important mechanism for remedying the injustice of contemporary workplaces – at least in investor-governed firms, but perhaps also in worker-governed firms – in Part I, I argue that collective bargaining can play an important role in reducing power imbalances at work. In Part II, I briefly emphasize the consonance with natural law theory of governance mechanisms that, in the absence of workplace democracy, could supplement collective bargaining as ways of ensuring that workers could affect decisions in investor-governed firms. In Part III, I suggest that fair collective bargaining can provide an efficient and flexible mechanism for setting workplace standards in investor-governed firms. In Part IV, I suggest that it can equip workers in LDCs to avoid exploitation while responding flexibly to market conditions. In Part V, I offer an overview of my observations about the limited steps toward justice in unjust workplaces outlined in this chapter.

I The value of collective bargaining

Collective bargaining is not a perfect substitute for democratic govern-ance at work, but it can help to secure workers' dignity, protect their well being, and ensure that their insights into organizational processes are taken into account. Thus, automatic collective bargaining (given teeth by the right to strike[1]) should play a crucial role in shaping the relationships between workers and, especially, investor-governed firms.[2] The institu-tion of collective bargaining is potentially remedial in investor-governed firms, in part because it can foster movement toward worker governance. It may be remedial in worker-governed firms because it can help to reduce the dominance of elite groups within some such firms.[3]

I argue in Section A for the moral importance of collective bargaining, underscoring its value as a means of helping to ensure the fairness of con-tract negotiations and terms. In Section B, I seek to respond to objections to collective bargaining.[4]

A The moral significance of collective bargaining

Collective bargaining is a crucial means of ensuring justice at work in the absence of workplace democracy. In Subsection 1, I suggest that collective bargaining is morally important because it can help to ensure that both the process leading to an employment agreement and the terms of the agreement are reasonable. In Subsection 2, I suggest that the purpose of collective bargaining can help to determine who is entitled to bargain collectively with a particular firm. In Subsection 3,

---

[1] See 2 GERMAIN G. GRISEZ, THE WAY OF THE LORD JESUS: LIVING A CHRISTIAN LIFE 760–61, 770–71 (1994).

[2] For an alternative view, see John A. Litwinski, *Regulation of Labor Market Monopsony*, 22 BERKELEY J. EMP. & LAB. L. 49 (2001).

[3] See Michael C. Harper, *Reconciling Collective Bargaining with Employee Supervision of Management*, 137 U. PA. L. REV. 1 (1988).

[4] For simplicity's sake, I focus throughout on the model of collective bargaining as under-taken by unions. Whether unions provide the only defensible institutional framework for collective bargaining is a different question. I propose an alternative in Gary Chartier, *Toward a New Employer-Worker Compact*, 9 EMPLOYEE RTS. & EMPL. POL'Y J. 51 (2005). However, in that article, I held constant, with relatively minor modifications, the existing structure of firm governance. Here, of course, I envision a much more substantial change in the structure of decision-making at the firm level. In any event, collective bargaining must involve representation for all hourly and salaried workers, both full-time and part-time, including most or all of those currently deemed "professional" or "managerial"; *cf.* William B. Gould IV, *Reflections on Workers' Participation, Influence and Powersharing: The Future of Industrial Relations*, 58 U. CIN. L. REV. 381, 386–88 (1989).

I suggest that bargaining collectively is a positive responsibility of the individual firm.

1   Collective bargaining and power imbalances

A just commercial agreement is one that is negotiated in a reasonable manner and that reaches an outcome which it is reasonable for the parties to accept. Collective bargaining helps to ensure both sorts of reasonableness. It can help to reduce disparities in bargaining power, and so ensure that workers are not forced to accept employment terms. And it can help to ensure that contract terms are beneficial to workers, so that outcomes are ones they can reasonably accept.

Significant disparities in bargaining power can render the processes leading to commercial agreements and the outcomes of those agreements unfair.[5] Consider the case of "a woman whose automobile breaks down in a rough neighborhood, and who fears that she might be attacked or [that] her car might be vandalized. ... [She] may willingly agree to the demand by the driver of a passing tow truck to pay him fifty dollars more than he usually charges."[6] She has chosen to accept certain contractual terms, but it is hard to regard her choice as, in any strong sense, free, or the outcome as fair, and the tow-truck driver almost certainly would regard a similar agreement with resentment were their roles reversed.

Employment negotiations often involve confrontations between individual workers and much larger and more powerful organizations (this may be less true in small worker-governed firms, but it will certainly be true in larger worker-governed firms just as it typically is in investor-governed firms). And a firm negotiating employment terms typically has significantly more bargaining power than the tow-truck driver,[7] "power

---

[5] *Cf.* Martijn W. Hesselink, *Capacity and Capability in European Contract Law*, 13 Eur. Rev. Private L. 491 (2005).

[6] Grisez, Living, *supra* note 1, at 324. Finnis discusses the point in more general terms in John Finnis, Aquinas: Moral, Political, and Legal Theory 201–3 (1998). Finnis seems to see a fair transaction as primarily one "in which all parties to the transaction are, so far as possible, compensated proportionately for what they are giving up." *Id.* at 203. He suggest that market price is "[t]he normal measure of something's value" (*id.* at 202), and suggests that, when one seeks to sell at a price excessively above the market price, one "is indeed selling what is not one's own to sell" (*id.* at 203). My focus, instead, is on the unfairness of the bargaining situation itself, on the amount of flexibility the bargainers' circumstances permit them to enjoy.

[7] *See* Keith N. Hylton & Maria O'Brien Hylton, *Rent Appropriation and the Labor Law Doctrine of Successorship*, 70 B.U.L. Rev. 821 (1990). *Cf.* American Steel Foundries v. Tri-City Cent. Trades Council, 257 U.S. 184, 209 (1921) (Taft, C.J.). *But cf.* Keith N. Hylton, *Efficiency and Labor Law*, 87 Nw. U.L. Rev. 471, 485–6 (1993) (questioning

to set terms [relatively] unconstrained by competition."[8] A worker characteristically finds herself concluding a take-it-or-leave-it bargain with a firm, with little or no room for negotiation. Background injustices as well as specific labor market conditions and personal circumstances may significantly constrain her options. By contrast, with more financial and informational resources, a firm can often afford to insist on terms favorable to its interests. As the United States Supreme Court said in 1921, before the advent of collective bargaining, an individual

> employee was helpless in dealing with an employer. He was dependent ordinarily on his daily wage for the maintenance of himself and family. If the employer refused to pay him the wages that he thought fair, he was nevertheless unable to leave the employ and to resist arbitrary and unfair treatment. Union was essential to give laborers opportunity to deal on equality with their employer.[9]

Thus, collective bargaining can help to ensure the reasonableness of the process leading to an employment agreement because it can help to ensure a level playing field,[10] reducing exploitation and limiting disparities in influence over contractual terms.[11] It "equalize[s] bargaining

the appropriateness on economic grounds of defending unions as means of rectifying inequalities in bargaining power, in the course of arguing that labor law can, indeed, be economically efficient).

[8] Daniel J. Chepaitis, *The National Labor Relations Act, Non-Paralleled Competition, and Market Power*, 85 Calif. L. Rev. 769 (1997). *Cf.* Keith N. Hylton, *A Theory of Minimum Contract Terms, with Implications for Labor Law*, 74 Tex. L. Rev. 1741 (1996).

[9] *Am. Steel Foundries*, 257 U.S. at, 209. Thanks to Charles Fried for bringing this passage to my attention; *see* Charles Fried, *Individual and Collective Rights in Work Relations: Reflections on the Current State of Labor Law and Its Prospects*, 51 U. Chi. L. Rev. 1012 (1984). *Cf.* Jay R. Mandle, Globalization and the Poor 116 (2003): "Avoiding collective bargaining and instead dealing with individual workers one at a time maximizes management's bargaining leverage in dealing with its labor force." Collective bargaining offers workers "parity in negotiations." *Id.* at 117.

[10] Support for collective bargaining as a means of ensuring equal bargaining power is the clearly established (official) policy of the United States. See 29 U.S.C. §151.

[11] *Cf.* Fried, *Rights*, *supra* note 9, at 1035; Roy J. Adams, *The North American Model of Employee Representational Participation: A Hollow Mockery*, 15 Comp. Lab. L. 4 (1993); Peter Levine, *The Legitimacy of Labor Unions*, 18 Hofstra Lab. & Emp. L.J. 529 (2001) (focusing not only on bargaining fairness but also on personal dignity, justice in distribution, and unions' roles in civil society).

Fried notes that power imbalances between the vulnerable and the strong are often evident in the tenant–landlord or consumer–producer relationship. Fried, *Rights*, *supra* note 9, at 1036–37. He observes that we do not use collective bargaining to deal with these power imbalances. And he asks why we should do so, by contrast, in the context of the worker–firm relationship. There are at least two responses. In the case of at least some tenant–landlord relationships, there might well be an argument for collective bargaining. And there would seem to be issues of efficiency that make collective bargaining

power by overcoming the incentive structure under which each worker is compelled to undercut fellow workers and by changing the setting from one in which only the employer can appropriate rent to one in which both parties, employer and … [workers], have this power."[12]

This equalized bargaining power reduces injustice in the negotiating *process*. But it also obviously has the potential to lead to better *outcomes*. When workers have more power, and when their insights can inform the determination of contract terms, their welfare is likely to receive more reasonable protection. Obviously, not every collectively negotiated contract will be free of exploitation and subordination (just as not every individually negotiated contract will be exploitative or subordinative). But, when employment agreements are collectively negotiated,[13] both the process and the outcomes are likely to be fairer.[14]

The requirements of practical reasonableness create a very strong presumption that firms should be democratically governed by workers. But at firms that are not democratically governed, collective bargaining, automatically available when a firm crosses an appropriate size threshold, can facilitate the protection of workers' interests and the transition to workplace democracy.

2   The scope of collective bargaining protections

Not all workers are employees: some work is performed by contractors who are genuinely not members of a firm. But the claim that someone qualifies in accordance with a narrow legal definition as a contractor does not justify depriving her of collective bargaining rights. Understanding the point of those rights helps to make clear when they ought to be available. What is most important is the worker's vulnerability to the firm's decisions. Someone who provides services for many different firms (say,

---

between particular final-stage consumers of products and the producers of those products impracticable.

[12] Hylton & Hylton, *supra* note 7, at 836. It may also, in fact, promote efficiency by reducing transaction costs in the internal labor markets of investor-governed firms. *See* Stephen Bainbridge, *Corporate Decisionmaking and the Moral Rights of Employees: Participatory Management and Natural Law*, 43 VILL. L. REV. 741, 816 (1998) ("Recognizing a natural right to collective action by workers is also justifiable on efficiency grounds. ..."); Michael L. Wachter & George M. Cohen, *The Law and Economics of Collective Bargaining: An Introduction and Application to the Problems of Subcontracting, Partial Closure, and Relocation*, 136 U. PA. L. REV. 1349 (1988).

[13] *But cf.* CHARLES FRIED, CONTRACT AS PROMISE: A THEORY OF CONTRACTUAL OBLIGATION 101 (1981).

[14] That is, likely to be consistent with the Golden Rule when it is applied to the choices of the actors in the actual bargaining situation.

someone who provides plumbing services to each of 150 firms 5 times each year) often need not be overly concerned about a particular firm's behavior. By contrast, someone whose putatively arms'-length contractual labor is performed for a single firm or a small number of firms has much more reason to be concerned about the behavior of the firm or firms. Her vulnerability makes it important that she participate in collective bargaining. Such a worker has also invested more in the firm or firms; reward as a criterion of justice in distribution provides a further reason for her to be entitled to the influence over the firm or firms for which she works that collective bargaining would afford her.

The degree to which a firm actually controls, or asserts the right to control, the way in which the worker does her job, rather than just the outcome of her work, is also important. To the extent that it controls her day-to-day (perhaps moment-by-moment) activities (likely in violation of the principle of subsidiarity), it is especially important that she be able to exert the countervailing power provided by collective bargaining. This power helps to ensure both that she has greater discretion to perform her own work and that the indignities associated with supervision and monitoring are reduced. On the other hand, when only the final outcome of someone's work is determined by a firm, she has less reason to regard the chance to bargain collectively with the firm as important.

3   Collective bargaining as a responsibility of individual firms

Conceiving of labor rights as intrinsically, rather than just instrumentally, important helps to insulate such rights from erosion in light of the calculus of productivity. Some defenses of collective bargaining focus on its capacity to give workers *a greater share* of a firm's profits. My argument here, however, has been that suitable collective bargaining arrangements ensure that workers will receive *a fairer share* of the profits and provides them with *a fairer opportunity* to participate in firms' decision-making processes. Therefore, under ordinary circumstances, when a firm fails to bargain collectively with workers it runs a serious risk of treating them in a way that is inconsistent with the requirements of practical reasonableness.

Thus, a firm ordinarily has an obligation to bargain collectively whether or not it is legally required to do so. It is not the responsibility of a firm to seek the incoherent goal of welfare maximization in the region or regions in which it operates, or in the world as a whole. The firm does have a duty to be fair to the workers it actually employs; and it is less likely to negotiate fairly and to reach fair terms if it fails to bargain with them collectively. There is thus a strong presumption in favor of collective bargaining.

B Criticisms of collective bargaining

Critics object to collective bargaining on a variety of grounds. I seek to respond here to several such objections: that it is unreasonable to criticize individually negotiated contracts as unfree because the negotiation of a contract is coercive only if a negotiator violates an independently specified right, and a contract offer doesn't ordinarily presuppose or involve the violation of any such right (Subsection 1); that some arguments for collective bargaining seem to make firms responsible for solving what should be seen as societal problems related to the overall distribution of wealth (Subsection 2); that collective bargaining unfairly imposes costs on workers as a group (Subsection 3); that it disadvantages particular subgroups of workers or individuals (Subsection 4); that it imposes particular costs on unemployed, and employed but vulnerable, workers (Subsection 5); and that it reduces resources available, through investment or wealth transfers, for poverty relief (Subsection 6).

1 Individually negotiated contracts are free because coercion requires the violation of an independently specified right

A central argument for collective bargaining is that, when individually negotiating with firms, workers are incapable meaningfully of effecting alternatives. On this view, freedom is constrained by circumstances: the presence or absence of certain options affects the extent to which people are relevantly free. One response to the charge that individually negotiated employment contracts are not appropriately free is to delimit carefully what counts as a lack of freedom in the relevant sense. Thus, for instance, Charles Fried proposes limiting the category of duress in contract law to those cases in which the person putatively exerting duress worsens another's situation by doing something – or threatening to do something – she doesn't have the right to do (say, using physical violence). "A proposal," he says, "is not coercive if it offers what the proponent has a right to offer or not as he chooses."[15] On this view, a firm has the right to offer a worker money that the firm already possesses, and the firm may

---

[15] FRIED, CONTRACT, *supra* note 13, at 97.

select any amount whatsoever to propose. Whatever the background conditions of the transaction,[16] the firm's proposal is not coercive.

But there are problems with this narrow concept of duress, as the example of the tow truck driver makes clear. Simply because there is a right, we cannot conclude that just any exercise of that right will be reasonable (or non-coercive). Perhaps, indeed, the right obtains precisely to the extent that it is non-coercive. Most rights are not all-or-nothing affairs. And determining the extent of a right will be a matter of asking, at least, about fairness. So it cannot be determined whether someone making a proposal has the right to make the proposal without asking about the fairness of the proposal.

To be sure, "[b]y casting the relation between a person and a thing in ... [the] form of a right, we withdraw it *pro tanto* from the domain of collective imposition."[17] But whether a firm has an obligation to bargain collectively (or to do anything else with its property) is a separate question from whether the legal system can rightly compel it to honor that obligation. The absence of a legally enforceable duty would not mean that there was no duty at all, or that performance of the duty could not be encouraged using various forms of nonviolent social pressure. Whether a *legal* remedy is available or not, the obligation to act in a practically reasonable manner will persist.

Further, it is not reasonable to suppose that, by, acknowledging the conventional property rationales, a community withdraws any particular putative piece of property from the reach of communal norms and rules in any *absolute* way. We cannot determine, even on Fried's own criterion, whether a property-owner acts appropriately without asking what conventions, norms, and rules govern her disposition of her property.[18]

---

[16] This is perhaps too harsh a statement of Fried's position. He grants that the liberal understanding of contract that he defends "assumes a well-functioning market and hardships caused only by the relative poverty of the parties and by general resource constraints." *Id.* at 107. And his understanding of justice in contract presupposes a reasonable system of social welfare provision; *see, e.g.,* CHARLES FRIED, RIGHT AND WRONG 128–30 (1978).

[17] FRIED, CONTRACT, *supra* note 13, at 101. Fried maintains that rights "in one's own person, talent, and efforts are nonconventional." *Id.* at 100. But this need not count against the point made in the text, both because these are not the sorts of rights at issue in the debate over the question whether someone may dispose of her money at will and because it is not clear that they are best spoken of as property rights. *See also* Carole Pateman, *Self-Ownership and Property in the Person: Democratization and a Tale of Two Concepts,* 10 J. POL. PHIL. 20 (2002).

[18] Fried is clear that "there are no ... [grave] problems about denying legal recognition to promises exacted in return for the performance of what the promisee was bound to do

And among these may be standards that create a strong presumption in favor of collective bargaining.

The rationales underlying a just property regime provide good reason for property rights not to be defined in ways that allow for frequent, unpredictable interference. Legal constraints designed to ensure fairness will be disruptive unless they are spelled out in advance of individual negotiations in non-arbitrary rules that allow workers and firms to govern their interactions predictably. More broadly, it certainly will sometimes make sense to cabin rights that are not inherently absolute with protections that do leave people free sometimes to do things they have good reason not to do. (Almost no one, for instance, wants to be the victim of sexual betrayal; but most people would nonetheless prefer that their homes be free from invasion even by those interested in detecting and preventing adultery.) But within these constraints a community's legal system or its conventions regarding property rights certainly need not be unjust simply in virtue of limiting property rights by requiring collective bargaining.

2   Expecting firms to bargain collectively treats them as responsible for remedying community-wide problems

It might be argued that expecting firms to bargain collectively – as a way of declining to take unfair advantage of current or prospective workers – means asking firms on their own to accept responsibility for the overall distribution of wealth.[19] But the defense of collective bargaining on which I have concentrated here is that firms which fail to bargain collectively act unfairly or, at least, run a significant risk of acting unfairly, in particular transactions with their own workers because of the power imbalance that misshapes the bargaining relationship.[20] They are not being asked to shoulder the task of sorting out general problems of wealth distribution, but only to bargain in a fair manner with their own workers. There may well be no way to craft precise but general *legal* rules that determine when

anyway," even if what the promisee was bound to do anyway was to perform a moral duty which is not itself legally enforceable. FRIED, CONTRACT, *supra* note 13, at 110. But this obviously leaves open the question whether a general requirement of fairness would not entail the conclusion that one thing a promisee is bound to do is not to take unfair advantage of the promissor's circumstances. There will be no way to specify what counts as "unfair advantage" except, obviously, in moral terms.

[19] *Cf. id.* at 13, at 107. *But cf.* JOHN FINNIS, NATURAL LAW AND NATURAL RIGHTS 173–77, 184–88.

[20] FRIED, CONTRACT, *supra* note 13, at 107.

the *outcomes* of particular transactions are fair (a Golden Rule test should be able to answer this question for the participants in particular cases). But negotiating contracts collectively can obviate the need to argue about such rules because, when bargaining power is equalized, workers' own judgments about contract terms will shape those terms to a significant degree. The likelihood that the substance of those terms will be reasonable will be dramatically increased because the negotiating process will be fair.

3   Unions unfairly disadvantage workers as a group

It also might be argued that collective bargaining arrangements cannot be seen as means of safeguarding fairness for workers because they in fact *disadvantage* workers. Among the potential problems for workers might be "the payment of union dues, the subjection to union discipline and to union officers, the involvement in union politics, the possibility of being called out on strike or being required to honor a picket line, and the more formal and adversarial nature of labor-management relations that unionization is thought to produce."[21] Union structures are sometimes perceived as undemocratic.[22] And unions have a history of corruption that rightly troubles not only opponents but also friends of workers' rights.[23]

There is no way to avoid the possibility of strikes and the challenges of picket lines if workers are to be capable of asserting their rights. Especially when firms are undemocratic, "the more formal and adversarial nature

---

[21] Fried, *Rights, supra* note 9, at 1027.

[22] *Cf.* Jeffrey S. Follett, *The Union as Contract: Internal and External Union Markets after Pattern Makers'*, 15 BERKELEY J. EMP. & LAB. L. 1, 3 (1994) (maintaining that "unions are perceived as large, undemocratic bureaucracies"); Michele Hoyman & Lamont Stallworth, *Suit Filing by Women: An Empirical Analysis*, 62 NOTRE DAME L. REV. 61, 63, 73–74 (1986) (observing that perceptions of unions as undemocratic affect women's legal responses to perceived sex discrimination); Richard L. Abel, Review, *Risk as an Arena of Struggle*, 83 MICH. L. REV. 772, 810 (1985) (noting workers' reported concern that unions are undemocratic).

[23] *Cf.* JOHN HUTCHINSON, THE IMPERFECT UNION: A HISTORY OF CORRUPTION IN AMERICAN TRADE UNIONS (1971); WHAT'S WRONG IN THE CARPENTERS' UNION? THE STORY OF ADMINISTRATION [*sic*] CORRUPTION AND EXPULSION OF MILITANTS IN THE CARPENTERS' UNION (1925); DAVID SCOTT WITWER, CORRUPTION AND REFORM IN THE TEAMSTERS UNION (2003); Michael J. Goldberg, *The Teamsters' Board of Monitors*, 30 LAB. HIST. 563 (1989); Barbara A. Lee & James Chelius, *Government Regulation of Labor-Management Corruption: The Casino Industry Experience in New Jersey*, 42 IND. & LAB. REL. REV. 536 (1989); Paul A. Weinstein, *Racketeering and Labor: An Economic Analysis*, 19 IND. & LABOR REL. REV. 402 (1966); David Scott Witwer, *The Different Meanings of Corruption in the Context of the Teamsters Union*, 21 J. LAB. RES. 287 (2000).

of labor-management relations" may be a persistent problem from some perspectives, but informal and adversarial arrangements are potentially quite costly for workers: such arrangements often provide them with too little leverage to safeguard their welfare satisfactorily. so it is hard to see formal and adversarial arrangements as especially troubling. Worker activism and communal norms, rules, and institutions can help to ensure that collective bargaining agents function democratically. And corruption is hardly a necessary feature of the collective bargaining process, and can largely be restrained by openness and democracy.

It is not clear, therefore, that the costs I have briefly considered are necessary features of collective bargaining. But, in any case, some costs are worth paying for the gains workers realize through collective bargaining. In principle, high compensation levels might be achievable without collective bargaining, though regulation seems likely to prove a most inefficient and intrusive alternative and individual negotiation quite unlikely to involve fair processes or to lead to fair outcomes. But some important gains, those directly associated with democratic self-determination, are difficult or impossible to realize when individual workers interact independently with investor-governed firms. When workers lack not only democratic freedom in the workplace but even the opportunity to bargain collectively they are, in general, unjustly subordinated, even if their compensation levels are high and the material conditions of their work appealing, because they are unable to participate in shaping the strategies and policies that govern their work lives.

4   Unions unfairly disadvantage particular workers or subgroups of workers

Historically, unions have too often been racist and sexist.[24] They have sometimes also promoted seniority systems which have perpetuated

---

[24] *Cf.* David E. Bernstein, Only One Place of Redress: African Americans, Labor Regulations, and the Courts from Reconstruction to the New Deal (2001); *but cf.* Davison M. Douglas, Review Essay, *Contract Rights and Civil Rights*, 100 Mich. L. Rev. 1541 (2002); Steven H. Kropp, Review Essay, *Deconstructing Racism In American Society – The Role Labor Law Might Have Played (But Did Not) in Ending Race Discrimination: A Partial Explanation and Historical Commentary*, 23 Berkeley J. Emp. & Lab. L. 369 (2002). Whatever may be the case historically as regards the racism of unions and the racial impact of labor legislation, there is a strong case to be made for the view that the civil rights project will be incomplete without a commitment to economic democracy; *see* Gary Chartier, *Civil Rights and Economic Democracy*, 40 Washburn L.J. 267 (2001). Whether the civil rights movement *historically* embodied such a commitment is a matter of dispute; *see* Jeffery M. Brown, *Black Internationalism: Embracing an Economic Paradigm*, 23 Mich. J. Int'l L. 807, 851 n.182 (2002); Jeffery M. Brown,

discriminatory patterns of employment[25] and which might hamper efforts to provide reasonable accommodations to disabled persons.[26] And it might also be argued that the idea of collective bargaining involves the erasure of difference, since it involves treating all workers as broadly similar.[27]

These criticisms are not clearly persuasive.[28] There is nothing about collective bargaining that *requires* it to be racist, sexist, heterosexist, ageist, or otherwise inattentive to difference in a problematic way. As long as antidiscrimination rules and norms and market pressures keep firms and workers alike from erecting inappropriate barriers to entry into a particular workplace, and monopolistic pressures are not exerted on behalf of such barriers, *all* workers will ultimately be able to participate in collective bargaining, and will thus be able to protect their own well being.

It is true that allowing group-to-group negotiation of contract details means that some individual differences and objectives may be ignored.[29] In that sense, representative structures will be deficient in their attentiveness to some differences. But it still seems clearly to the benefit of most to

---

Deconstructing Babel: Toward a Theory of Structural Reparations, 56 RUTGERS L. REV. 463, 483 n.112, 511 n.244 (2004); *but cf.* Risa L. Goluboff, *"We Lives in a Free House Such As It Is": Class and the Creation of Modern Civil Rights*, 151 U. PA. L. REV. 1977 (2003). *Cf.* William E. Forbath, *Civil Rights and Economic Citizenship: Notes on the Past and Future of the Civil Rights and Labor Movements*, 2 U. PA. J. LAB. & EMP. L. 697 (2000).

[25] *Cf.* Bruce Fehn, *Chickens Come Home to Roost: Industrial Reorganization, Seniority, and Gender Conflict in the United Packinghouse Workers of America, 1956-1966*, 34 LABOR HIST. 324 (1993); Julius G. Getman, *The Changing Role of Courts and the Potential Role of Unions in Overcoming Employment Discrimination*, 64 TUL. L. REV. 1477, 1480–82 (1990); Simon Jeffreys, *Sex Discrimination: ECJ Closes Seniority Loophole*, 108 ACCOUNTANCY 49 (1991); Stephen Pass, *Dualism and Overlooked Class-Consciousness in American Labor Law*, 37 HOUS. L. REV. 823, 854–57 (2000); Gangaram Singh & Frank Reid, *Are Seniority-Based Layoffs Discriminatory?*, 53 IND. REL. 730 (1998).

[26] *Cf.* Estella J. Schoen, Note, *Does the ADA Make Exceptions in a Unionized Workplace? The Conflict Between the Reassignment Provision of the ADA and Collectively Bargained Seniority Systems*, 82 MINN. L. REV. 1391 (1998).

[27] This concern seems to lie beneath much of the work of Harry Hutchison. *See, e.g.,* Harry G. Hutchison, *Toward a Critical Race Reformist Conception of Minimum Wage Regimes: Exploding the Power of Myth, Fantasy, and Hierarchy*, 34 HARV. J. on LEGIS. 93 (1997); for a specific example, *see, e.g., id.* at 125–26.

[28] For a critique of right-to-work legislation, see Raymond L. Hogler and Robert LaJeunesse, *Labor Policy and Civic Values: The Curious Contradictions of Right to Work*, 54 LAB. L.J. 214 (2003). And *cf.* Roger Ebert's pithy characterization of right-to-work laws as offering "the right to work cheap." Roger Ebert, *The Corporation* (review, CHICAGO SUN-TIMES, July 16, 2004), http://www.suntimes.com/ebert/ebert_reviews/2004/07/071604.html.

[29] *See, e.g.,* Ellyn Moscowitz & Victor J. Van Bourg, *Carve-Outs and the Privatization of Workers' Compensation in Collective Bargaining Agreements*, 46 SYRACUSE L. REV. 1 (1991).

occupy the relatively level playing field afforded by collective bargaining. The Golden Rule suggests, then, that it is not unreasonable to ask the few who might be disadvantaged to live with the trade-off between additional benefits for themselves and greater freedom from exploitation for their co-workers. The problem of attention to difference can be significantly reduced by ensuring that collective bargaining mechanisms are genuinely and fully democratic. And, in any case, a collectively negotiated agreement can provide for considerable particularization of the employment terms offered to particular people.[30]

5   Collective bargaining imposes unreasonable costs on the unemployed and on vulnerable employed workers

Collective bargaining is likely to raise the compensation and otherwise improve the circumstances, of employed workers. An objector might allege, however, that it could also increase the difficulty that an unemployed person confronts in finding a job, and may make layoffs more likely, because it raises the cost of hiring or retaining a worker.[31] On this basis, the objector may maintain, collective bargaining is disadvantageous to unemployed workers and perhaps also to some vulnerable employed workers.

But whatever the indirect impact of collective bargaining at a given firm on workers not employed by the firm, a firm runs a significant and unnecessary risk of acting unfairly in relation to its own workers if it fails to bargain collectively with them. By contrast, it has no general duty with regard to the incomes of all other workers. It *does* have responsibilities to those of its own workers who are the most likely to be laid off in financially difficult circumstances. However, concern for their welfare provides no justification for the firm to avoid bargaining collectively: it can fulfill these responsibilities by bargaining collectively with their welfare in mind.

6   Collective bargaining limits opportunities to reduce poverty through wealth transfer or investment

Guarantees of labor rights can help to foster market-based wealth reallocation, shifting wealth from investors to workers. A critic might maintain,

---

[30] *Cf.* Bertrand-Marc Allen, *"Embedded Contract Unionism" in Play – Examining the Intersection of Individual and Collective Contracting in the National Basketball Association*, 35 Conn. L. Rev. 1 (2002).

[31] Thanks to an anonymous reviewer for helping me to see the importance of addressing this point here and in connection with my response to the problem of sweatshops.

however, that, because collective bargaining will likely increase workers' share of profits, it will reduce firms' incentives to be productive. The reduction in productivity incentives, in turn, according to the critic, will lead to a decline in the resources available to promote the well being of the poor, whether through direct gifts from or investments by firms and shareholders that will putatively benefit poorer communities.

Suppose, *arguendo*, that the critic is right that, with collective bargaining protections in place, a larger share of the product of a given firm or sector would go to workers. This need not have a negative influence on overall productivity, however, if structural changes brought about in virtue of collective bargaining increased productivity. Collective bargaining *can* enhance investor-governed firms' productivity if it leads to increased participation by workers in decision-making and in firms' productivity gains, to increased worker loyalty and commitment, and so to enhanced firm performance. With more discretion and more incentives to perform, workers may do better, more profitable, work.

Perhaps, however, the net impact of respecting workers' collective bargaining rights on a firm's profits will be negative. In this case, there will likely be less money for investment by the firm or its investors in other enterprises that might indirectly benefit poor people, and less wealth in excess of the investors' public trust thresholds to be shared with poor people in accordance with the requirements of practical reasonableness.

Practical reason does not necessarily require that an investor use resources in excess of her public trust threshold exclusively or primarily to benefit poor people or communities. So reducing the resources of an investor committed to meeting the requirements of justice would not necessarily reduce the resources allocated specifically toward the relief of poverty. Perhaps, however, the investor might be constrained by a communal norm designed to channel resources specifically into poverty relief. In this case, there would be less available for distribution to the poor if collective bargaining reduced firm profits and so the investor's income. But the money available to workers might serve to relieve the poverty either of the workers themselves or, through consumption expenditure or investment, of their communities. Collective bargaining, presuming it actually boosts workers' well being, could thus ensure efficiently that many people had direct access to resources in a way that wealth transfers might not.

The attempt to resolve this kind of factual question is obviously beset with uncertainty, much like most questions about long-term consequences. To know how to respond to these consequences morally, we would have to know more about them than we do or can. We do know, however, that when deciding to bargain collectively with workers, firms are doing what practical reason requires of them in relation to those who actually work for them. The ripple effects of their choice to treat *these* workers fairly – effects which are indeterminate, epistemically uncertain, and causally distant from their actions – are not, in an important sense, their responsibility.

II Worker participation in the direction of investor-governed firms

Firms should often or always be democratically governed by workers. Even when it would be inconsistent with practical reason for a firm to deny workers the opportunity to govern themselves democratically, however, it may be difficult to achieve democracy within a firm. On an interim basis, in tandem with collective bargaining, significant opportunities for participatory management can serve some of the values democratic worker governance would honor and promote[32] and facilitate the emergence of genuine workplace democracy by increasing the influence of workers over firm strategy and policy. In Section A, I note the complementary relationship of collective bargaining and participatory management in investor-dominated firms. In Section B, I highlight some possible mechanisms that could be used to make possible extensive worker participation in firm management.

A Collective bargaining and participatory management as complementary

Participatory governance and collective bargaining can play complementary roles in investor-governed firms. The availability of opportunities for participation does not obviate collective bargaining.[33] Workers integrally involved in an investor-governed firm's decision-making structures will

---

[32] *Cf.* Walther Müller-Jentsch, *Industrial Democracy: From Representative Codetermination to Direct Participation*, 25 INT. J. POL. ECON. 50 (1995). These mechanisms would be especially crucial were there a case in which, as I doubt, worker self-government proved impossible or impracticable, since their creation would almost certainly be required in this case as a second-best option.

[33] *See* Harper, *supra* note 3.

often, understandably, be more inclined to favor decisions that enhance
the well being of the firm as a whole than they would be were they not
participants in firm governance processes.[34] This collaborative attitude
on the part of workers may reasonably be seen as among the important
benefits accruing *to firms* in virtue of their adoption of participatory
management schemes.[35] However, while workers' well being can sometimes be furthered by the same strategies and policies that further the
well being of other stakeholders, sometimes it can't. It is thus important,
at minimum, that participatory decision-making structures be aug-
mented by the provision of opportunities for collective bargaining. These
opportunities serve to protect the priorities of a firm's workers that are
not so clearly aligned with those of the firm or its elites.[36]

   The co-existence of collective bargaining and participatory management
in investor-governed firms is also important because of the value of diverse
avenues for workers to use to influence decisions in their workplaces. Not
only does this diversity of options ensure that collective bargaining can
continue to play an effective, independent role in protecting workers, separate from the role played by participatory management structures; it also
expands the number of opportunities workers have for direct involvement
in shaping their work environments, and thus increases the participatory, democratic character of workplace governance.[37] In addition, it likely
expands the range of perspectives available to inform firm decisions.

B   *Alternative participatory mechanisms*

Many different sorts of mechanisms could help to foster worker
participation in decision-making within undemocratic firms,[38] including

[34] *See id.* at 6.
[35] *Cf.* John Simmons, *Participatory Management: Lessons from the Leaders*, 79 MGMT. REV.
   54 (1990).
[36] *Cf.* Harper, *supra* note 3, at 18–38, 49–75, 79–95.   [37] *See id.* at 11.
[38] *Cf.* Rudolf Buschmann, *Workers' Participation and Collective Bargaining in Germany*,
   15 COMP. LAB. L. 26 (1993); Ronald J. Gilson & Mark J. Roe, *Lifetime Employment:
   Labor Peace and the Evolution of Japanese Corporate Governance*, 99 COLUM. L. REV.
   508 (1999); Raymond L. Hogler, *Worker Participation and Representation in the United
   States and the European Union: A Comparative Analysis*, 47 LAB. L.J. 586 (1996); Sanford
   M. Jacoby, *Employee Representation and Corporate Governance: A Missing Link*, 3
   U. PA. J. LAB. & EMP. L. 449, 485 (2001); Marleen O'Connor, *Labor's Role in the American
   Corporate Governance Structure*, 22 COMP. LAB. L. & POL'Y J. 97 (2000). Among the most
   intriguing alternative participatory mechanisms are the various boards envisioned in
   RUSSELL L. ACKOFF, THE DEMOCRATIC CORPORATION: A RADICAL PRESCRIPTION FOR
   RECREATING CORPORATE AMERICA AND REDISCOVERING SUCCESS 117–41 (1994).

democratically elected enterprise committees,[39] work teams,[40] and the practice of open-book management.[41] Worker stock ownership,[42] like the appointment of workers to a firm's board of directors,[43] would also

[39] *See generally* HARRY C. KATZ & THOMAS A. KOCHAN, AN INTRODUCTION TO COLLECTIVE BARGAINING AND INDUSTRIAL RELATIONS 397–98 (1992); Kirsten S. Wever, *Learning from Works Councils: Five Unspectacular Cases from Germany*, 33 IND. REL. 467 (1994); *but cf.* David Brody, *Why No Shop Committees in America: A Narrative History*, 40 INDUST. REL. 356 (2001).

[40] *Cf.* Mark R. Dixon et al., *Changing Conceptions of Employee Compensation*, 23 J. ORG. BEH. MGMT. 95 (2003); Hans Pruijt, *Teams between Neo-Taylorism and Anti-Taylorism*, 24 ECON. & IND. DEMOCRACY 77 (2003).

[41] *Cf.* JOHN CASE, OPEN-BOOK MANAGEMENT: THE COMING BUSINESS REVOLUTION (1996) Rai Aggerwal & Betty J. Simkins, *Open Book Management – Optimizing Human Capital*, 44 BUS. HORIZONS 5 (2001); John Case, *Opening the Books*, 75 HARV. BUS. REV. 118 (1997); Tim R. V. Davis, *Open-Book Management: Its Promise and Pitfalls*, 25 ORG. DYNAMICS 7 (1997); David Drickhamer, *Open Books to Elevate Performance*, 251 INDUSTRY WEEK 16 (2002) (interviewing Jack Stack); Gould, *supra* note 4, at 392–93; Rick Maurer, *Open-Book Management*, 24 J. QUALITY AND PARTICIPATION 64 (2001); Rick Maurer, *Making a Strong Case for Change*, 26 J. QUALITY AND PARTICIPATION 41 (2003); Charles A. O'Reilly III & Jeffrey Pfeffer, *PSS World Medical: Opening the Books Boosts Commitment and Performance*, 20 J. ORG. EXCELLENCE 65 (2001); Phil Perry, *Opening Your Books to Profit*, 87 IND. DISTRIBUTION 104 (1998); Gary J. Tulacz, *Compensation: Top Talent Still Top Dollar*, 246 ENR 86 (2001). *Cf.* CHARLES C. HECKSCHER, THE NEW UNIONISM: EMPLOYEE INVOLVEMENT IN THE CHANGING CORPORATION 169–71 (1996) Howard Gospel, Graeme Lockwood, & Paul Willman, *A British Dilemma: Disclosure of Information for Collective Bargaining and Joint Consultation*, 22 COMP. LAB. L. & POL'Y J. 327 (2001); *But cf.* Robert R. Falconi, *Too Many Cooks Spoil the Books*, 11 FINANCIAL EXECUTIVE 15 (1995); Richard J. Schonberger, *Open-Book Management: Less than Meets the Eye*, 16 COST MGMT. 12 (2002).

    Open book management may seem to be simply one example of the ways in which firms might embody in their governance structures a clear commitment to worker participation. But it is not simply a contingent, optional feature of organizational design. When a worker is denied access to information about a organization for which she works, it is clear that she is being excluded from intimate involvement in decision-making and that she is not a full member of the organization. Denial of access to information places the worker in a subordinate, arms'-length position in relation to the firm: it ensures that she is not a partner, but a servant.

[42] *See* PAUL OSTERMAN, SECURING PROSPERITY – THE AMERICAN LABOR MARKET: HOW IT HAS CHANGED AND WHAT TO DO ABOUT IT 155–56 (1999) (explicating and assessing the views of MARGARET M. BLAIR, OWNERSHIP AND CONTROL (1995) and MARK J. ROE, STRONG MANAGERS, WEAK OWNERS (1994)); Jeffrey M. Hirsch, *Labor Law Obstacles to the Collective Negotiation and Implementation of Employee Stock Ownership Plans: A Response to Henry Hansmann and Other Survivalists*, 67 FORDHAM L. REV. 957 (1998); Jacoby, *Representation*, *supra* note 38, at 486 (noting workers' "heavy investments – both financial and human capital – in the[ir] employing compan[ies]"). Roughly one quarter of Sears Roebuck's stock was held by the firm's worker profit-sharing plan in the mid twentieth century; *see* SANFORD JACOBY, MODERN MANORS: WELFARE CAPITALISM SINCE THE NEW DEAL 110, 122 (1997); *cf.* CASE, MANAGEMENT, *supra* note 41, at 104–10.

[43] *See* Charles B. Craver, *Mandatory Worker Participation is Required in a Declining Union Environment to Provide Employees with Meaningful Industrial Democracy*, 66 GEO.

provide valuable opportunities for participation in firm decision-making. And of course there are other options investor-governed firms might take to move at least partially toward democracy.[44] Governance boards, like those recommended by Russell Ackoff,[45] for instance, have been instituted at firms including Kodak, Anheuser-Busch, National Life of Vermont, Alcoa Tennessee, Super Fresh, Metropolitan Life, and Armco Latin America.[46] The precise form of a firm's participatory management structure is not crucial. Mechanisms of multiple kinds can offer genuine opportunities for extensive involvement in management and autonomous decision-making by workers and help firms move toward full-fledged democratic governance.

III   Setting workplace standards using collective bargaining

In democratically governed firms, workers would obviously set compensation levels. Because they would bear many of the costs and reap many of the benefits of the relevant decisions, it would also make sense for them to determine working hours and to set health and safety standards.[47] But even in investor-governed firms, answering questions about compensation, hours, and working conditions flexibly, on the basis of firm-by-firm contracting,[48] would be consistent with the Golden Rule's

---

WASH. L. REV. 135, 164–68 (1997); Jacoby, *Representation, supra* note 38, at 486; Gould, *supra* note 4, at 387–91; ACKOFF, *supra* note 38, at 57, 121.

[44] A range of other mechanisms for participatory management, like the one created by Polaroid founder Edwin Land, would be worth considering as well. *See* Paul C. Weiler, *A Principled Reshaping of Labor Law for the Twenty-First Century*, 3 U. PA. J. LAB. & EMP. L. 177, 198 (2001) ("Back in the late 1940s, Land … developed a system of full-blown employee democracy in his workplace. Every Polaroid employee, from the CEO down to the janitor, had a secret ballot vote to elect the board members who addressed a broad array of employee concerns").

[45] Ackoff conceives of boards that may, at least under some circumstances, include stakeholders – including contractors, suppliers, and representatives of the public – who are not workers. *See* ACKOFF, *supra* note 38, at 118–20.

[46] *See id.* at 120, 138–41.

[47] Of course, it might sometimes be important in such firms for the determination of such standards to reflect the influence of collective bargaining, if this helped to prevent or reduce unreasonable differential impacts of firm decisions on some workers.

[48] It is somewhat puzzling to find Fried arguing that regulation is a preferable means of securing legitimate worker goals; *see* Fried, *Rights, supra* note 9, at 1036–37. Where collective bargaining is strong, it seems that health, safety, and other standards can be adapted more satisfactorily to specific local conditions by workers.

requirement of fairness *if* collective bargaining and due process rights were respected.[49]

In Section A, I discuss the negotiation of compensation. Then, in turn, I consider negotiated approaches to health and safety standards (Section B) and working hours (Section C). In each case, I argue that collective bargaining could protect workers' well being while enhancing flexibility and the development of firm-sensitive standards.

A   Negotiating compensation

If workers can bargain collectively, compensation levels can be set in accordance with collectively negotiated contracts.

The consequences of minimum-wage rules continue to be hotly debated.[50] The conventional wisdom has been that increasing minimum wages will tend to limit the availability of low-wage employment: firms providing such employment will be able to fund fewer positions, and because they may be unable to deliver desired products and services, they may cease operations, thus eliminating even more positions.[51] By contrast,

---

[49] *Cf.* Karl E. Klare, *Critical Theory and Labor Relations Law, in* THE POLITICS OF LAW: A PROGRESSIVE CRITIQUE 554 (David Kairys ed., 1999) ("Collective bargaining offers the advantage of flexible adaptability to local conditions and problems. ... In principle, collective bargaining represents a decentralized, activist alternative to clumsy or antagonistic bureaucratic power").

[50] *See, e.g.,* John T. Addison & McKinley L. Blackburn, *Minimum Wages and Poverty,* 52 IND. & LAB. REL. REV. 393 (1999); Diego F. Angel-Urdinola & Quentin Wodon, *The Impact on Inequality of Raising the Minimum Wage: Gap-Narrowing and Reranking Effects,* 18 LAB. 317 (2004); Stephen Bazen & Velayoudom Marimoutou, *Looking for a Needle in a Haystack? A Re-Examination of the Time Series Relationship between Teenage Employment and Minimum Wages in the United States,* 64 OXFORD BULL. ECON. & STAT. 699 (2002); John F. Gaski, *Raising the Minimum Wage is Unethical and Immoral,* 109 BUS. & SOC. REV. 209 (2004); Omer Gokcekus & Edward Tower, *An Efficiency Enhancing Minimum Wage,* 6 J. ECON. POL'Y REFORM 247 (2003); David Neumark et al., *Minimum Wage Effects throughout the Wage Distribution,* 39 J. HUM. RES. 425 (2004); Paul Wolfson & Dale Belman, *The Minimum Wage: Consequences for Prices and Quantities in Low-Wage Labor Markets,* 22 J. BUS. & ECON. STAT. 296 (2004). An important recent attempt to overturn the established orthodoxy in this area is DAVID CARD & ALAN B. KRUEGER, MYTH AND MEASUREMENT: THE NEW ECONOMICS OF THE MINIMUM WAGE (1995).

[51] *See, e.g.,* Daniel Shaviro, *The Minimum Wage, the Earned Income Tax Credit, and Optimal Subsidy Policy,* 64 U. CHI. L. REV. 405, 406 (1997) ("Most economists of all ideological persuasions have long agreed that it is self-defeating: it destroys jobs in the low-wage sector of the economy and thus hurts many of the people it is intended to help") (citing sources including J. R. Kearl et al., *A Confusion of Economists?,* 69 AM. ECON. REV. 28, 30 (1979); Bruno Frey et al., *Consensus and Dissension Among Economists: An Empirical Inquiry,* 74 AM. ECON. REV. 986, 991 (1984)).

one recent economic analysis contends that, because workers are likely to respond to higher pay by working harder, minimum-wage rules will likely "affect[] wages over a range that exerts relatively small employment effects."[52] Whatever the actual effects of minimum wage rules, however, strong collective bargaining protections would obviate them.

The argument for a negotiation-based approach is twofold. First, this approach offers greater flexibility. Practicing open-book management, firms could clarify their financial circumstances and reach realistic conclusions in negotiations with workers. They could propose compensation packages consistent with their financial capacities and argue for them persuasively. Even if they were not always able to be persuasive, the collective bargaining environment would give them the freedom to negotiate flexibly, changing their offers with economic conditions and addressing the different circumstances of different groups of workers.[53] This level of flexibility is obviously crucial, since it would allow businesses to respond sensitively to diverse conditions.

However, though collectively negotiated compensation levels could reflect environment-specific conditions and could be shaped flexibly in light of factors including firm resources, workers wouldn't be likely to lose out, as long as resources were available: "the quantity effect in the case of a … [collective bargaining] premium is predictably higher (in an absolute sense) compared with the minimum-wage model."[54] Collective bargaining would allow workers to negotiate from a strong position for high compensation.[55] And, to the extent that most or all communities

---

[52] Richard A. Ippolito, *The Impact of the Minimum Wage if Workers Can Adjust Effort*, 46 J. LAW & ECON. 207, 223 (2003).

[53] While traditional collective bargaining has specified compensation levels fairly precisely, greater flexibility seems to be typical of white-collar employee unions; *see* HECKSCHER, *supra* note 41, at 66.

[54] Ippolito, *supra* note 52, at 221.

[55] No doubt this is why not all European labor law regimes have featured minimum wage requirements. *See, e.g.,* Samuel Estreicher, *Labor Law Reform in a World of Competitive Product Markets*, 69 CHI.-KENT L. REV. 3, 16 (1993); Gregor Thusing, *Recent Developments in German Labor Law: Freedom of Association, Industrial Action, and Collective Bargaining*, 9 IND. INT'L & COMP. L. REV. 47, 62 (1998) (emphasizing that while "[t]he German government has never had to fix a minimum wage," "most employment contracts continue to refer to a collective agreement and … there are collective agreements for almost every branch of industry"); Cara Waldman, *The Future of German Labor Relations: Lessons German Unions Can Learn from American Failures*, 19 CONN. J. INT'L L. 689, 704 n.131 (2004) (citing Otto Jacobi et al., *Germany: Codetermining the Future? in* INDUSTRIAL RELATIONS IN THE NEW EUROPE 237, 247–48 (Anthony Ferner & Richard Hyman eds., 1992)); Aditi Bagchi, Note, *Unions and the Duty of Good Faith in Employment Contracts*, 112 YALE L.J. 1881, 1906 (2003) (observing that Germany's

recognized the collective bargaining rights flowing from practical reason, in most cases there would be no downward pressure on compensation exerted by the wages offered by comparable firms whose workers lacked the freedom to bargain collectively. Even if not all firms recognized this right, however, workers who bargained collectively could still take appropriate advantage of relevant economic conditions; if there were inter-firm compensation differences among otherwise comparable firms that did bargain collectively, they would be explicable largely in terms of firms' financial conditions and regional cost-of-living variations.

Firms and workers alike will tend to equilibrate their behavior in ways that appear to be fair rather than single-mindedly pursuing their own well being.[56] Given the evident impetus toward fairness, "a minimum wage requirement may be less necessary to raise wages than might otherwise be thought,"[57] because at least in some cases "employers and employees may find their way to an equilibrium with higher wages entirely on their own."[58] This drive operates even in the absence of collective bargaining.[59] When the fairness dynamic and the influence of collective bargaining are combined, therefore, the odds are even greater that compensation levels will be reasonable.

In some cases, of course, compensation unfairness could result over the short term from the tendency of collective bargaining to lead to arrangements favoring current over prospective employees. Suppose a firm plans to hire a new group of workers. These workers may be covered in unfavorable ways in a collectively negotiated contract, because in

---

"system of industrial regulation attempts to achieve worker protections almost exclusively through private negotiation"); Patrick McCarthy, Book Review, 14 Comp. Lab. L.J. 99, 102 (1992) (noting that French Socialists opted for negotiated, specific increases in pay scales in particular sectors rather than an across-the-board increase in the minimum wage); Martin Behrens et al., *Unions in Germany: Searching to Regain the Initiative* 22 (Hans-Böckler-Stifting Project Nt. 2000-205-2, 2001) *available at* http://www.expertbase.net/forum/reader/wsi.pdf.

[56] *See* Christine Jolls, *Fairness, Minimum Wage Law, and Employee Benefits*, 77 N.Y.U. L. Rev. 47, 51–57 (2002) (referring to sources including Ernst Fehr, George Kirchsteiger, & Arno Riedl, *Does Fairness Prevent Market Clearing? An Experimental Investigation*, 108 Q.J. Econ. 437 (1993)).

[57] Jolls, *supra* note 56, at 57.

[58] *Id.* at 58. Jolls emphasizes the distinction between environments in which workers monitor themselves (in which the "fairness dynamic" to which she refers seems more evident) and those in which high levels of supervisor monitoring take place (in which the fairness dynamic may be supplanted); *see id.* at 58–68.

[59] Jolls does not seem to distinguish between cases in which workers benefit from collective bargaining and cases in which they don't, but many of the cases to which she refers are clearly ones in which workers' salaries have not been set through collective bargaining.

the nature of the case negotiators represent existing workers. If the new worker group is different in some way from the current worker group, its concerns and goals may be underserved. However, the new workers will be able to participate in the election of subsequent bargaining representatives once they are hired, and the new workers should therefore be able to make their voices heard and alter the disadvantageous arrangements relatively soon.

B   Negotiating workplace health and safety standards

Workers should be able to shape workplace health and safety standards cooperatively through collectively negotiated contracts.

The current regulatory maintenance of health and safety standards in the United States

> depends on a good working relationship between [the National Institute for Occupational Safety and Health] and [the Occupational Safety and Health Administration], adequate budgets and personnel for each agency, and insulation of the decision makers from the political pressures that invariably arise when new regulations are proposed. The rulemaking process is protracted, detailed, cumbersome, expensive, and adversarial. The reviewing courts have required detailed analyses of significant risk and technological and economic feasibility. The courts also have shown a reluctance to uphold the validity of emergency temporary standards, and have required, at times, a precise and an almost cataclysmic showing of "grave danger."[60]

By contrast, rules that are collectively negotiated at the workplace level can be tailored to particular firms' economic conditions and workers' tolerance for risk. They can be adopted and adjusted quickly and, in principle, cooperatively.

Such a model seems unlikely to work in an environment in which individual workers negotiate with employing organizations. In such settings, workers, with little power, will be more likely to accept unreasonably unsafe working conditions. So it is not surprising that, under current conditions, being a non-unionized worker makes it more likely that one will find oneself exposed to significant risks in return for relatively low pay. "[N]onunion workers in dangerous jobs are, in many cases, simply unlucky: they have found their way into situations of high risk and low

---

[60] Mark A. Rothstein, *Substantive and Procedural Obstacles to OSHA Rulemaking: Reproductive Hazards as an Example*, 12 B.C. ENVTL. AFF. L. REV. 627, 698 (1985).

pay and would presumably move to ... better job[s] ... [if] they could."[61] By contrast, the influence of workers who bargain collectively should enable them to adopt and enforce reasonable standards.

The employment at-will doctrine also reduces the capacity of workers to demand reasonable health and safety levels. Under the at-will doctrine, a firm is, in practice, free to dismiss a worker who objects to workplace safety conditions (despite a contravening provision of the Occupational Safety and Health Act).[62] OSHA can intervene without a worker complaint to correct workplace safety violations. But universal collective bargaining and the elimination of the at-will doctrine could render the need for this kind of intervention less obvious.

There is some precedent elsewhere for a negotiation-based approach to setting health and safety standards. "Canada treats safety and health policy as a bargain between labor and management, with government facilitating negotiation."[63] "The success of labor-management efforts to provide a safe working environment [in Sweden] has caused some to question the need for national legislation."[64] And in the United States, negotiation already plays a more substantial role in the development and implementation of health and safety standards than it once did.[65]

Current negotiated approaches sometimes rely not on agreements among the primarily affected parties, but on the "contracting-out" of rule-making authority by governmental agencies to putatively neutral third parties, and such arrangements suffer from obvious liabilities.[66] The

[61] Peter Dorman & Paul Hagstrom, *Wage Compensation for Dangerous Work Revisited*, 52 INDUS. & LAB. REL. REV. 116, 133 (1998) (quoted in Sydney A. Shapiro, *The Necessity of OSHA*, 8 KAN. J.L. & PUB. POL'Y 22, 25 (1999)).

[62] *See* Shapiro, *Necessity, supra* note 61, at 25.

[63] Randy S. Rabinowitz & Mark M. Hager, *Designing Health and Safety: Workplace Hazard Regulation in the United States and Canada*, 33 CORNELL INT'l L.J. 373, 433 (2000).

[64] Julie E. Korostoff, Linda M. Zimmermann, & Carolyn E. Ryan, Comment, *Rethinking the OSHA Approach to Workplace Safety: A Look at Worker Participation in the Enforcement of Safety Regulations in Sweden, France, and Great Britain*, 13 COMP. LAB. L. 45, 52 (1991).

[65] *See* Charles C. Caldart & Nicholas A. Ashford, *Negotiation as a Means of Developing and Implementing Environmental and Occupational Health and Safety Policy*, 23 HARV. ENVTL. L. REV. 141 (1999); Jody Freeman, *Collaborative Governance in the Administrative State*, 45 UCLA L. REV. 1 (1997); Philip J. Harter, *Negotiating Regulations: A Cure for Malaise*, 71 GEO. L.J. 1 (1982); Philip J. Harter, *The Political Legitimacy and Judicial Review of Consensual Rules*, 32 AM. U.L. REV. 471 (1983); Thomas O. McGarity, *Some Thoughts on "Deossifying" the Rulemaking Process*, 41 DUKE L.J. 1385 (1992); Sidney A. Shapiro, *Outsourcing Government Regulation*, 53 DUKE L.J. 389 (2003).

[66] *See* Shapiro, *Outsourcing, supra* note 65, at 406–11. Shapiro identifies a range of liabilities here. Private standard-setters may be unduly concerned about their own profits (*id.*

direct negotiation of standards among affected parties already appears in the contemporary work environment to yield potential benefits and to be subject to fewer liabilities than this approach.[67] It certainly appears capable of prompting creative thinking even when, as at present, the parties know that they are not ultimately responsible for a projected standard, which will be determined by a public agency.[68] The evidence that workers and firms can indeed engage in thoughtful, responsible conversations regarding health and safety issues when their exchanges are being assisted by a facilitator[69] suggests that, under the pressure of contract negotiations,[70] they could be expected to perform even more effectively.[71] "Both political theory and practical experience, therefore, point to exploring the possibility of basing regulations on negotiations among

at 406); they may not share a regulatory agency's objectives (*id.* at 406–7); and they may take advantage of information asymmetries (*id.* at 408). But negotiations between firms and workers regarding workplace safety standards would not be subject to these liabilities. Those most directly affected – workers – would be at the table and in a position to bargain effectively.

[67] *See id.* at 411–13. Shapiro suggests that "regulatory negotiation" will pose a smaller risk of opportunistic behavior than will the contracting-out of regulation. He suggests that "[a]gencies … may find it difficult to rely on regulatory negotiation to establish certain types of regulatory standards because of the difficulty of specifying in advance a set of policy parameters that will lead to the resolution of information deficiencies and value conflicts in a manner acceptable to the agency" (*id.* at 412). But this concern is somewhat question-begging when the issue is precisely who ought to set the relevant parameters and whether the relevant concerns (in this case, primarily those of workers) will be adequately protected if the affected parties are left free to negotiate these parameters.

[68] *Cf.* Freeman, *supra* note 65, at 49–55 (describing negotiations involving OSHA and representatives of firms and workers from the steel industry).

[69] *See id.* at 49–53.

[70] There is perhaps a stronger argument here for industry-wide collective negotiation than there is with respect to wages and working hours, though the model I elaborate here does not entail a commitment to industry-wide or firm-specific negotiation regarding safety issues.

[71] This conclusion assumes, of course, that the parties would not become more combative and opportunistic if they knew they would actually be responsible for the final outcome of the negotiation. Freeman points to a number of problems with regulatory negotiation as currently conceived that would not obtain in the case of contractual negotiations regarding health and safety issues among affected parties. When governmental agencies convene negotiating, they may tend to limit the scope of negotiations to ensure their manageability (*id.* at 67–69). Firms and workers would have no similar incentive to reduce the range of issues on the table; they could respond more flexibly to creative ideas. Negotiations may be hampered by the perception that they are elements in zero-sum games (*id.* at 69–73). But, as Freeman notes, negotiations can also breed trust; and trust would likely be easier to create and maintain when parties knew each other and had to work with each other, as in a firm-specific negotiation regarding safety rules.

representatives of the affected interests, resulting in a broad-based consensus and the procedure to implement such participation."[72]

To argue for the potential viability of fully negotiated workplace health and safety standards is not to deny that communal health and safety norms can be very useful to workers. Such norms can "stimulate an employer to action" in a way that "does not depend upon the workers' knowledge of occupational risks or bargaining power."[73] Collective bargaining provides workers with the bargaining power they need to ensure that workplace safety standards are adequate. But it may not provide them with all of the information they need to make informed judgments regarding appropriate safety standards to include in contracts.

There is thus a continued role for communal norms and conventions related to workplace health and safety. They need not mandate particular workplace health and safety standards. Rather, they could serve to make clear – especially to workers, who might otherwise lack adequate information about risks – what the consequences of particular health and safety arrangements might be. Information that might not be readily available to negotiating workers – even, perhaps, to firms – could be embodied in model contract provisions. These model provisions could serve as starting-points for negotiation; they could be altered in the course of fair negotiation, but their availability would mean that negotiators could assess alternatives with both eyes open.

This approach would increase firms' flexibility and responsiveness to local conditions. However, collective bargaining would help to ensure a level playing field on which health and safety issues could be discussed and resolved.[74] Thus, it could reasonably be anticipated that

[72] Harter, *Legitimacy, supra* note 65, at 476. Harter suggests that the model of consensual rule-making he elaborates can work only if interests are adequately represented; the number of represented interests is limited; no interest has overwhelming influence; the issues to be discussed are live ones, ready for negotiation; no party should be expected to compromise a fundamental value; participants should be able to express their preferences in rankings; there should be a deadline for decision; and the parties should be open to negotiation. *Id.* at 479–80. I think it is clear that, at least in the context of determining safety regulations, firm–worker negotiation (when conducted in the context of collective bargaining) should be able to meet these requirements at least as well as firm–worker–agency negotiations.

[73] Thomas O. McGarity & Sydney A. Shapiro, *OSHA's Critics and Regulatory Reform*, 31 WAKE FOREST L. REV. 587, 608 (1996).

[74] According to Caldart and Ashford, "when OSHA abdicates its policy-making responsibility by making clear to industry and labor that it will accept a negotiated settlement as the basis for occupational safety and health standards, the chances that negotiation will produce meaningful safety and health gains are reduced considerably"; Caldart & Ashford, *supra* note 65, at 202. But this seems likely to depend not on the fact that the

a firm-specific or industry-wide consensus would respect the relevant values in play, protecting worker safety[75] as well as firm profitability.[76]

C   Negotiating work hours

Work hours can be regulated fairly by contract – provided contractual terms result from reasonable collective bargaining procedures.[77] Providing workers with the collective opportunity to negotiate regarding work hours would give them the freedom to craft working arrangements reflective of their distinctive circumstances and needs, and sensitive to firms' needs as well.

When legislation limiting work hours was being considered in the United States during the Great Depression, the American Federation of Labor, in line with a position it had taken for some time, was initially "opposed to legislation that would take the place of collective bargaining in setting work hours."[78] Of course, a community-wide norm in accordance with which work hours were reduced across the

outcome results from a bargain, but from the lack of satisfactory bargaining strength. Because a negotiating team can negotiate about health and safety issues with a guaranteed right to strike if bargaining about them leads to an impasse, it is not clear that Caldart and Ashford's doubts are entirely warranted.

[75] *Cf.* Arlin R. Crisco, *Fighting Outside the Ring: A Labor Alternative to the Continued Federal Regulation of Professional Boxing*, 60 OHIO ST. L.J. 1139, 1175 (1999) (noting that industry-specific health and safety standards might be among the topics to be negotiated by an envisioned boxers' union and representatives of boxing promoters).

[76] Philip Harter observes that "it would not be too far fetched to imagine a negotiation resulting in a weak occupational safety standard in return for a higher rate of pay. That option is simply not acceptable under the Occupational Safety and Health Act, however, and OSHA would reject the proposal out of hand." Philip J. Harter, *In Search of Goldilocks: Democracy, Participation, and Government*, 10 PENN ST. ENVTL. L. REV. 113, 129 n.59 (2002). However, collective negotiation, backed up by the right to strike, would make it less likely that workers would accept unreasonable contract terms. And if there is no single right answer to the question of the degree to which a potentially undesirable outcome should be tolerated, it does not seem in principle unreasonable that negotiation be used to determine risk levels, provided adequate information is available and bargaining strength reasonably equal.

[77] Hours are a focus of growing concern among those seeking to humanize workplaces in the United States; *see, e.g.*, JULIET SCHOR THE OVERWORKED AMERICAN: THE UNEXPECTED DECLINE OF LEISURE (1993); L. Camille Hebert, *The Fair Labor Standards Act: "Updating" the "White-Collar" Employee Exemptions to the Fair Labor Standards Act*, 7 EMPL. RTS. & EMP. POL'Y J. 51 (2003).

[78] Seth D. Harris, *Conceptions of Fairness and the Fair Labor Standards Act*, 18 HOFSTRA LAB. & EMP. L.J. 19, 103 (2000) (citing Elizabeth Brandeis, *Organized Labor and Protective Labor Legislation, in* LABOR AND THE NEW DEAL 199 (Milton Derber & Edwin Young eds., 1957) (footnote omitted)).

board might be a reasonable response to mass unemployment. But it seems clear in general that a fair collective bargaining process could set satisfactory firm-by-firm standards for work hours. Work-hour reductions in France and Germany have been significantly influenced by collective bargaining.[79] And "[c]ollective bargaining agreements in Germany, Italy, and Australia have frequently reduced workers' work hours at the enterprise level while providing employers with greater flexibility in scheduling work through innovations such as annualized hours of work, time banking schemes, individual working time contracts, and flexible starting and finishing times."[80] Determining work hours by contract need not mean a return to the 60- or 72-hour work-week. In the context of collective negotiation, firms and workers can opt for arrangements regarding work-hours that are simultaneously flexible and fair – though collective bargaining *is* crucial if workers are to resist firms' encroachments on their time and excessive demands for productivity.[81]

In one firm, "boards at the shop-floor level" opted "to eliminate time cards and time clocks,"[82] and there would be good reason for others to follow suit. In any case, the availability of collective bargaining and opportunities for meaningful workplace participation and the availability of strikes and lawsuits to enforce workers' rights could ensure that, in an environment in which work hours were determined by collective bargaining, workers were not exploited.

IV   Collective bargaining and sweatshop labor

Collective bargaining can provide an appropriate and flexible means of setting fair labor standards, especially (whether or not exclusively) in investor-governed firms. And, especially in the absence of workplace

[79] Scott D. Miller, *Revitalizing the FLSA*, 19 HOFSTRA LAB. & EMP. L.J. 1, 116 (2001) (citing ANDERS HAYDEN, SHARING THE WORK, SPARING THE PLANET: WORK TIME, CONSUMPTION, AND ECOLOGY 133–49 (1999)) (footnotes omitted).

[80] Peter Berg, Eileen Appelbaum, Tom Bailey, & Arne L. Kalleberg, *Contesting Time: International Comparisons of Employee Control of Working Time*, 57 IND. & LAB. REL. REV. 331, 332 (2004) (citing FRANCESCA BETTIO ET AL., WORKING TIME PATTERNS IN THE EUROPEAN UNION: POLICIES AND INNOVATIONS FROM A GENDER PERSPECTIVE (1998)) (footnote omitted).

[81] *Cf.* Maury Gittleman, Michael Horrigan, & Mary Joyce, *"Flexible" Workplace Practices: Evidence from a Nationally Representative Survey*, 52 IND. & LAB. REL. REV. 99, 102 (1998).

[82] *See* ACKOFF, *supra* note 38, at 126.

democracy, it can play an especially important role in helping to eliminate sweatshops in an economically rational manner and helping to increase the availability of worker governance in sweatshop firms. Workers are often forced into sweatshop labor, as they have been throughout history, because their land has been stolen or their employment opportunities limited by law. Neither workplace democracy nor collective bargaining can resolve the problems created by the deprivation produced by centuries of injustice and ongoing violence. But even before those problems have been rectified, collective bargaining can help to protect workers' freedom, dignity, and well being.

In Section A, I argue that sweatshop labor is not a necessary feature of the economic environment, even in LDCs. In Section B, I maintain that collective bargaining can be seen as a second-best alternative to workplace democracy that is preferable to more common responses to the problem of sweatshops. In Section C, I suggest that guaranteeing collective bargaining rights will not lead to injustice in LDCs, and reject the claim that communities should not encourage, and firms should not afford, collective bargaining rights because recognizing these rights will reduce the resources available to promote the well being of poor people. In Section D, I argue that protectionism is not a helpful response to violations of labor rights. I maintain in Section E that special obligations may preclude outsourcing by IC firms, even when sweatshop labor is not an issue. I emphasize in Section F that, at least in the absence of workplace democracy, collective bargaining rights can play a key role in ensuring justice at work and, by implication, justice in global trade.

A *The contingency of sweatshop labor*

Many mainstream economists, including ones concerned about global poverty, suggest that the nature of the global economy makes current abysmal working conditions around the world unavoidable. Some critics of the model of globalization evidently preferred by many investor-controlled corporations evidently believe that the reality of sweatshop labor justifies protectionist behavior by ICs. I suggest that both are wrong. I emphasize the awfulness of working conditions in many environments in Subsection 1, note the apologia for the existence of these conditions advanced by many economists in Subsection 2, and emphasize the potential of collective bargaining to address the problem of sweatshop labor in Subsection 3.

1   The prevalence of sweatshop conditions

Labor conditions in many parts of the world are miserable. Businesses from ICs sometimes partner with entities that use slave labor.[83] But even people who work in some sense voluntarily, for wages, do so in wretched conditions – in settings that certainly deserve the label "sweatshops." A sweatshop worker may be paid less than $1 per day.[84] Sweatshop workers are expected to work in unsafe and unhygienic environments, sometimes without bathroom access or needed sleep. Especially pronounced abuses have included mandatory contraception for women workers and twenty-hour work days.[85]

2   Economists' understanding of sweatshops as unavoidable

Reporting on a visit to the apparel factories of Dhaka, Bangladesh, Jeffrey Sachs notes that "[s]ome rich-country protestors have argued that Dhaka's apparel firms should either pay far higher wage rates or be closed." Sachs begs to differ: "closing such factories as a result of wages forced above worker productivity would be little more than a ticket for … [the] women [who work in the factories] back to rural misery."[86] Tim Harford argues that people seek sweatshop employment "voluntarily, which means – hard as it is to believe – that whatever their alternatives are, they are worse."[87] And Douglas Irwin contends that critics "of sweatshops have failed to consider what alternative opportunities for employment can be created."[88]

---

[83] *See* Maria Ellinikos, *American MNCs Continue to Profit from the Use of Forced and Slave Labor Begging the Question: Should America Take a Cue from Germany?*, 35 COLUM. J.L. & SOC. PROBS. 1 (2001); Douglas S. Morrin, *People Before Profits: Pursuing Corporate Accountability for Labor Rights Violations Abroad through the Alien Tort Claims Act*, 20 B.C. THIRD WORLD L.J. 427 (2000).

[84] Nicholas D. Kristof and Sheryl WuDunn, *Two Cheers for Sweatshops*, NEW YORK TIMES MAGAZINE, Sept. 24, 2000, at 70–71, *quoted in* DOUGLAS IRWIN, FREE TRADE UNDER FIRE 215 (2002).

[85] Andrew Ross, *Introduction* to NO SWEAT: FASHION, FREE TRADE, AND THE RIGHTS OF GARMENT WORKERS 25, 25 (Andrew Ross ed., 1997). Thanks to Julia Fisher for this reference; *see* Julia Fisher, *Free Speech to Have Sweatshops? How* Kasky v. Nike *Might Provide a Useful Tool to Improve Sweatshop Conditions*, 26 B.C. THIRD WORLD L.J. 267, 273 (2006).

[86] JEFFREY SACHS, THE END OF POVERTY: ECONOMIC POSSIBILITIES FOR OUR TIME 12 (2005). Sachs is clear that "safer working conditions" are needed at such factories. *Id.* at 11.

[87] TIM HARFORD, THE UNDERCOVER ECONOMIST: EXPOSING WHY THE RICH ARE RICH, THE POOR ARE POOR – AND WHY YOU CAN NEVER BUY A DECENT USED CAR! 222 (2005); *cf. id.* at 223, 252.

[88] IRWIN, *supra* note 84, at 215.

Jagdish Bhagwati responds dismissively to claims that global corporations "exploit" workers in LDCs. It is nonsense, he maintains, to demand that these companies pay such workers "living wages." They regularly pay more than their domestic competitors in LDCs. And "[f]ew workers are going to work, except under duress or in the gulag, for a 'dying wage.'" Anti-sweatshop activists are dupes of self-interested unions, Bhagwati asserts. They incorrectly label as sweatshops "firms and factories paying low wages that *naturally* reflect the fact that … [the regions in which the firms and factories are located] are poor and have low wages." Sweatshops, he insists question-beggingly, are "properly defined as those in violation of safety standards, minimum wage laws, legislated working conditions, etc."[89] Bhagwati skirts the question whether the relevant laws and standards are themselves reasonable.

Martin Wolff is less dismissive, but no less critical, of challenges to employment practices in LDCs. "The fact that wages paid by investors are lower in developing countries than in rich ones is a perfectly reasonable response to local conditions," he observes.[90] Wolff seeks carefully to defend this conclusion. He imagines a critic maintaining "that if foreign companies are far more productive than domestic ones, they can also afford to pay far more. Otherwise, the pay is unfair."[91] Wolff responds that "cheaper labour … [is what attracts] investments in the first place," so "it will not make sense, either for the economy as a whole or for the employer, to pay a huge multiple of … [the] best alternative" wage for a worker. And it makes sense for global companies to pay them less than workers in the companies' communities of origin to the extent that their productivity levels are genuinely lower than those of these workers.[92] In "the classic 'sweatshop' industries … , it seems clear that … workers are better off than if … [their] jobs did not exist . …"[93] And because "conditions in domestically oriented factories (let alone the informal sector) tend to be worse than in export-oriented plants," it follows that "[a]ttacking the latter is mere tokenism."[94]

[89] JAGDISH BHAGWATI, THE WIND OF THE HUNDRED DAYS: HOW WASHINGTON MISMANAGED GLOBALIZATION 320–22 (2000) (my italics).
[90] MARTIN WOLFF, WHY GLOBALIZATION WORKS 242 (2004).   [91] *Id.* at 237.
[92] *Id.*; *but cf. id.* at 186 (observing that plants in, say, China may be operated just as efficiently as those in ICs, but defending compensation disparities because "it makes no sense for workers with similar skills to be paid very differently in any given labour market").
[93] *Id.* at 238; *cf.* IRWIN, *supra* note 84, at 215.
[94] WOLFF, *supra* note 90, at 239.

3   Justice for sweatshop workers

There is no reason, of course, to take "local conditions" that occasion sweatshop labor for granted. Behind the conditions that generate sweatshop working conditions are often not benign or unavoidable economic dynamics but rather a range of violent dispossessions and infringements, both legal and extra-legal, on people's safety, their property, and their opportunities for market entry.[95] Political power and organized violence have frequently created the "local conditions" from which attractive alternatives to sweatshop labor are absent. Often these are the responsibility of local elites, though IC firms have certainly encouraged and facilitated them as well. Perhaps, for instance, peasants have been forced from their land by the consolidation of rural farms into large estates owned by rich absentee landlords. And perhaps, therefore, they or their descendants have been compelled to seek available urban employment as an alternative to poorly remunerated, backbreaking work as tenant farmers on land formerly owned by their families. In a sense, their willingness to accept sweatshop employment reflects local economic conditions, but those conditions are hardly innocent or unavoidable.

Ultimately, therefore, a just solution to the problems that force people to accept positions in sweatshops will require the redress, in diverse forms, of the injuries that have actively constrained the options of sweatshop workers. As I have already suggested, practical reason does not *automatically* require that current land titles be vacated when they are rooted in injustice. But justice *may*, indeed, often require that they be vacated. And even when it does not, it surely does require that those whose lives have been stunted, whose opportunities have been dramatically contracted, by dispossession or oppression of other kinds receive appropriate compensation, preferably from those responsible for their injury or their victimizers' successors in interest.

Thus, respecting collective bargaining rights is not an alternative to redress for the violence, exclusion, and subordination from which LDC workers have suffered, any more than it is a finally adequate substitute

[95] This point is made nicely at the general level in Ellennita Muetze Hellmer, *Establishing Government Accountability in the Anti-Sweatshop Campaign: Toward a Logical, Activist Approach to Improving the Working Conditions of the Poor*, J. LIBERTARIAN STUD., Sum. 2005, at 33–47, though there are concerns, acknowledged by the author, regarding the accuracy of details related to the use of slave labor in manufacturing in Burma: *see* Sheldon Richman, *Burma and Forced Factory Labor: No Evidence, No Allegations*, http://sheldonfreeassociation.blogspot.com/2006/04/burma-and-forced-factory-labor-no.html (featuring both the results of Richman's own careful investigation and comments from others, including Hellmer) (last visited Sept. 28, 2008).

for democratic firm governance. Ultimately, of course, LDC firms, like IC firms, must be democratically organized, and poor people in LDCs must be compensated directly for the injustices they or their ancestors have suffered. But instituting and respecting workers' collective bargaining and due process rights could begin to help workers achieve justice at work – and, perhaps, ultimately (to the extent that, once organized, they can exert some influence on communal norms, rules, and institutions), redress for past dispossession.

B   Competitive advantage and collective bargaining

Given the way they have framed the issue, Sachs, Harford, Bhagwati, Irwin, and Wolff might seem obviously right. It is not *merely* "a lack of organized labor and weak government regulations [that] reduce the cost of manufacturing"[96] in LDCs. Rather, as I note in Subsection 1, the lower cost of living in an LDC (no doubt often inexplicable without reference to various sorts of injustice) gives workers in the LDC an advantage in comparison with those in some other regions in which production facilities might be located: workers in LDCs can afford to work for less than workers in ICs. To the extent that labor costs are significant, their competitive advantage can help LDCs to seek investment more successfully. At the same time, I suggest in Subsection 2, collective bargaining provides a means by which this competitive advantage can be realized more fairly (if not as fairly as it would be if LDC workers democratically governed their firms).

1   Cost of living as a source of competitive advantage for LDC workers

It should be clear that production workers in LDCs would not want to be compensated at IC levels *in the short term*.

A worker in an LDC who opts to work in a manufacturing facility despite unsafe and oppressive working conditions presumably does so because of economic benefits she perceives as unavailable elsewhere.[97]

---

[96] Jeffrey Hollender & Stephen Fenichell, What Matters Most: How a Small Group of Pioneers is Teaching Social Responsibility to Big Business, and Why Big Business Is Listening 43 (2004).

[97] The question of just how free choices to work in such facilities actually are is obviously vital to the moral issue with which I am concerned, and I trust it is clear from what I have said here and elsewhere that I do not regard the simple conclusion of a contract as satisfactory evidence of free choice, and that I believe background injustice has significantly constrained the options of sweatshop workers.

Given the alternatives available to her (ones often shaped by desperate poverty and background injustice), she seemingly prefers the compensation available to her at the facility to the compensation available elsewhere. This suggests that – unless she is (as she may be) a slave – the compensation she receives for working at the facility, however miserably low, is better than what is available to her elsewhere. And, if an IC firm operates the facility, it evidently judges that it makes the most efficient use of its resources when it hires this worker and others like her rather than hiring IC workers at IC compensation rates.

If LDC and IC compensation levels were identical, few firms would judge that it was reasonable to employ the LDC worker rather than her IC counterpart, at least when labor costs played a significant role in determining overall production costs. Firms based in ICs would be more likely to base their production operations as well as their management activities in ICs. The result would be fewer jobs and less wealth for LDCs. It seems unlikely that this is an outcome most workers in LDCs would prefer: they would be impoverished for the benefit of workers in ICs. Workers in a typical LDC would not want wages for jobs they could perform set at IC levels. They would wish to retain their jobs and to see money enter their region from others.

I emphasize that, by suggesting that workers would seek to realize the global advantage afforded by their costs of living, I do not intend to imply that it is irrelevant that injustice is often deeply implicated in workers' poverty. I do not intend to excuse this injustice or ignore the need for systemic remedies. I simply want to suggest that many LDC workers will have at least some reason to treat their circumstances, resulting as they often do from dispossession and oppression, as sources of competitive advantage.

2   Collective bargaining as a means of realizing LDC workers' competitive advantage

Globally recognized labor rights – including automatic collective bargaining rights, the right to strike, and the right to have access to relevant information – could help to secure minimal fairness for LDC workers while allowing them to realize the competitive advantage afforded by their costs of living.

It is clear that LDC workers with the leverage afforded by collective bargaining would not accept oppressive and riskily unsafe working conditions, excruciatingly long work periods, and painfully low compensation levels. Bargaining as a group, they would doubtless – once confident of their ability to articulate and effect decisions – insist on safe working conditions, respect for their dignity and privacy, reasonable work hours, and suitable compensation.

What is equally clear, however, is that they would wish to *use* their competitive advantage. While the suitable wages on which they would insist would undoubtedly be higher than those they are currently paid, they would surely not insist on compensation at IC levels. Taking into account their cost of living, they would bargain for wages and working conditions at levels that would enhance their financial positions while ensuring the continuation of their jobs. Collectively bargained wages in what were formerly sweatshops would not be "wages forced above worker productivity."[98]

However, even if (as I suspect) IC firms and LDC firms alike could often pay higher salaries than they now do, increases in compensation *will* be limited by profitability. At some point, a firm will either close or relocate if its costs become too high. Recognizing that firms' resources are not infinite, collectively bargaining workers will seek *realistically* high compensation levels. Even though workers in different environments would almost certainly bargain to different compensation levels in order to realize their respective competitive advantages,[99] the existence of varying compensation levels could be just. These compensation levels would reflect workers' responsiveness to different economic conditions, including their own costs of living and their productivity. Workers are not foolish. There is no reason to think that, given opportunities to bargain collectively, they would not take actual market conditions into account, seeking a reasonable share of profits while declining to abandon the competitive advantage created for them by their often unjustly depressed cost of living.

They would doubtless lack perfect information. (So do workers in other settings, a fact which does not seem to make collective bargaining impossible elsewhere.) They could, however, determine viable working conditions through the process of bargaining, just like IC workers. Provided that at least a second-best alternative to a just workplace governance regime is in place globally, and that collective bargaining and due process rights are thus generally acknowledged, they would not need to be concerned that firms might relocate to other environments in which people currently lack the freedom to bargain collectively. But even in a global environment marked by the persistence of widespread injustice

[98] SACHS, *supra* note 86, at 11.   [99] *Cf.* MANDLE, *supra* note 9, at 109–13.

they could use the leverage available to them to reduce manipulation and secure better compensation and conditions. They would need to be realistic about their productivity and their employers' costs, but they would be able to insist on decent treatment.

C   Labor rights and intra-region inequity

One challenge to the fairness of respecting LDC workers' collective bargaining rights is that it would lead to inequities within LDCs. Thus, Wolff effectively acknowledges that a transformation of labor rights might provide an alternative to the legal imposition of constraints on working conditions. But he doubts that "activist trades unions or the panoply of worker rights treasured in Europe are inevitably appropriate for a labour-surplus developing country (or for a rich one, for that matter)."[100]

Wolff maintains that, if unions "were successful in raising wages and conditions for the lucky minority of workers employed in modern factories to levels closer to those westerners consider reasonable," the result would be that "[t]he price of labour to modern enterprises would rise above its opportunity cost."[101] But if the price of labor actually rose above its opportunity cost in a given region, it is not clear that IC firms would continue to operate in that region at all. Wolff seems to assume that workers would extract IC-level wages from firms even if doing so led to the closure of the local companies that directly employed them. It is unclear why he thinks workers are so unreasonable.

Perhaps in fact he thinks that workers are not unreasonable, but that they simply lack market knowledge. But effective bargaining by workers does not ordinarily depend on careful market research. Like firms setting prices, they can find appropriate compensation levels through the give and take, the mutual adjustment, of the bargaining process itself.

Wolff's fundamental concern seems to be with the impact of higher compensation on local economies. Suppose workers succeeded in raising compensation levels at companies producing for export in partnership with IC firms. There would, Wolff implies, be an enormous compensation gap between what other local workers at these companies received and what workers elsewhere earned. As a result,

> the labour market would ... be dualistic, with low incomes for the great
> majority and relatively high incomes for the organized few. Both profitability in the modern sector and the labour-intensity of production

---

[100] WOLFF, *supra* note 90, at 186.   [101] *Id.*

would be lower. The modern sector would then grow more slowly. People would queue for these high-paying jobs, creating more open unemployment. Migration from the countryside would also slow, delaying, perhaps indefinitely, the time when labour shortages began to raise rural wages rapidly. All these unions would have achieved is to have created an island of privilege in an ocean of misery.[102]

Collectively bargaining workers will be sufficiently self-interested, in Wolff's view, that they will increase their own wages at significant cost to poor people in their communities and to the economies of those communities more generally.

On the proposal I am offering here, of course, the labor-market dualism Wolff envisions would not obtain. Wolff envisions a market in which collective bargaining is quite limited. However, the labor rights I suggest should be recognized globally would include the right to bargain collectively at all enterprises, not merely those operated by IC firms, and in rural areas as well as cities. And collective bargaining in the countryside would lead to increases in wages for rural workers in some settings as well.

In any event, firms cannot determine whether to treat their workers fairly on the basis of calculations regarding the macro-level impact of collective bargaining on an LDC's economy. Bargaining collectively with workers is a way of ensuring that the process of determining *particular workers'* compensation and working conditions is equitable and that the terms resulting from this process are fair. Firms need to treat particular workers in ways that are fair, or that will make fair outcomes likely; their primary concern cannot be with the spillover effects of their own collective bargaining choices.

D   The responsibilities of industrialized countries

There is good reason for firms to give decision making power to workers rather than managers. Absent workplace democracy, there is good reason for workers to seek collective bargaining rights and for firms to engage in collective bargaining against a background of workplace procedural protections. It is clear that employment relations in *our* world do not, in general, meet standards of justice consistent with practical reasonableness. But action at multiple levels could help to ensure that sweatshop workers' labor rights were recognized, even in the absence of a global consensus in support of labor rights. I consider two possible approaches

[102] *Id.*

here: the enforcement of labor rights in LDCs by IC courts (Subsection 1), and the use of tariffs to raise the prices of goods manufactured in LDCs and imported into ICs to IC levels (Subsection 2).

1   Enforcement of labor rights by IC courts

One targeted and potentially effective approach, if LDC courts cannot or will not hold IC firms or their local subsidiaries or partners accountable for ignoring labor rights, would be for courts in ICs to hold individual businesses accountable for respecting the rights of workers in LDCs.[103] Enforcement of collective bargaining requirements by the courts of individual communities need not be protectionist in nature. Enforcement actions could target specific firms and yield compensation for workers denied collective bargaining rights by those firms.

2   Protectionism as a response to violations of labor rights.

Lawsuits targeting individual firms that fail to respect labor rights can simply require these firms to accept responsibility for their actions. They need not discriminate against any firm on the basis of its geographic location or its cultural or ethnic identity. By contrast, a range of unapologetically protectionist measures do just this. Thom Hartmann, for instance, suggests that tariff levels be set to force companies based in the United States to pay overseas workers American wages:

> If there's a dollar's worth of labor in a pair of shoes made here, and you can make the shoes in some other "cheap labor" country with 10 cents' worth of labor, there will be a 90-cent import tax (tariff) when you bring them into the country, to protect our domestic industries and our manufacturing jobs. Tariffs level the field for both American business and American labor.

---

[103] Of course, an LDC could clearly take steps to address the problem of sweatshop labor as well. Cambodia's example suggests that this is possible even in a relatively poor region: "The Cambodian Government has decided instead to continue a program of independent factory monitoring carried out by the ILO, which appears to have genuinely improved factory conditions and labor compliance. Though Cambodia still faces enormous problems associated with corruption and bureaucratic inefficiency, foreign buyers appear to have responded well to Cambodia's attempts to improve labor and factory conditions. The higher labor standards offered by Cambodian producers, it appears, is attractive to Western buyers sensitive to accusations that their products are manufactured in sweatshop conditions. Indeed, Cambodia appears to have directly benefited from media reports of poor labor standards elsewhere, and its reputation as a safe-haven for fair labor standards has attracted international retailers concerned about consumer backlash." John A. Hall, *"China Casts a Giant Shadow": The Developing World Confronts Trade Liberalization and the End of Quotas in the Garment Industry*, 5 J. INT'L Bus. & L. 43 (2006).

[If the United States abandons multilateral free trade agreements,] [o]ffshore labor can … be set in price – by adding tariffs to it – to equal a living wage in the United States.

If a company wants to hire people to answer the phone in India for $2 per hour, fine. Let them do it – and pay a $10-per-hour tariff on top of the $2 hourly wage. If somebody wants to manufacture a computer in China with $10 worth of labor that would be worth $100 in the United States, no problem – just impose a $90 tariff on it when it's imported. Most companies will simply return to the United States for their labor.[104]

Hartmann's proposal seems objectionable both because it discriminates against LDC workers and because it is likely to yield limited benefits for IC workers.

Members of LDCs need help and ICs have been and continue to be complicit in the exploitation of LDCs. Thus, in accordance with the Golden Rule, ICs have clear responsibilities to help to enhance the economic conditions of LDCs' residents. Ending IC complicity in oppression and dispossession in LDCs is a crucial part of improving these conditions. Members of ICs can fulfill their duty to eliminate poverty and promote prosperity in LDCs through wealth transfers. They can also do so by respecting the freedom of members of LDCs to migrate.[105] But job-creating investment in LDCs is surely an effective way of fulfilling ICs' responsibility to redistribute resources to the global poor, as is the elimination of trade barriers that exclude LDC goods and services from IC markets. ICs may not have the *same* responsibility for the well being of residents of LDCs as for their own residents. However, their responsibilities to the world's poor must mean, at minimum, ending their support for unjust policies in LDCs and avoiding discrimination against residents and products of LDCs.

To the extent that fair production in LDCs reduces prices and so lowers living costs, it will be most beneficial to the most vulnerable persons in ICs. It is the well being of these people that welfare protectionist measures are often touted as defending. However, they clearly benefit from low consumer prices, which would rise substantially if measures like those proposed by Hartmann were adopted. It seems that "if consumers were blocked by protectionist measures from seeking cheaper end products manufactured abroad, what we would have is, at best, a redistribution

[104] THOM HARTMANN, SCREWED: THE UNDECLARED WAR AGAINST THE MIDDLE CLASS – AND WHAT WE CAN DO ABOUT IT 178–80 (2006).
[105] MANDLE, *supra* note 9, at 99–100, notes that freedom of global migration would be an especially effective means of enhancing the well being of the global poor. He seems to me clearly to be right.

from consumers to employers and workers and, at worst, a deadweight loss that is insulated from the competitive pressure that should squeeze it out."[106]

Hartmann is right, of course, that global trade has led to significant disruptions in ICs. But protectionism is neither fair nor effective as a response to these disruptions. A fairer and more effective response would be for communities to expect wealthy people to share the disproportionate benefits they reap from increased global trade. Their communities might expect them to support projects designed to provide assistance for the unemployed, to enhance the productivity of workers whose standards of living might decline as a result of trade,[107] and to support efforts intended to protect people from losses associated with compensation reductions or overall economic downturns.[108] Provided that the wealthy in ICs fulfilled their responsibilities to support projects like these, manufacturing in LDCs in which labor rights are acknowledged would be an appropriate, indeed attractive, means of redistributing global wealth to LDCs.[109]

E   Firms' responsibilities to current workers and local communities

Protectionism and other means of preventing outsourcing from ICs to LDCs are often unreasonable. But it does not follow from this fact that firms currently producing in ICs should, or even may, relocate production activities to LDCs (any more than that a firm currently operating in a given LDC should automatically relocate if collective bargaining raises costs *there*). A firm has particular responsibilities to workers: not to treat them as dispensable and to ensure that their lives are not disrupted simply because, though already profitable, it has the opportunity to increase its profits. It may also have responsibilities in virtue of its ties to a particular community: it may have contributed to the creation and sustenance of a way of life that many members of the community may find valuable and worth preserving, not only because of the economic benefits resulting from it but also because of its contributions to their identities. The firm's role in the history of the community and the community's vulnerability to its actions, as well as commitments it may have made, may obligate it

---

[106] Fried, *Rights, supra* note 9, at 1023.
[107] *Cf.* ROBERT B. REICH, THE WORK OF NATIONS (1991).
[108] *Cf.* JACOB S. HACKER, THE GREAT RISK SHIFT: THE ASSAULT ON AMERICAN JOBS, FAMILIES, HEALTH CARE, and RETIREMENT – AND HOW YOU CAN FIGHT BACK (2006); ROBERT J. SHILLER, THE NEW FINANCIAL ORDER: RISK IN THE 21st CENTURY (2003).
[109] My dependence will be obvious here on MANDLE, *supra* note 9, at 111–20.

not to leave the community when it might otherwise be free to do so and, indeed, when there might be reason for it to do so.

Such considerations will not always be decisive. But concern for and loyalty to workers and communities will often provide good reason for an IC-based firm to continue operating where it has a history of doing so rather than outsourcing its operations to one or more LDCs. To be sure, a firm's operations in a given community may cease to be financially viable at some point. In each particular case, a firm's decision-makers will need to ask what the Golden Rule requires – what costs they themselves would be willing to tolerate if their roles and those of community members and workers were reversed.

Many IC firms currently benefit from a wide range of subsidies and monopoly privileges in their home communities. Particularly relevant in this case are the multiple subsidies afforded to long-distance transportation. If firms were expected to internalize the costs currently covered by subsidies, they might be more inclined to produce and distribute locally, and the outsourcing of production tasks to LDC firms might be less likely. Elimination of direct and indirect subsidies could lead firms to be more responsible to communities in which they were rooted, whether they acknowledged duties to those communities or not.

F   Collective bargaining and justice for sweatshop workers

Presuming that collective bargaining and due process rights are acknowledged, the salaries, benefits, and working conditions of LDC workers may be sufficiently fair that firms employing them need not be exploiting them by doing so. But their salaries, benefits, and working conditions will not be identical with those of IC workers. Instead, they will have used their competitive advantage to secure both jobs and compensation levels they might not otherwise have had. With workers' rights acknowledged, the fairness of the global trade environment would not be compromised by differentials in pay and working conditions. Calls for boycotts or tariffs designed to influence pay and working conditions in settings in which these rights were observed would be unnecessary and unreasonable. By contrast, when compensation levels and working conditions are not determined by free collective bargaining, the production activities of an LDC firm are presumptively unjust. Mechanisms that permit and facilitate lawsuits against those who ignore the demands of fairness, rather than tariffs and embargoes, will be the best way to help those paid unfair wages and subjected unreasonably to unsafe working conditions.

Collective bargaining would not eliminate compensation differentials between sectors or regions. It would, however, raise wages to fairer levels and ensure that working conditions were more reasonable. Collective bargaining can help to lay the groundwork for just trade and the development of workplace democracy across the globe.

V   Limited justice in unjust workplaces

There is good reason for most or all workplaces to be democratic. But pursuing a combination of participatory management and collective bargaining can be an effective remedial response to the absence of workplace democracy (and, of course, collective bargaining can play a remedial role even within a democratically governed firm).

Collective bargaining is crucial if the fairness of the employment contract, at least in the investor-governed firm, is to be assured. Unions can withstand a range of criticisms, and can help to develop fair and flexible compensation packages, working hours, and workplace health and safety standards. They can help to minimize disregard for workers' interests in worker-governed firms while providing the backbone of worker participation in the governance of investor-dominated firms. Along with unions, institutions including enterprise committees and work teams – not as inclusive and powerful as democratic structures, but capable, in principle, of affecting firm policies and strategies in ways that will help to protect workers' well being and, quite possibly, improve firm performance – can enhance worker participation in the management of investor-dominated firms.

Bargaining collectively with workers helps firms to address the problem of sweatshop labor more fairly. Abandoning global production and mechanically imposing global parity are not the only options. Giving workers a chance to set standards through collective bargaining is another, and better, alternative – though practical reasonableness may still require workplace democracy in most settings around the world, and the background injustices that contribute to sweatshop workers' poverty and reduce their options must still be addressed.

~

Conclusion

Natural law theory provides a set of supple, powerful tools for the inves-tigation of a range of problems in economic life. Built on an awareness of the diversity of the aspects of flourishing and fulfillment and the import-ance of a limited number of practical principles, the natural law approach to moral, social, and political life leaves open a wide range of options among which morally responsible actors can select, while shaping their choices in accordance with the character of well being and the demands of reason.

The *assignment* of property rights is basic to any economic system. There is no single just system of property rights. Natural law theory does not dictate how property rights ought to be assigned, but it constrains judgments about them in several ways. It highlights rationales – per-sonal and communal – that ought to be respected when property rights are assigned. It stresses the contingent character of such rights, and so undermines inflated claims about their absolute status. And it empha-sizes that a community's system of property rights is reasonable only to the extent that it actually benefits the community's members and their shared projects, and that such a system may sometimes rightly constrain the ways in which people use their property in light of the principles of practical reasonableness and the underlying rationales that justify the existence of a property system in the first place. At the same time, it also stresses that the failure to recognize stable property rights at all, or to deny recognition to certain specific kinds of rights, would likely be unjust.

Each person has a responsibility to assist others, using the wealth in excess of her public trust threshold to benefit other people or to support common projects or shared goods. In turn, community norms, stand-ards, and organizations can and should foster economic security and the relief of poverty, both domestically and globally, clearly calling people to contribute to these endeavors and coordinating their participation. A well-ordered property system – one which was free of the effects of mon-opoly, tariff, license, patent, subsidy, and restrictions on access to capital, one in which people were no longer impoverished or rendered econom-ically insecure because of the consequences of the large-scale and violent dispossession of their ancestors – might well provide economic well being for most people. But even in an environment fully shaped by the demands of justice, some people – victims of illness, accident, disability, or decline, or in search of bohemian freedom – might still require assistance from others; and, in any event, *our* system of property rights and holdings is not well ordered, not structured in accordance with the requirements of practical reason.

Practical reasonableness leaves open a variety of ways in which we can meet our obligations to distribute wealth justly. And it does not impose on anyone an overwhelming burden of responsibility for the public weal. Among the ways of meeting the requirements of justice in distribution might be community-wide sharing of the costs of health care and basic income support. Certainly, it would be inconsistent with those requirements for an entire community to refuse to invest and transfer wealth in ways designed to benefit the global poor. It would be similarly inconsistent with people's responsibilities regarding justice in distribution to cooperate purposefully with trading partners responsible for unreasonable harm or to ignore appropriate limits on substantive cooperation with those such partners.

Communities' legal systems can sometimes reasonably foster the well being of tenant farmers, other workers, and other people by reassigning property titles. Focusing on decisions to reassign property titles and the principles governing them serves as a useful illustration and test of the natural law approach to norms, rules, institutions, and rights I outline in this book. The varied rationales underlying a just property system preclude arbitrary and overreaching property reforms. But because the victims of injustice deserve remedies, because varied interests in property are sometimes reasonably honored, because subordination is unjust, because transferring title may sometimes be a just remedy for impoverishment or the deliberately non-productive use of property, and because property rights are not absolute (and some are vitiated by their unjust roots), reassignments of title will sometimes be appropriate. Urban redevelopment efforts that displace people from their homes often ignore the importance of people's and groups' deep attachments to places and the relationships made possible by association with those places. A satisfactory natural law understanding of property rights gives us good reason to be skeptical about such efforts. But – when they empower people, offer them tools they can use to escape from poverty, help to recompense them for past expropriation, equip them to make effective use of property unjustly acquired by others, compensate them for their "sweat equity," and enable them to retain valued connections – reassignments of title to peasants and other workers can be seen, not as antithetical to, but as expressions of, the natural law understanding of property.

While a central *function* of economic life is the production and distribution of the goods and services to which communities, families, and persons are entitled – *property* – the *means* by which this function is most often accomplished is *work*. Work occupies an enormous fraction of a typical person's life, and our work lives provide opportunities for creativity, friendship, discovery, and service – but also for tedium, meaninglessness, and subjection to arbitrary power. Natural law theory is compatible with multiple forms of industrial organization. But practical reasonableness requires that worklife be structured in a way that frees people from subordination and capricious exclusion and gives them the power to direct their own lives. At minimum, practical reasonableness entails the rejection of arbitrary dismissal and discrimination. It also requires that all or almost all workplaces should be thoroughly participatory, and provides good reason to believe that all or almost all should be democratically governed by workers. It also strongly supports collective bargaining – appropriate in investor-governed and worker-governed workplaces alike – as a means of fostering contractual fairness and facilitating the transition to workplace democracy, and the adoption of sensible, broadly endorsed, workplace-specific standards for working conditions, set, at least in investor-governed firms, through collective negotiation. Collective bargaining can also help to provide the beginnings of a solution to the problem of sweatshop labor, which obviously demands a range of legal and economic responses.

Natural law theory offers a framework that enables us to understand economic justice and so to be more just. In this book, I have only sketched the outlines of what practical reasonableness might be thought to require in the sphere of economic life and provided a three-part overview focused (with some overlaps) on property, work, and consumption. But I hope the fruitful and provocative character of natural law theorizing as it is described and (I trust) exemplified here will prompt continued engagement with the task of understanding and enacting justice.

INDEX

retired persons 162
reward
    distribution 54
    see also compensation
risk
    distribution 55
    minimization
        due process 78
Rudy, Jesse 81

Sachs, Jeffrey 213
savings 66
self-employment 119, 161
self-esteem 8
self-respect and basic income 166
selfhood *see* identity
share ownership, worker 201
slave labor 213, 217
small firms
    consumer service and worker-
        governed 119
    health insurance 161
    large firms compared with 92, 95,
        97–99, 103, 113, 115–16
social order and natural law 26–31
social science model, standard
    rational decision-making 23–24
South Africa 88, 137
specialization 52
    capacity 53–54
    managerial 92
sphere sovereignty and workplace
    democracy 116–18
squatters
    property rights
        abandonment 45–46
        compensation rationale 36
        identity rationale 42
stateless society 29, 117
stewardship
    rationale for property rights
        38–39, 45
        private developers 149
        reform 128, 139, 142–43
stock ownership, worker 201
strike, right to 186, 217
subordination
    democracy, workplace 93–94

property reform 127–28, 153
subsidiarity 29–31, 103–04, 113
subsidies 98, 224
    transportation costs 97, 224
Super Fresh 202
sweat equity
    property reform 127, 142
        sweat equity purchase 132, 134
sweatshop labor and collective
        bargaining 211–12, 224–25
    competitive advantage 216–19
    contingency of 212–16
    firms' responsibilities 223–24
    ICs, responsibilities of 220–22
    labor rights and intra-region
        inequity 219–20
Sweden 207

taxation 179
tenant farmers / peasants
    comparison of claims: private
        developers and 151–54
    productivity rationale for property
        rights 38
    property reform 127–28
        homesteading, radical 132,
            133–35
        homesteading abandoned
            property (moderate) 132, 133
        nonstandard purchases 132
theory, natural law 6–7, 31
    basic aspects of well being 7–8
    identification of 8–10
    irreducible, incommensurable,
        and non-fungible 10–13
    practical reasonableness *see*
        practical reasonableness
    social order 26–31
Thomas Aquinas, St. 45
tort of wrongful or abusive discharge
    73
transportation costs 97, 224

underutilization/abandonment
    property rights 45–46
        moderate homesteading 132, 133,
            146
        reform and productivity 126–27